BRITISH MILITARY LONGARMS 1715–1865

BRITISH MILITARY LONGARMS 1715–1865

by

D. W. BAILEY

ARMS AND ARMOUR PRESS
NEW YORK LONDON SYDNEY

To
Howard Blackmore and Christopher Roads,
who started it all.

Special Note

The present writer has for some time been working on an exhaustive study of all the records concerning the design, production and distribution of British military firearms, including handguns, from 1690 to 1815, which is scheduled to appear in 1988. It is therefore hoped, indeed requested, that any information about or photographs of arms that are included in this work as unknown or unidentified will be forwarded to the writer for inclusion in the work now in progress.

Published in Great Britain
in 1986 by Arms and Armour Press Limited,
2–6 Hampstead High Street, London NW3 1QQ.

Distributed in the USA by Sterling Publishing Co. Inc.,
2 Park Avenue, New York, N.Y. 10016.

Distributed in Australia by
Capricorn Link (Australia) Pty. Ltd., P.O. Box 665,
Lane Cove, New South Wales 2066, Australia.

First published in two-volume form, 1971 and 1972.

British Library Cataloguing in Publication Data:
Bailey, D. W.
British military longarms, 1715–1865.
1. Great Britain. *Army*—History
2. Firearms—Great Britain—History—18th century
3. Firearms—Great Britain—History—19th century
I. Title
355.8′24′0941 U820.G7

ISBN 0–85368–835–4

Printed and bound in Great Britain by
Richard Clay (The Chaucer Press) Ltd,
Bungay, Suffolk

Contents

Acknowledgments

The kind cooperation of the entire staff of the Royal Armouries, H.M. Tower of London, has made this work possible. I should particularly like to express my gratitude to A. R. Dufty, Esq., A.R.I.B.A., F.S.A., former Master of the Armouries, for permitting me to research for many months in the Tower collections: this volume is one of the unexpected results. I am also most grateful to A. N. Kennard, Esq., B.A., F.S.A., former Assistant Master of the Armouries, for the benefit both of his years of experience and of his knowledge of arms, and for his friendship and encouragement. My thanks also to H. J. Woodend, Esq., Custodian of the Pattern Room Collection at the Royal Small Arms Factory, Enfield Lock, for his help and for his knowledge of the arms in his charge. To Jeremy Hall, Esq., I am indebted for the superb photography which illustrates this volume, an unsurpassed example of what can be done in the field of firearms photography. All the photographs were taken at the Armouries of the Tower of London, and are Crown copyright; they appear by kind permission of the Department of the Environment.

I would also like to express my gratitude to the staff of the Public Record Office at Kew and Chancery Lane who have given me every assistance in my examination of the Ordnance and other relevant records since 1967.

All who study British military firearms are in the debt of Howard L. Blackmore, Esq., and Christopher H. Roads, M.A., Ph.D., for their classic works *British Military Firearms, 1650–1850* (1961), and *The British Soldier's Firearm, 1850–1864* (1964). I would like to express my warmest thanks to them both for their encouragement and many kindnesses which were behind the production of this volume, and for access to their knowledge and notes in the preparation of this work.

Despite the assistance of the many who have guided and encouraged me along the path leading to this volume, any faults which may be found must be laid at my door alone.

De Witt Bailey
Battersea, London
1986

Introduction

Since the publication of classic works by Blackmore and Roads in the early 1960s, no large scale study of British military firearms has been undertaken.

Information uncovered as the result of documentary research over the last fifteen years, and of examining weapons in America and Europe as well as Britain, has not significantly altered any of the background material offered in the original publications. A great deal of detail about the processes of manufacture, and about the guns themselves (including several modifications of dates of introduction), has been located. Almost two dozen unknown or unidentified distinct patterns have emerged before 1815. Some of these are not described in the sort of detail that will allow of positive identification, while others are clearly defined but almost certainly do not survive, due either to the small numbers made, or to the nature and location of the service where they were used. As might be expected, most of these unidentified pieces are most likely to be found in North America or on the continent of Europe.

Selected new material, located since the original publication of this work in two volumes in 1971 and 1972 has been included as far as space will allow in the Addenda on page 158. It has not been possible to correct all captions in alignment with the new material; where differences occur, use the Addenda as a guide. Selection has been balanced between relevance to the history of the arms and items of particular collector/student interest. Wherever possible corrections to the original text appear in their appropriate place, and others will be found in the final chapter.

The limited size of the present volume requires that a largely technical approach be adopted. Only 'issue' weapons manufactured in Great Britain (with the exceptions of the P/53 Windsor Rifle Musket and the Model 1855 Sharps carbines), will be dealt with here. But it should be clearly understood that the purchase of weapons made abroad, primarily in Liège, usually to Ordnance patterns, was a normal occurrence in the early stages of every conflict that occurred during the period covered. In 1793 this practice was expanded, for the first time, to include large numbers of non-Ordnance-pattern arms.

To obtain a balanced understanding of any antique firearm, it is of the greatest importance to consider the military, industrial and commercial background against which the arm was produced.

Attempting to write firearms history purely on the basis of examination of wood and metal has been proven to be a largely futile and highly misleading exercise—never more so than with military small arms. Firearms are, first and foremost, social instruments, the creations of man: of a time, place and society. Without an understanding of these factors, it is all too easy to make assumptions that lead to a complete failure in assessing a weapon, its manufacture and its use. The entire concept of government in 18th-century England was such that to apply standards of 20th-century classification and technology to any of its operations leads to probable misinterpretation of the methods of design, manufacture and distribution of small arms. While such methods unquestionably make it easier for the collector to identify a piece, they make it equally easy to mis-identify the weapon and to draw inaccurate conclusions about the methods of its manufacture, which lead inevitably to mis-identification of other examples. Despite the changeover in 1714–16 to the 'Ordnance System' which increased the degree of centralization and control, older usages—as much in the Army as within the Ordnance—continued to thwart the new system until mid-century. Situations were met—or not met—as they arose. Long-term planning was neither thought about, nor financially feasible. Even when, by the mid-19th century, towards the very end of our period, such planning was possible, it was not implemented. Military small arms production in Great Britain was always very much of an 'ad hoc' operation, due largely to the political and financial organization of the government, and the insistance upon avoiding all consideration of public expenditure until the need for it actually occurred.

The gradual introduction of machinery and factory methods, dating from the beginnings of the armoury at Enfield Lock in 1804, and especially from its expansion in 1816–18, did not greatly change the outlook of the men who governed what Enfield would do; it merely introduced an alternative method, which caused a great deal of in-fighting between the contractors and their supporters, and those who felt that a government-owned and operated national armoury was a better proposition for the nation's defence. The English gun trade, including military manufacture, was one of the last trades to be substantially affected by the Industrial Revolution. Despite the valiant efforts of George Lovell, beginning in the mid-1830s, the centralized 'Government Armoury' concept played second-fiddle to the traditional decentralized system until just after the end of our period. The vast bulk of Pattern 1853 arms were made under the same system as the first of the Land Pattern muskets in the 1720s.

BRITISH MILITARY LONGARMS 1715–1815

Duke of Cumberland's Sharp Shooters, 1808

Background

The year 1715 has been selected as the starting point for several reasons. In 1715 a new system of manufacture of military firearms for the British government was organized and set in motion which came to be known as 'the Ordnance system of manufacture'. The year 1715 is also considered by most historians as the real beginning of the eighteenth century rather than the titular date of 1700; it was the end of the long era of the wars of Louis XIV and the beginning of an era of relative peace—the longest the eighteenth century was to know—during which time the manufacturing and commercial processes of this country and those of the Continent were modernized and often reorganized along new, more efficient, lines. From this date the system of national armouries came into being generally in Europe and on the Continent the production of specific patterns of military arms developed rapidly, whereas between 1700 and 1715—roughly the period of the War of the Spanish Succession—the old systems of supply had predominated. The monarchs of the last century were dead and those of the major powers were just beginning their reigns: the House of Hanover in Great Britain, the Regent for Louis XV in France, Philip V in Spain, Charles VI in Austria, Frederick William I in Prussia. It was in many ways the end of the old period and the beginning of the new.

Prior to 1715 it had been the normal practice for the Board of Ordnance to purchase complete weapons from a large number of private contractors in England, Ireland and (particularly) Holland. The details of construction were decided by the contractors within very wide limits but, so long as they were of similar calibre and stood both proof and a minimum standard of inspection by British Ordnance agents, they were accepted. The result was a confused mass of non-standardized weapons of indifferent quality. The length of the War of the Spanish Succession, and the considerable extent to which England had committed her financial and military resources, had aggravated the evils of this system to the point where—when peace was at last obtained and England found herself in a favourable and secure position in her relationships with the Continental powers—definite steps were taken to establish a new system of manufacture. The new system was expected to ensure a reasonably steady flow of parts, the manufacture of which could be more closely supervised and inspected and the finishing of which would be under the virtual direct control of the agents of the Board of Ordnance. This did not mean that the purchase of arms from abroad ceased: throughout the entire period covered by this volume it continued a practice resorted to in times of acute shortage of arms, and there were many of those. The new system itself had much to recommend it, but the perennial shortage of funds often caused the execution of it to lag well behind requirements, so that when an emergency occurred arms were obtained from outside sources to fill the gap.

Of the one hundred years with which this volume deals, Great Britain was at war—that is, officially declared war—for fifty-one of them. In addition, until the American War broke out in 1775, she was responsible for the supply of arms to the North American colonies for their defence against the incursions of the French and their almost constant minor warfare with the Indians. Particularly during the French Revolutionary and Napoleonic Wars Britain also undertook to supply not only money but arms to her Continental allies, and to the many foreign corps enrolled in the British service. It is important to bear this background in mind when considering the operation of the Ordnance system.

As it developed and operated from about 1720 until well into the nineteenth century, the system was simply that officials designated by the Board of Ordnance signed contracts on behalf of the Ordnance for the supply of the various components required to set up a complete weapon. The size of the order would depend largely upon the amount of money available at the time and the requirements for bringing the number of weapons in store up to a predetermined figure. The contracts were separately negotiated with each of the several makers of parts concerned, although they tended to work together, and disputes which wasted time and effort were not uncommon even in the face of emergencies. Patterns were furnished by the Ordnance to the makers of the parts, and the finished parts were delivered either to the Ordnance contractors or directly to the central depot, the Tower of London. From this central point sets of components were despatched to a relatively small number of London gun makers known as 'rough stockers and setters up', located in most instances in the Minories and generally close to the Tower, who finished up the rough stock blanks and set up the completed weapons including, where applicable, the fitting of the bayonets. The finished weapons were then delivered to the Tower and issued against specific requisitions. There were four groups of contractors who supplied the parts for Government weapons: the barrelmakers, lockmakers, furniture makers (brass founders) and small-work men who supplied the pins, screws and triggers. The former two groups were concentrated largely in the Birmingham area during the period, while the latter two were divided between London and Birmingham.

It was not until 1803 that anything was done to tighten up the system of contractors and deliveries by the establishment of a centrally-controlled group of workmen. In that year a staff of rough stockers and makers of the small parts began to be assembled at the Tower. At the same time the facilities of the Armoury Mills at Lewisham were taken in hand and, in 1808, the entire force was moved to Lewisham. The Lewisham armoury—designed to manufacture barrels, locks, ramrods and bayonets—continued in operation (much reduced in scale after 1814) until 1818 when the facilities were again divided up between the Tower and a new factory at Enfield Lock.

The system was extended to Birmingham where, from 1804 (when contracts with eleven gun makers were signed) until 1818, complete arms were assembled. The staff of the central Birmingham depot was halved in 1814, so that the primary period of production may be considered as the first ten years. From March 1804 until September 1815 a total of 1,743,382 complete arms were set up in Birmingham, comprising 1,682,610 muskets, 14,695 rifles, 38,778 carbines and 54,474 pistols. The same Parliamentary Report gave a grand total (with no individual details) of 2,673,366 arms fabricated 'in the Royal manufactory and by individuals in London' from 1803 to 1816.

There is a great tendency amongst modern collectors of antique military firearms to extend the system of classification and model designation which holds good for most nineteenth century weapons (e.g. Pattern 1853, Second Model Rifle-Musket) back into the eighteenth century. In some few instances, such as Austrian and French arms, this system is both practical and justifiable but in the case of British military firearms it is neither. So far as British weapons were concerned the conscious attempt to classify and designate different models and types did not make its appearance until the adoption of the percussion ignition system in the late 1830s. Any attempt to analyse production on the basis of a series of models and types is, therefore, unsound, even though it may be workable in terms of the weapons themselves—which is only rarely the case. The system under which arms were procured for the Ordnance, the conditions under which the separate pieces were manufactured and set up, the circumstances under which they were issued and returned into store, and the manner in which they were repaired when in service and refurbished subsequently—none of these elements in the life cycle of an individual weapon permit a rigid classification. If it were possible for the average collector of antique arms to keep this historical distinction clearly in mind when discussing the structural evolution of a particular British military weapon, then there would be less objection to the existence of a dual system of identification—the old, or Pattern system, and the new, or Typological system, e.g. Militia or Marine Pattern, Second Model, Type II. While this system may be appropriate when discussing the actual construction of a particular piece, its use leads to the assumption that the weapon was deliberately designed in specific detail, and this ultimately creates a host of misunderstandings and inaccuracies. It also creates a complete misunderstanding of the system of manufacture and use, which in turn leads to incorrect identification and inaccurate historical supposition. Given the operation of the original system, it would not be possible to date any weapon to closer than a decade had not the locks been dated until 1764. Unfortunately most of the structural changes which have been assigned significance by modern collectors occurred after the dating of locks ceased and there is no infallible means of dating most of these changes.

Muskets

British flintlock muskets of the 1715–1815 period fall into five major categories:

1. Pattern of the 10,000 and Colonel's Patterns, 1715–35.
2. Land Pattern, 1730–97.
3. India Pattern, 1793–1815.
4. New Land Pattern, 1802–15.
5. Sea Service, entire period.

The above datings are approximate and overlap, the introduction dates being more precise than termination dates. It must also be noted that, although the India Pattern musket was taken into use by the Government in 1793, it did not become an accepted pattern to guide manufacture of Government muskets until 1797.

The pre-Land Pattern muskets of the first twenty years of this study were structurally a combination of Dutch features from earlier muskets and more modern ideas taken from contemporary sporting weapons and from French military arms. Typical of these weapons were the flat lockplates held by three sidenails (with or without sideplate), the early form of flat ring-neck cock with the thin forward reinforce, and the dog-catch. The tops of the steels were usually flat as on Continental arms and there was no bridle between the pan and the steel screw, a feature which produced what was known as the 'single-bridle lock'. On the earliest weapons of this period, mostly before 1720, the furniture was generally iron, sometimes rounded but more usually flat in contour, and often simply screwed to the surface of the wood rather than inlet. During the 1720s there was a growing use of rounded, semi-inlet brass furniture, and by 1730 brass furniture was well established as the standard—even though an occasional iron-mounted musket will be found dated during the 1730s. Most of the features which we now consider denoting a typical Brown Bess developed during this period; there was no sudden change in the design of the Government musket. The 'handrail' or 'stair-rail' shape of butt with the long narrow comb and round wrist extending back over half the length of the butt, the 'banana lockplate' with the pronounced downward curve of the tail of the plate, the swell of the stock at the tailpipe to afford a better grip, the form of the stock carving round the barrel tang and around the lockplate and sideplate flat, the rounded contour of the lockplate surface and the rounded swan-neck cock with its jaws nearly rounded in shape when viewed from above—all of these features occurred increasingly on muskets made from the early 1720s. The double border lines engraved round the edges of the lockplate and the body and top jaw of the cock appeared during the first five years of the period to become standard decoration by the late 1720s, and the dating of the locks changed from only the final two figures of the date on the earliest locks to the use of the full date by about 1725. The pattern of the furniture was the last of the several features to assume a settled form and, while appearing in the early 1730s as a complete set of 'typical Brown Bess mounts', variations in the form of the sideplate, trigger guard finials, buttplate tangs or escutcheons continued to appear during the same period. The Plates indicate all of the salient features of the Land Pattern series, which served as the basic pattern for the British musket until the unparalleled demands of the outbreak of the French Revolutionary Wars in 1793 called for drastic measures which brought about a basic alteration in the overall pattern of the British service musket. Within the Land Pattern series there were three major types, and one of these was but a variation of the second type, thus: the Long Land Pattern (with a 46inch barrel), the Short Land Pattern (with a 42inch barrel) and the Marine & Militia Pattern—which was actually a Short Land Pattern with a flat sideplate, no escutcheon and a shortened buttplate tang. In July 1775 the furniture of the Marine & Militia Pattern was made standard for the Short Land series, but with the reintroduction of the escutcheon and the normal pin-and-stud arrangement for holding the tang of the buttplate. It seems very probable that the original Marine & Militia Pattern, of which so much has been made, was a short-term wartime production expedient which did not long outlast the end of the Seven Years War in 1763, for while a great many Short Land muskets are seen with flat sideplates, they have the pin-held buttplate tang and the escutcheon—whereas completely correct Marine & Militia Pattern muskets with the screw-fastened buttplate tang and no wrist escutcheon are very rarely seen.

Basically there are two patterns within the Land Pattern series, the Long and the Short; structurally it is purely a matter of barrel length which distinguishes the two for when the Long Land muskets were later cut down owing to wear, damage or a desire to up-date them, there is no telling which may have originally been a Long Land and which was made as a Short Land. There were, however, a number of structural changes applied to the Land Pattern muskets which should be noted, as they applied to both lengths and were chronological in nature.

The introduction of the 'double-bridle' lock in the early 1740s was the first change which was widely applied to the British service musket as a whole. This consisted of a connexion or link between the pan and the steel screw, giving the latter much greater support; it is quite rare to find a lock dating later than 1745 which is of the older 'single-bridle' type except on Sea Service muskets.

The second basic change was much more gradual, occurring over the years from 1724 until 1776; it was in some cases a deliberate change, in others one of up-dating while in for repair and, in some instances, the old form was kept for specific reasons—particularly in the use of the steel ramrod as opposed to the wooden, brass-tipped rod. The original Long Land musket was made with the wooden ramrod until about 1750, when new production weapons were made with the steel rod and correspondingly small-diameter pipes, the upper pipe being longer and of trumpet-shape, and the stock being fitted with a cast brass fore-end cap. The conversion from wooden to steel rod was not carried out with any apparent regularity or system; as earlier Long Land muskets came back into store or were sent in for repair they were up-dated. The conversion took the form of a sleeve being fitted into the upper pipe and a small flat spring being riveted or screwed into the tailpipe; the opportunity was also taken of adding a fore-end cap.

The Short Land musket, which appears to have begun life as a Dragoon weapon, made its appearance in the early 1740s, and had a wooden ramrod of the old type until its supersession by a carbine in 1770. From this it would appear that Short Land Muskets with wooden ramrods classify as dragoon muskets, and would not have been used by infantry, who would have had the Long Land musket. What is considered as the Short Land musket with steel ramrod probably made its first appearance as the Marine & Militia Pattern *c.* 1758, but the true Short Land musket with steel ramrod would not have appeared until after 1770 as the result, first of all, of the gradual conversion of dragoon muskets, and then as the final form of the Marine & Militia Pattern with its steel rod, escutcheon and shortened buttplate tang. From 1768 the 42inch barrel became standard, but this was only on paper and should not be confused with any consideration of the weapons in the hands of the troops at a given date. From *c.* 1770 there was a hodge-podge of Long and Short Land muskets in issue, very few of them with wooden ramrods, but beyond this it is folly to attempt precise enumeration beyond what some companies of some regiments may have had on a given date. Long Land muskets were being set up until 1790, even though the Short Land was by then being used in most regiments.

The third change which can be considered as applying to all new production arms of either Long or Short Land type is the introduction, on paper from 1777, of Pratt's funnel-shaped second ramrod pipe and of his ramrod stop which was simply a small square plate driven into the stock beneath the front finial of the trigger guard at the rear of the rod channel.

The remaining changes may best be described as evolutionary modifications which occurred at unspecified times and for no specific reason. They doubtless became generally accepted as cheaper, stronger and easier means of accomplishing an end within the general working pattern of the weapon concerned, and may have been the result of one finisher's idea or the joint effort of some obscure Ordnance committee whose deliberations were not recorded or have not survived to inform us of the date and value of their decision. Into this category—annoyingly broad—fall the following list of items, to which wherever within reason a tentative date of general acceptance has been added:

1. The evolution of the swell of the fore-end at the tailpipe; on the earliest examples this was a lump quite localised and pronounced, but gradually it spread out and became less pronounced over the years. There was little change from *c.* 1750.
2. A modification of the shape of the trigger guard bow to include a forward curl on its inside rear bend took place about 1740 and was standard thereafter.
3. A simplification of the stock carving round the lockplate and sideplate, from a long flat 'arrow-head' pattern at front and rear to a plain rounded pattern at front and much shorter 'teardrop' shape at rear, took place in the early 1740s.

Lock Changes

1. A lessening of the 'banana' profile of the plate, accomplished primarily by straightening the lower line of the plate, from 1756.
2. A change in the pattern of the steel-spring finial from a trefoil shape to a teardrop style, *c.* 1768.
3. The appearance of the tip of the sear-spring screw through the plate behind the cock, *c.* 1770.
4. The replacement of the thin, curled cock spur (as seen from the side) with rounded jaws by the thicker, straighter spur with the forward curl at the top, and the oval jaw which was slotted and slid along the spur, *c.* 1770. This change was probably accompanied by the piercing of the jaw screw in addition to the usual slotting. At this time also, the engraving of the top jaw with double border lines was dropped.

It must be emphasized that none of the above changes, particularly those relating to the lock and which occurred after the abolition of the practice of dating in 1764, should be dogmatically accepted as occurring on all production at any one date. It should be clear from the conditions and circumstances described in the foregoing chapter that this could not have happened.

The India Pattern is probably the most common of British flintlock muskets; its period of manufacture for Government use extended from 1793 until the close of 1815, and the total production probably approached three million. Technically it was not considered as a forward step in the design of the British musket at the time of its adoption for the service: quite the contrary, it was accepted as a cheaper, simpler weapon to meet a sudden vast increase in demand at a time when supplies in store were sadly inadequate. For almost five years the Ordnance vacillated in accepting the inevitable and foreign muskets, trade muskets, India Pattern and Short Land muskets were all taken into store between 1793 and 1797 but, by the latter date, it was obvious that the high standards required for the Short Land arm were not consistent with the need for a vastly increased number of arms on the shortest possible notice, and so the India Pattern became a regulation arm.

The India Pattern musket contained a number of changes in design from the Short Land musket. In addition it was generally of somewhat poorer finish, although this is often difficult to detect where pitting and wear have brought finish to low levels for either type. The wood used for the stocks was of inferior heart and sap walnut and it is curious to note that the stock carving round the lockplate, sideplate and barrel tang were still insisted upon despite other simplifications in design.

India Pattern furniture consisted of three ramrod pipes rather than four: a long trumpet-shaped upper pipe, a trumpet-shaped middle pipe and shorter tailpipe of Short Land pattern; the rounded contour sideplate had no tail and was a close copy of the contemporary French Model 1777, being a sort of loosely-curved S- shape. The buttplate had a fairly wide tang with two steps and a rounded tip and the trigger guard had a very plainly moulded front finial resembling a poorly formed pineapple, with a solid base at the rear of the bow rather than a forward curl inside and the rear finial held by two wood screws rather than a screw and a cross-pin. There was no escutcheon at the wrist.

The single significant change in the design of the India Pattern musket during its production was the substitution of a rounded ring-neck cock for the rounded swan-neck design, the change being authorized late in 1809. It was not cheaper, but was considered to be stronger and more durable; it had been used briefly on the New Land musket when the first group of these arms had been made in 1802–4, and was then being used for rifle and carbine locks in a flat version.

The New Land musket chronologically belongs to this period but, with the exception of the years 1802–04 and a short time in 1814–15, it was a production model of the post–1815 period. Until 1815 the pressure created by wartime needs prevented the production of high quality weapons with rigorous inspection and proof. The New Land series was the legitimate successor to the Land Pattern arms, being a deliberately improved and modernized weapon constructed and finished to normally high Government standards. There were a number of important changes in design over all previous British muskets, reflecting many of the trial and experimental arms which had been made in small numbers since the 1780s.

Two features in the design of the New Land musket were immediately apparent: the plain 'modern' look of the stock with its standard style of comb and butt, and the flat lockplate with its flat ring-neck cock. The barrel length was 42inches rather than the economy-dictated 39inches of the India Pattern, and the barrel was held by three flat keys rather than pins. There were three ramrod pipes, the upper one long and trumpet-shaped, but no tailpipe. The breech of the barrel was finished plainly without the traditional baluster turning, and there was no carving round the barrel tang. The trigger guard was much shorter—the rear finial held by a single screw—and the finials were plainly rounded at the ends. The buttplate had a plain rounded tang. The many improvements to the lock are described in the caption to the illustration.

Considering the tremendous importance of naval warfare during the many wars of the eighteenth and early nineteenth centuries and the number of amphibous landings and small-boat expeditions which were carried out, the Sea Service musket as a primary weapon in all these operations has been singularly neglected. Often described as being made up of inferior parts, defective and out of date weapons, the picture created is hardly in accordance with the facts and needs extensive reinterpretation and specialized study.

Sea Service muskets as made throughout the period were heavily and strongly built largely of specificially manufactured parts rather than leftovers—even in the case of flat locks, which are often looked upon as outdated relics of the seventeenth century. Through the period of the Napoleonic Wars these muskets were characterized by the presence of a thick, flat, brass buttplate with a plain short tang, fastened by a woodscrew through the tang and two through the plate itself, and also by a heavy brass trigger guard with a front finial circular in form and well-rounded in profile. The flat lock was used long after it had been superseded by the rounded lock in army muskets possibly because it was larger (and therefore less easily damaged and easier to repair under primitive shipboard conditions) and because it was cheaper to produce. The strength and obvious value of the flat lock, and ring-neck cock common to the flat lock, were acknowledged by the Ordnance when it returned to them in the design of the New Land series arms, and by the adoption of the ring-neck cock for the India Pattern muskets in 1809 after almost a century of using the weaker, cheaper, but more attractive swan-neck cock. Sea Service muskets were not highly finished weapons for sound reasons: a highly finished weapon is far more susceptible to salt-water corrosion and rusting, costs far more to produce while adding nothing to its serviceability and is far more likely to catch the light when not being seen is indispensable to the success of an operation. The extent and importance of nocturnal expeditions is emphasized by the issue, after 1752, of equal numbers of Sea Service muskets with blackened and with bright finished barrels. At this same time it was decreed by the Admiralty that all Sea Service muskets should be fitted with bayonets and sling swivels became standard features as well.

The normal length for Sea Service musket barrels was between 36 and 38inches and the thickness of the barrels indicated that they were not made from cut down Land Pattern barrels. In addition to the peculiar buttplate and trigger guard, Sea Service muskets normally had plain barrel-type ramrod pipes and no tailpipe, and some also had rod-retaining springs fitted inside one of the pipes. Fore-end caps were rarely fitted and the sideplates were almost always flat until the period of the India Pattern musket, when they were of rounded pattern. The use of a wooden ramrod rather than one of steel paralleled the Land Pattern arms.

As the frequency and extent of naval warfare increased during the century so did the demands upon the Admiralty for greater quantities of weapons, and it is surprising to note that very few later Sea Service muskets were made up of 'cut down' India Pattern or other Army muskets but continued to be fabricated from the usual components peculiar to Sea Service weapons. It may be pointed out also that the blacking of the barrels was a special additional process and that the process was expedited by leaving the surface of the barrel in a typical, finely draw-filed, state.

Great care should always be taken when attempting to identify any musket of nonstandard design and proportions. So large a trade developed during the nineteenth century for the supply of cheap weapons for commercial trading purposes that vast numbers of guns were made up from ex-Government parts, and too many of this class of weapons have come to be classified as 'Sea Service' or 'Extra Service' weapons because one or more parts bears an old Government property stamp. While in periods of emergency the Government were often forced to accept arms of less than normal standards, these arms were of far more standard pattern in their basic description than is generally credited.

---

2. *A George I Musket of pre-Land Pattern by Richard Wolldridge, dated 1715*

Brass furniture of Sea Service design, with thin brass barrel bands, no ramrod pipes and a wooden, brass-tipped ramrod. The lock is of flat, three sidenail pattern with dog-catch and flat reinforced or ring-neck cock. The pan lacks a bridle. The plate is engraved ahead of the cock, crown over GR and across the tail of the plate R. WOLLDRIDGE over 15. The top of the steel is squared-off. Wolldridge's name also appears as Wooldridge on some examples. *Overall length 62in, barrel 46in, calibre 0.78in.*

3. *A George I Musket of pre-Land Pattern, dated 1720*

It is stocked to 4in of the muzzle with the bayonet stud acting as a foresight. The barrel is held by three pins and an upper swivel screw. Three brass baluster-turned ramrod pipes retain a wooden ramrod which has a brass tip, and there is a pronounced swell in the fore-end at the tailpipe, visible either from top or bottom. The furniture is brass. The trigger guard is pinned at the front and held by two screws in the rear finial. The flat sideplate has three sidenails and the buttplate is similar to the Land Pattern, but with a longer, narrower finial extending 7in along a thick rounded comb. The lockplate is flat with a bevelled edge with a detachable iron pan without a bridle and a squared-off top to the steel. Note also the spear-head finial of the steel spring and the large hole in the jaw screw. Notice that the comb of the cock on this musket (and that shown in the previous plate) is straight and narrow with the top jaw slotted to slide along it. The lock measures $7\frac{9}{16}$in × $1\frac{1}{4}$in. Engraved ahead of the cock is a crown over GR and, across the tail of the plate, TOWER over 20. A growing resemblance to the familiar Land Pattern is clearly visible in this musket. *Overall length 62in, barrel length 46in, calibre 0.79in.*

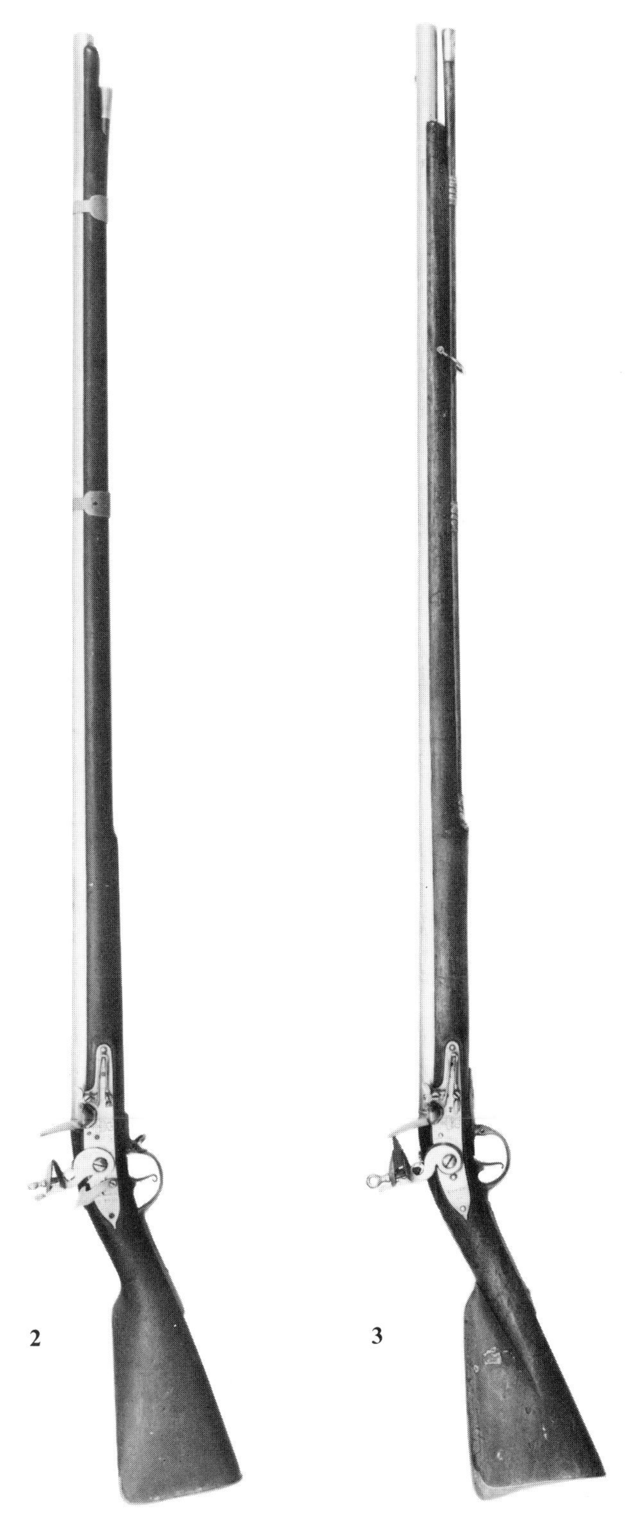

2

3

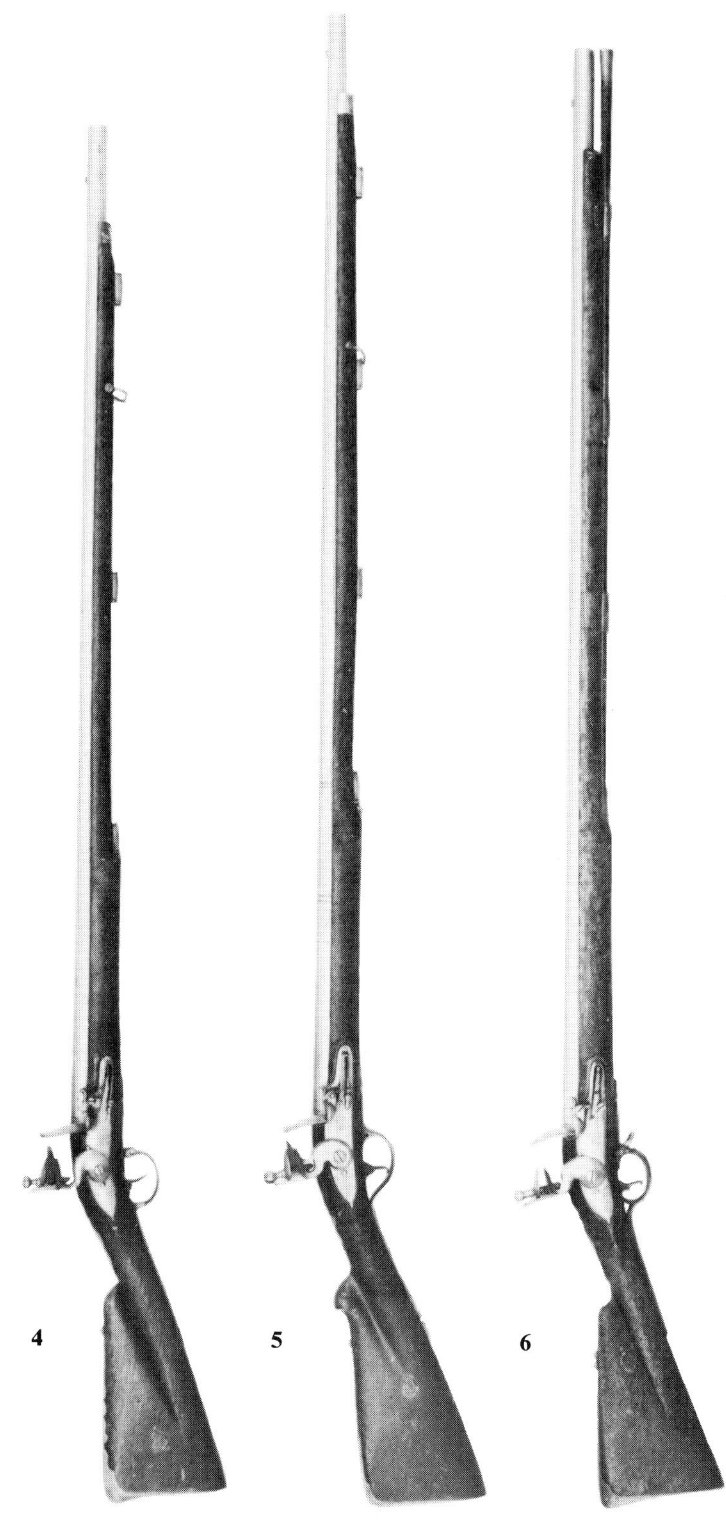
4
5
6

4. *A George I Musket of pre-Land Pattern by Richard Wolldridge, dated 1722*

Because of its dimensions this may be an early carbine, but it is shown here as a developmental example. It is stocked to 4in of the muzzle and there are three barrel-shaped brass ramrod pipes with the tailpipe having a long, tapering finial. The trigger guard and the sideplate are of iron, the guard being of Continental style with wavy finials in the French manner and grooves along the guard bow in the Prussian style. The rounded iron sideplate is of the Land Pattern, as is the wrist escutcheon or 'thumbpiece'. The iron buttplate has a long, very ornate tang. A thin brass fore-end cap has been fitted. The rounded lock and rounded swan-neck cock are of early Land Pattern, the lock being held by two sidenails. The lockplate has a rounded integral pan and the steel has a rounded tip. The steel spring has a trefoil finial and the plate has the familiar banana appearance. The jaws of the cock are nearly round as seen from above, with the comb being narrow and curled inward at its tip when viewed in profile. The familiar double border line engraving is present on the plate, cock and top jaw. Ahead of the cock is engraved a crown over GR and, across the tail of the plate, R. WOLLDRIDGE over 22. From about 1725 the date is engraved in full. *Overall length 58in, barrel length 42in, calibre 0.80in.*

5. *A George I Musket of pre-Land Pattern by Joseph Clarkson, c. 1726*

It is stocked to 3⅜in of the muzzle. The iron furniture includes four barrel-shaped ramrod pipes, one or two of whose cross-pins also retain the barrel, along with the upper swivel screw. The furniture is completely atypical when related to the Land Pattern and is very Continental in style. The barrel is turned 14in and 9½in from the breech and the barrel tang is pointed rather than squared-off. The barrel tang has a deep groove cut along it for a backsight. The knob formed at the comb of the butt is probably to afford a better grip when using the musket as a pike with the bayonet fixed. The lock is atypical, especially considering the development shown in Plate 4. The present lock is far more modern in design, having a bridle to the pan and a strongly constructed ring-neck cock with a straight comb and slotted top jaw: both the steel and steel spring screws enter from inside the lock and the finial of the steel spring is of the later tear-drop form. Engraved ahead of the cock is a large crown only and, across the tail, CLARKSON. The musket represents the result of private purchase by the colonel of a regiment rather than arming from Government Stores. It was purchased by General Sir Richard Kane after he became Colonel of the 9th Regiment in 1725, judging by the engraving on the escutcheon which reads KANE A No. 1. *Overall length 62in, barrel length 46in, calibre 0.78in.*

6. *A Land Pattern Musket also known as the 'Long Land Pattern', dated 1746*

This is a sealed pattern and represents a typical example of the Long Land musket as produced between 1740 and the early 1750s. It is stocked to 4½in of the muzzle, with the barrel retained by three pins and the upper swivel screw. Four barrel-shaped brass ramrod pipes retain the wooden, brass-tipped ramrod. The handrail, or stair-rail, butt is fully developed, and the furniture is entirely typical of the series. The lockplate measures 6⅞ × 1¼in and is rounded with a pronounced banana appearance towards the tail. The rounded integral pan has a bridle and the top of the steel is also rounded. The steel-spring has a trefoil finial, and the lockplate, cock body and top jaw have the typical engraved double border lines. Engraved ahead of the cock is a crown over GR and, across the tail, TIPPIN over 1746. *Overall length 62in, barrel length 46in, calibre 0.78in.*

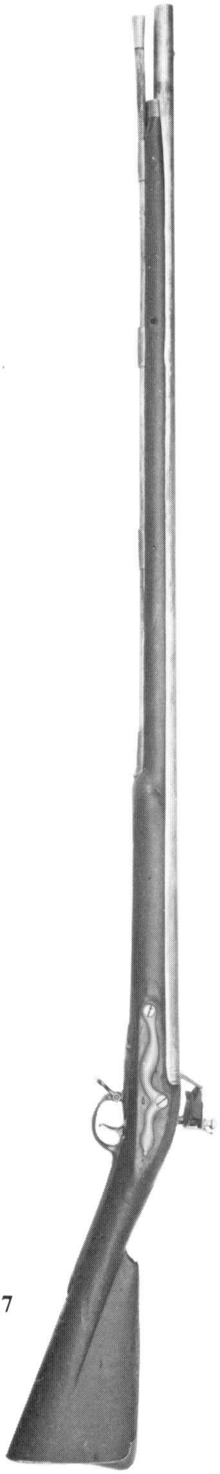

7. *A Land Pattern Musket set up at Dublin Castle, left side*

Entirely typical of the series in its major outline, with two exceptions shown here for reference, although not because they are typical of Dublin Castle arms. The thin brass fore-end cap is usually found on those muskets converted from wooden to steel ramrods, and the trigger guard with a solid rear section to the bow (as opposed to a forward curl inside) is typical of earlier arms made prior to about 1740.

8. *Early Land Pattern Lock*

Typical of the 'Brown Bess' muskets until the 1760s, only two major changes were made during the first thirty years of production. These were the introduction of the double-bridle design in which a bridle was added between the pan and the steel screw (in the years following 1740) and the gradual straightening of the lower edge of the lockplate at about the same period to eliminate the banana shape of the plate. The rounded swan-neck cock has a thin comb with its tip curled inwards and the top jaw moving in a tiny groove along the face of the comb. The jaw screw (top jaw screw, flint screw or cock screw) is slotted only and not pierced. The small stamp to the right of the Royal Cypher of a crowned Broad Arrow is standard for all Government locks, intended simply as a sign of Government ownership. Many minor variations will be found in the design of the crown and in the engraving.

7

9. *Long Land Pattern buttplate and breech construction*

Notice the three-step taper of the buttplate tang with the tiny ball at its tip, the formation of the hand-rail comb, the typical shape of the escutcheon (which is held in place by the single screw through the rear of the trigger guard), the carving of the stock round the squared-off barrel tang, the baluster-turning of the breech, the shape and engraving on top of the top jaw of the cock, shape of the pan and the steel, and the Government proof marks stamped on the breech of the barrel: all are typical features of Land Pattern muskets.

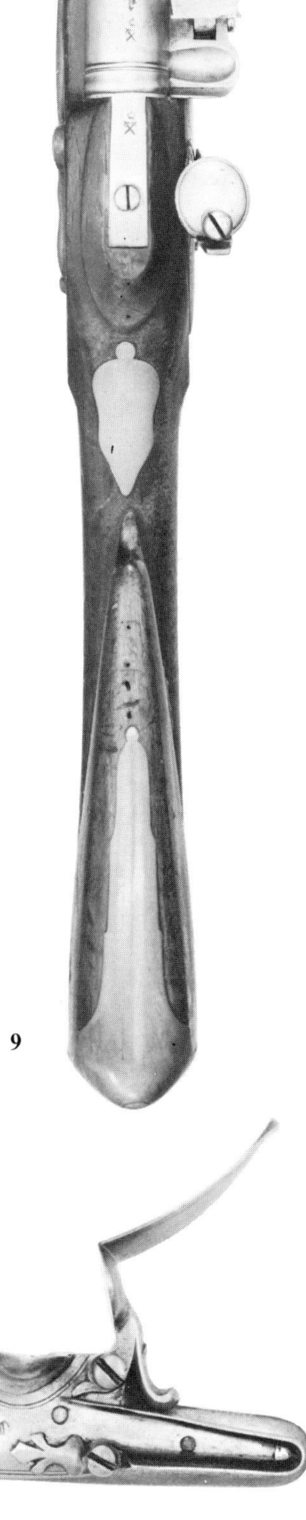

9

8

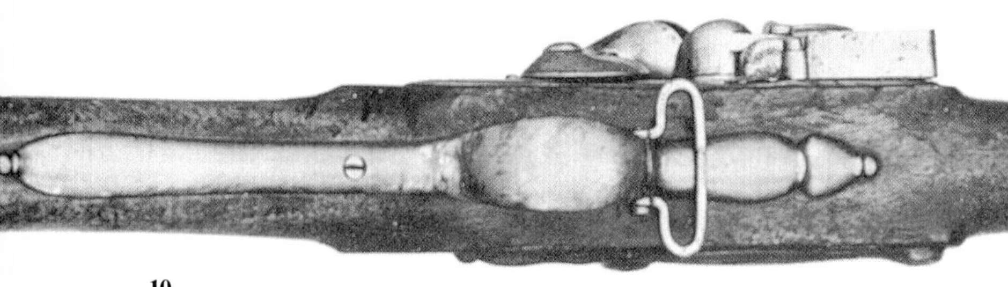

10

10, 11. *Land Pattern trigger guard and ramrod pipes*

This form was used on all Land Pattern muskets, whether Short or Long, wooden or steel ramrod, and whether or not they had a rounded or flat (Marine or Militia) sideplate. The overall contour is rounded and the front finial is secured by a cross-pin, as is the rear section of the rear finial. The screw at the rear of the bow holds the escutcheon in place. Notice also the rounded contour of the sideplate and the shape of the steel spring. The three upper ramrod pipes are of identical form and almost cylindrical. On those muskets converted for a steel ramrod the pipes retain the same form but are smaller in diameter, and the tail-pipe has a small flat spring either screwed or riveted inside it to hold the rod in place. The upper swivel on this example is missing. Note the shape of the ramrod head.

12, 13, 14. *Militia or Marine Musket, dated 1762*

It is stocked to $4\frac{3}{8}$in of the muzzle. The differences between this and the Land Pattern are found in the barrel length (42in rather than 46in) and the furniture. The escutcheon at the wrist is omitted and the tang of the buttplate is made wider and shorter—and is held with a screw rather than a cross-pin. The sideplate is of the same outline as the Land Pattern but it is flat in contour and flush with the surface of the wood. Note that the form of the butt does not vary. The use of the long trumpet-shaped upper ramrod pipe is not typical of the present pattern of arm, but was introduced for new-production steel ramrod Land Pattern muskets. Until 1768 the Long Land Pattern musket with its 46in barrel was the universal issue arm for infantry. During the Seven Years War the Militia or Marine musket was introduced as an economy measure and some Land Pattern muskets had their barrels cut down to 42in. What is now called the 'Short Land Pattern' with its 42in barrel did not become a regulation issue weapon for other than Dragoons, until 1768, when the shorter (42inch) barrel was approved for issue to the infantry. From 1775, at least on paper, the flat sideplate and shortened tang of the Marine or Militia Pattern became standard on all Short Land Pattern muskets, but the escutcheon at the wrist and the cross-pinning of the buttplate tang were reintroduced. *Overall length 58in, barrel length 42in, calibre 0.78in.*

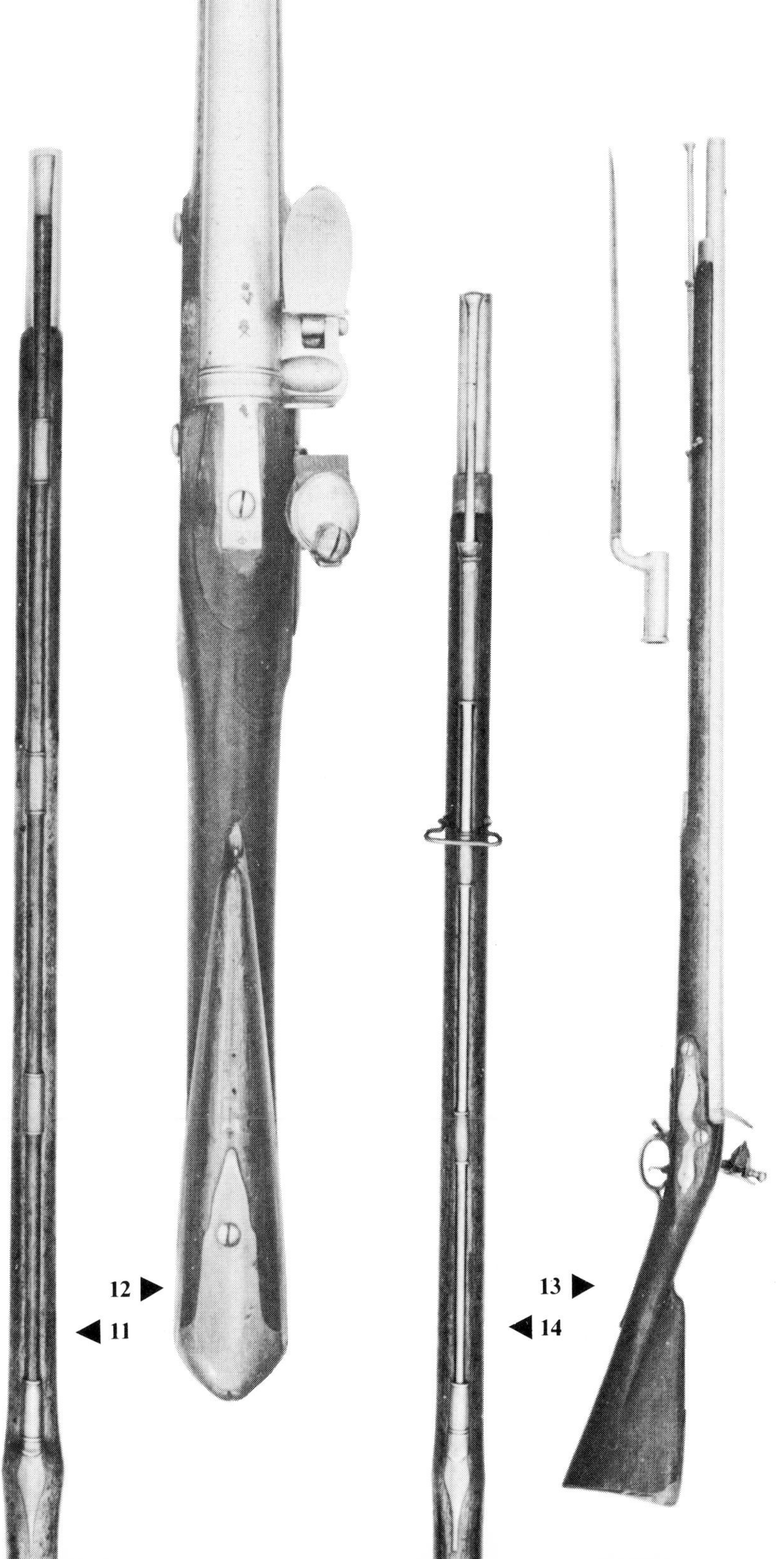
12 ▶
◀ 11
13 ▶
◀ 14

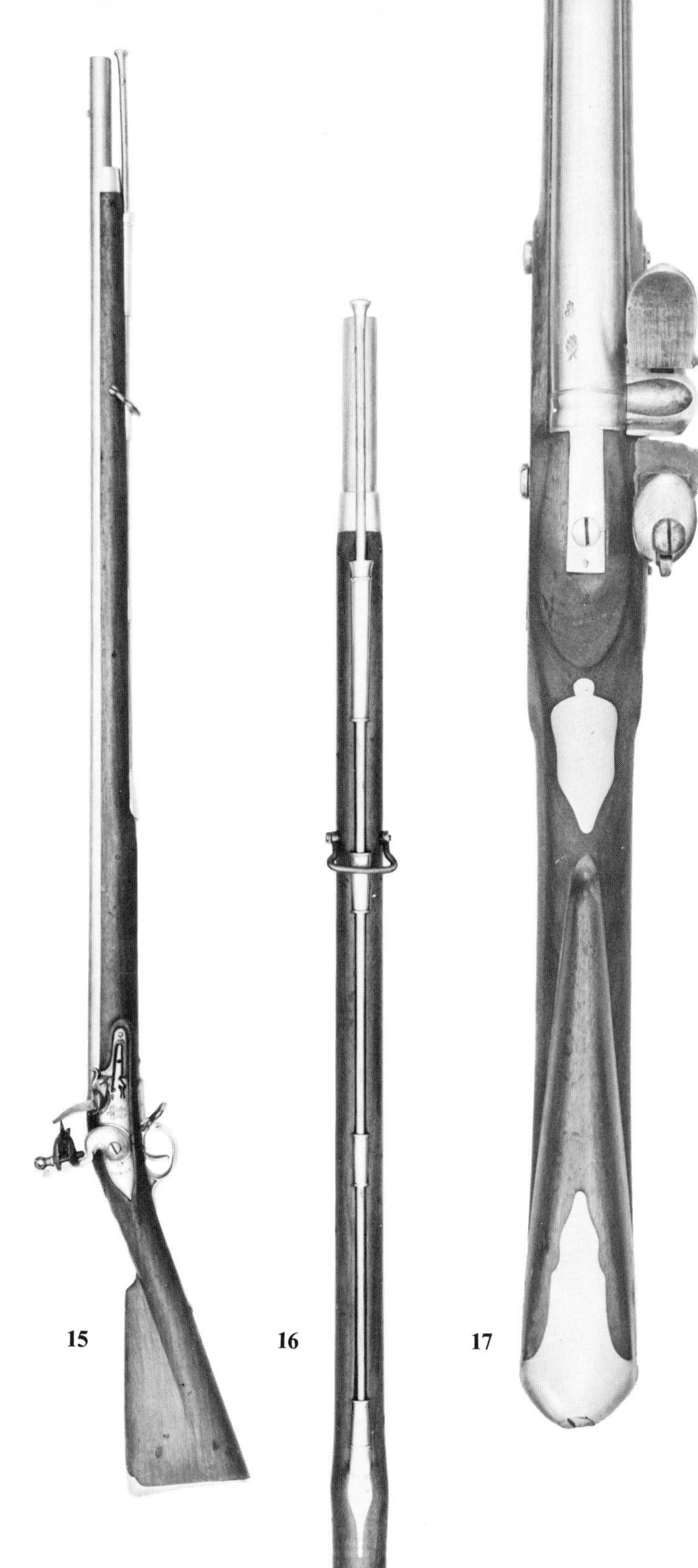

15

16

17

15. *Short Land Pattern Musket, c. 1785*

Stocked to 4in of the muzzle, the barrel is retained by three pins and the upper swivel screw. There are four brass ramrod pipes, the upper one long and trumpet-shaped, the second one coned or straight-tapered, the third one and the tailpipe barrel-shaped. The sideplate is flat as shown in Plate 13 and the trigger guard is of the design shown in Plate 10. The Short Land Pattern musket had been in use at least since the early 1740s as the carbine for dragoons, made with a wooden brass-tipped ramrod (Plate 43). It was officially sanctioned as an infantry musket by the Royal Warrant of 11th June 1768 and between that date and about 1776 could have been produced with either a rounded Land Pattern sideplate or the cheaper flat Militia or Marine sideplate which became standard for this pattern in 1775. *Overall length 58⅛in, barrel length 42in, calibre 0.78in.*

16, 17. *Short Land Pattern Musket furniture*

The shape of the butt remains unchanged throughout the several modifications from Long Land to Militia or Marine, to Short Land Pattern and—finally—to India Pattern. Compare with Plate 12 and note that the form of the buttplate tang is retained, but cross-pin fastening is reintroduced and the escutcheon of standard Land Pattern also reappears. Notice also that the position of the stamping of proof marks has been moved to the left side of the breech by *c.* 1785. With the exception of the second ramrod pipe, which on early examples will be of the same shape as the third pipe (barrel-shaped), there is no change from the style of pipes introduced for Land Pattern muskets with steel ramrods. It is not until the India Pattern was accepted for service that any significant change took place in form and arrangement of ramrod pipes. How many Short Land Pattern muskets may have been made with the trumpet-shaped second pipe introduced by John Pratt in 1777 is not known. Some muskets are found with this trumpet-shaped pipe in the third position as well. It appears to be one of those minor variations in assembly to which no particular significance may be attached, save that the presence of such a pipe will date a piece as post-1777.

18. *Land Pattern Lock from the 1760s*

To date any of the several structural changes which were made in the Land Pattern lock after the close of the Seven Years War is virtually impossible, since in 1764 it was decreed that no further locks were to be dated. There is also reason to believe that earlier locks sent in for repair may have been re-engraved without the date. Comparing with Plate 8 it is plain that a number of changes have been made in this post-1764 lock. The pan has a bridle (and will have had since about 1740) and the bottom edge of the lockplate is straighter. The steel spring now has a teardrop finial rather than one of trefoil pattern and the spring itself is shorter, no longer covering the forward sidenail. The sear spring screw is now externally visible. The body of the cock has not undergone any significant change although there is a subtle difference in contour. The comb, top jaw and jaw screw have changed completely, the latter now being pierced as well as slotted. The top jaw, slotted to slide on the narrow comb, is now more oval in form (see Plates 10 and 17) and is no longer engraved. The comb itself is now wider in profile and narrow from behind with the tip having a pronounced inward curl in profile. TOWER is engraved across the tail without the maker's name or the date.

19. *The Duke of Richmond's Musket, Rammer-to-the-Butt Pattern, c. 1792*

It is fitted with a break-off patent breech of Henry Nock's design and is stocked to $3\frac{3}{16}$in of the muzzle. The barrel is retained by four thick rounded-end pins and the upper swivel screw. The upper section of the fore-end is reduced in thickness and the ramrod channel begins $19\frac{1}{4}$in from the rounded brass fore-end cap. There is one large trumpet-shaped ramrod pipe and a tailpipe which is also trumpet-mouthed. The heavy iron ramrod is threaded in the face of the head for a jag. The rod extends downward to rest against the inside of the buttplate. There is no sideplate, merely a circular cup for the one sidenail which secures the Nock screwless lock. The trigger guard is rounded and held in front by a large screw, which also acts as the stud for fastening a lock cover, and at the rear by a single cross-pin. The buttplate is of the pattern later adopted for the New Land Pattern series (Plate 32). Nock's screwless lock is fitted with a flashguard as found on Harcourt's Carbine, and is engraved with a large crown over GR. The lockplate, which measures $6\frac{1}{4}$in $\times$ $1\frac{1}{4}$in, has a point at the tail and is engraved H. NOCK. This complete departure from previous patterns was produced in limited

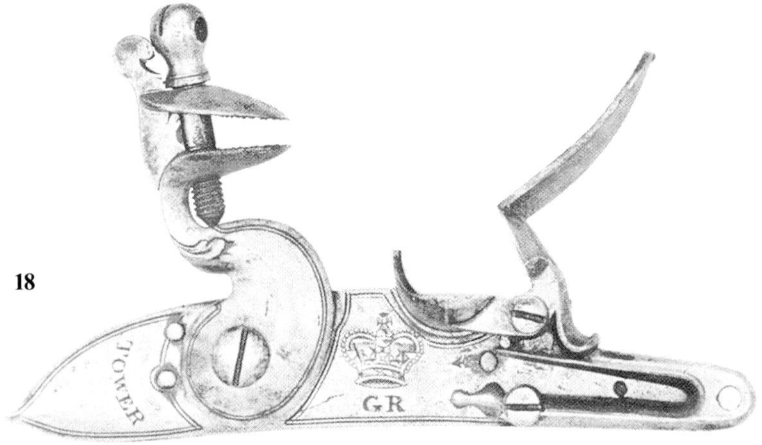

18

quantities during 1791-2. The records are not clear on how many were made or to whom they were issued. It is certain, however, that they were intended as an issue musket and not merely as an experimental arm, hence their inclusion here. The difficulties of manufacture caused them to be dropped in favour of the more conventional but still very superior Rammer-to-the-Muzzle Pattern (Plate 20) by the end of 1793. It is highly probable, had the French Revolutionary Wars not broken out at the critical period of initial manufacture, that one of these Nock muskets would have become the standard issue weapon of the British infantry. *Overall length 58in, barrel length 42in, calibre 0.76in.*

20. *The Duke of Richmond's Musket, Rammer-to-the-Muzzle Pattern, 1794*

This musket is also fitted with a break-off patent breech of Nock's design. It is stocked to $3\frac{3}{16}$in of the muzzle and the barrel is retained by three thick, rounded-end pins and the upper swivel screw. There are four brass pipes of wide diameter to retain the heavy iron ramrod. The upper pipe is long and trumpet-shaped while the second and third pipes are of the straight-taper type; the tailpipe has a flat spring riveted inside to retain the ramrod. The barrel is browned and the reduction of its bore from 0.76in to 0.73in was one of the important features of the new arm, as it reduced windage and thereby increased potential accuracy. The heavy rod was no doubt intended to assist loading when fouling accumulated more quickly in the tighter bore. The brass furniture is, except for the ramrod pipes, the same as that for the Rammer-to-the-Butt Pattern: there is no sideplate, and the buttplate is the Duke of Richmond's design as later adopted for the New Land Pattern. The trigger guard varies slightly from the other pattern

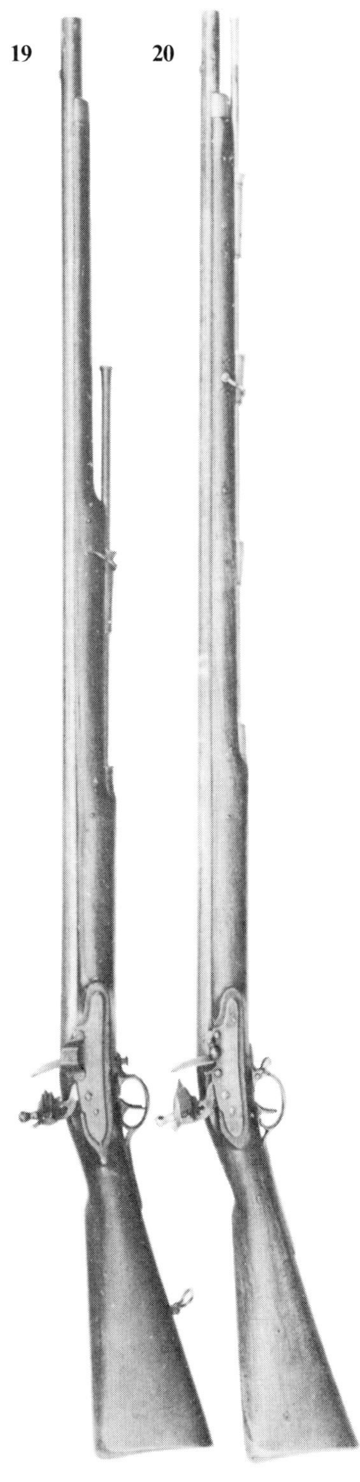
19 20

in having its rear finial secured by one screw and the cross-pin as on Land Pattern arms. The off-setting of the trigger in its box-housing, used on the Rammer-to-the-Butt Pattern, is retained. The Nock screwless lock of this example is not fitted with the flash guard and the tail of the lockplate is rounded rather than pointed. The plate measures $5\frac{5}{8} \times 1\frac{1}{8}$in (making it the middle size of Nock lock) and came to be standard on muskets and carbines, the larger size being dropped. The records show that 3,350 of this pattern were delivered by Henry Nock during the years 1794–7, but it is not known to which regiments they were issued. Within the conventional limitations of the age, this musket represents the highest degree of perfection attained by the British military flintlock and force of circumstances seems to have been the factor which prevented its general adoption by the British Army. *Overall length 58in, barrel length 42in, calibre 0.73in.*

21, 22. *The India Pattern Musket with swan-neck cock, c. 1800*

It is stocked to $4\frac{1}{8}$in of the muzzle, the barrel being retained by three pins and the upper swivel screw. There are three brass ramrod pipes, a rounded sideplate and a trigger guard of a simpler pattern than the Land series. This musket retains the general outline of the Short Land musket but is shorter and not so well finished. They are by no means of poor quality, despite the introduction of cheaper, simpler furniture. The stock carving of the Land Pattern and the form of the lock and butt are all retained—features which disappear on the New Land series. This pattern was first taken into Government service as an emergency measure in 1793 and was later accepted as a pattern for Government muskets in 1797. *Overall length $55\frac{1}{4}$in, barrel length 39in, calibre 0.75in.*

23. *The India Pattern Musket with ring-neck cock, c. 1810*

It is stocked to $4\frac{1}{8}$in of the muzzle, with the barrel retained by the usual three pins and the upper swivel screw. The ramrod is technically incorrect for the India Pattern—being of the swelled-throat type used on the New Land series—but it is quite possible that the rod would have been fitted under the stress of wartime assembly. The trigger is also of the later form used on New Land Pattern arms and late India Pattern muskets. The shape of the cock is the single major change made in the design of the India Pattern musket during its entire production period for Government use. The change was approved late in 1809 on grounds of economy and added strength. Note the heavier appearance of this musket as compared to that in Plate 21. *Overall length 55in, barrel length 39in, calibre 0.75in.*

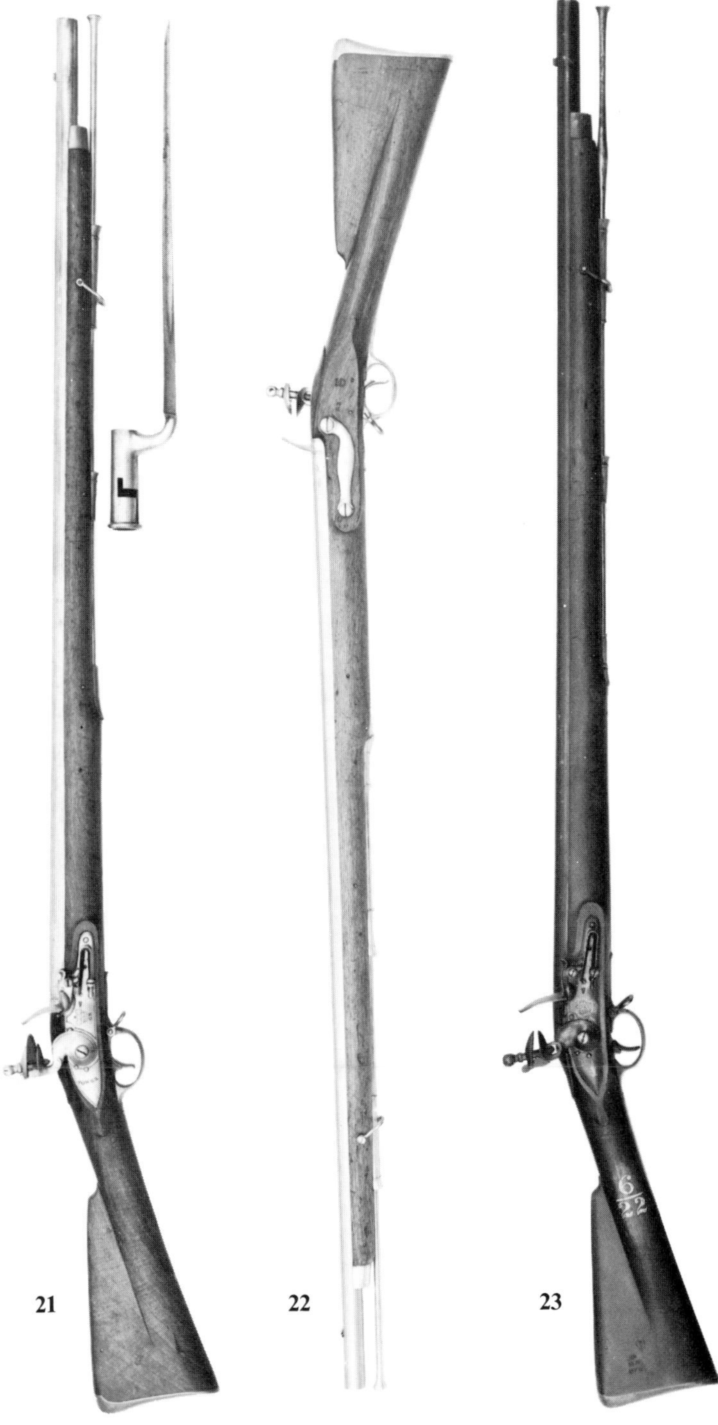

21 22 23

24, 25, 26. *India Pattern furniture*

It is in this respect that the India Pattern differs most from earlier types (compare with Plate 17)—although the form of the butt is unchanged, even to the carving round the barrel tang and lock and sideplate. The sideplate is now copied from the French Model 1777, rounded in contour but having no extension to the rear of the rear sidenail. The buttplate has a narrower tang of the same length as the Short Land Pattern but with a more rounded tip. The trigger guard varies considerably in several particulars: it is far less round in contour than the Land Pattern, the forward finial has no real shape aside from its outline, the forward curl of the rear part of the bow is replaced with a solid section and the rear finial is no longer cross-pinned but simply held by two screws. The escutcheon is eliminated. The ramrod pipes have been reduced by one in number and relocated. The upper, trumpet-shaped, pipe is moved back from the fore-end cap which, with the reduction of length in the barrel, enables the second pipe to be placed where the third pipe was formerly located. The second pipe is of the pattern introduced in 1777 by John Pratt, the London gunmaker. It is merely a shorter trumpet-pipe and obviously an improvement in aiding the rapid return of the rod during loading. The tailpipe remains of the Land Pattern, though often the contours are not so finely cast or finished. Note the position of the upper sling swivel, almost at the mid-point of the upper pipe.

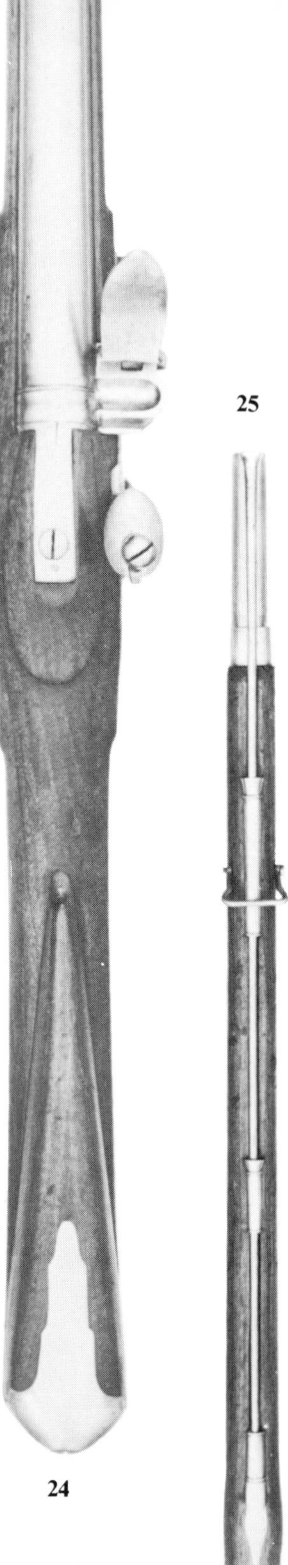

25

24

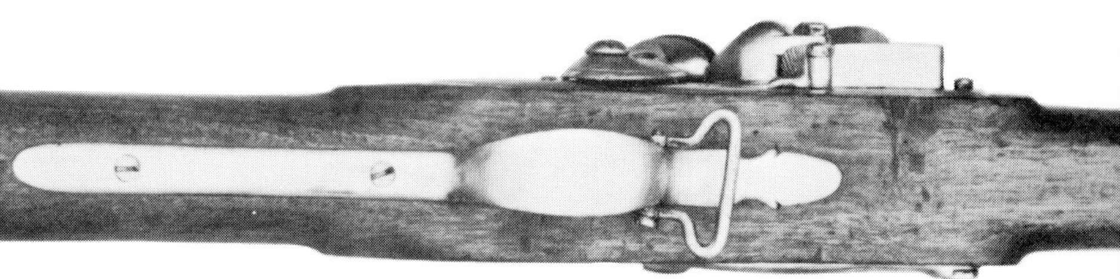

26

27. *Late Land Pattern and pre-1809 India Pattern lock*

This is the final development of the British military Government-issue flintlock in the eighteenth century. In the form shown it probably dates from *c.* 1785. Variations in finish and engraving occur to somewhat alter its appearance, especially during wartime production. Comparing it with Plate 18, it will be seen that the primary change occurs in the form of the comb of the cock, which is now straight and narrow as seen from the rear and very much straighter when seen in profile. The curl at the tip, more pronounced in some examples, is outward rather than inward. The engraving at the throat and the file cuts on the lower inside of the comb are omitted. Whether the shape of the curve on the back of the pan-cover portion of the steel may be considered a subject of deliberate change is questionable. Later examples do tend to have a more even curve compared to the slight upward curve at the hinge section of earlier specimens. The teardrop form of the steel spring finial is simpler.

28. *India Pattern ring-neck cock lock, of the pattern used from 1810*

Basically identical to the late Land Pattern lock, which was also used on India Pattern Muskets until 1810 (Plate 27), except for the introduction of the ring-neck, double-throated, or reinforced cock. Locks of this design tend to be the worst finished and poorest quality of any issue flintlock of this period, since they were produced entirely under wartime conditions. Engraving is replaced by stamping on the great majority of India Pattern locks of either pattern. One wonders if the slight forward tilt of the pan was a deliberate—if half-hearted—attempt to copy the tilted pans of the French Model 1777 and Year IX locks, or simply bad filing!

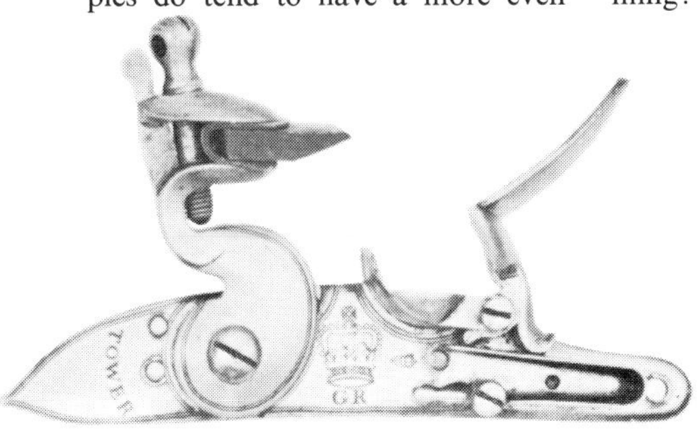

27

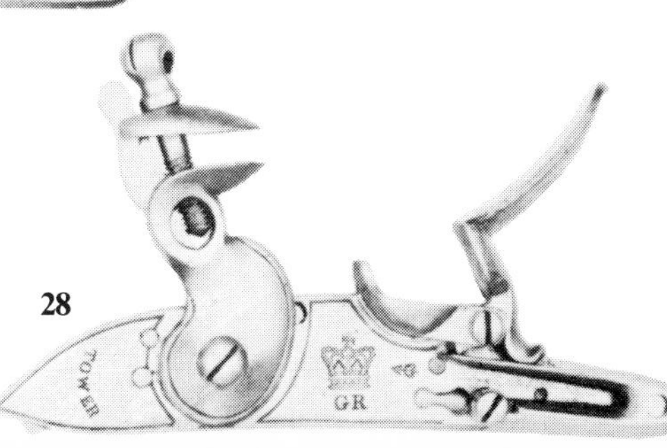

28

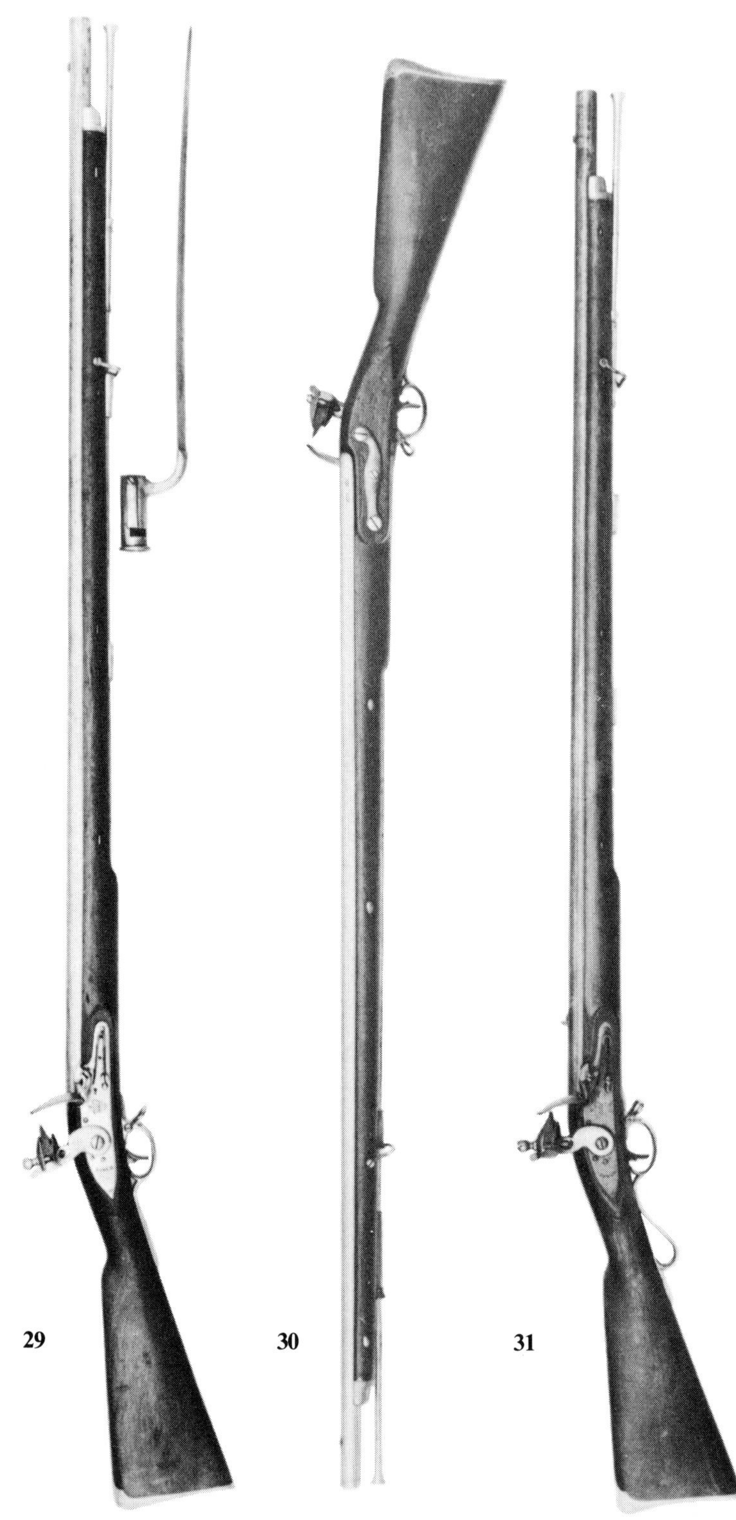

29

30

31

29, 30. *The New Land Pattern Musket, c. 1802*

This is stocked to 4in of the muzzle, and the barrel is retained by three flat keys or slides and the upper swivel screw. The brass furniture is of a new design, including three ramrod pipes but omitting a tailpipe. The ramrod is now made with a slightly concave button-head and a swell at the throat with a corresponding widening of the ramrod channel to help retain it in position. The lines of the stock are completely changed, modernised and simplified. The hand-rail butt and the carving about the barrel tang, lock and sideplate are all discarded, and the sideplate is no longer inletted into the wood but held in position by the two sidenails and a woodscrew through its centre. Intended to follow directly in the footsteps of the much improved Duke of Richmond's muskets, but on a more sensible production-line basis, the New Land series was introduced shortly after the signing of the Peace of Amiens in 1802 when the possibility seemed high of a return to peacetime levels of production and inspection. Unfortunately peace lasted just long enough for this first of the series to get into production and for its companion arm, the Light Infantry Musket, to be approved in pattern. Except for the period between the spring of 1802 and May 1803, and some months in 1814 before the Hundred Days, the New Land series was not produced during the pre-1815 period. *Overall length 58½in, barrel length 42in, calibre 0.75in.*

31. *A New Land Pattern Light Infantry Musket, c. 1810*

The browned barrel is retained by three flat keys and the upper swivel screw. Although the bayonet stud is still the only foresight, a notched block backsight is brazed to the barrel 3 in from the breech. Although the design for this musket was approved in mid-1803 for use by the 52nd and other Light Infantry Regiments, it was not until the middle of 1810 that any were produced. The earliest of these used the standard size of lock with a 6½in lockplate, but this was subsequently replaced with a smaller 6in lock of identical pattern. Some 20,000 New Land Pattern Light Infantry Muskets were ordered to be set up during 1811 and this may be the only production of this pattern during the pre-1815 period.

33

32

32, 33, 34. *New Land Pattern furniture*

The contrast between this and earlier types is striking for the simplicity of style. The buttplate has a plain rounded tang, the escutcheon at the wrist has been eliminated and there is no carving round the barrel tang. This tang is now parallel-sided and rounded at the end. The comb of the butt is lower and wider. The side-plate is of the India Pattern with a rounded contour, but is held in the centre by a woodscrew and not in-letted into the wood. The rounded trigger guard is, like the buttplate, of the Duke of Richmond's pattern, having a short rear finial held by a single screw. The trigger is of a new, stronger, design and swings in a box trigger plate housing. Note the bevel on the lower limb of the steel spring and that the lockplate is just proud of the stock surface. The upper ram-rod pipe remains the standard trum-pet pattern, while the remaining two return to the earlier Land Pattern. The second pipe is a straight-tapered type and the third pipe is barrel-shaped. The omission of the tailpipe is a holdover from the Duke of Richmond arms and the 1796 Car-bines. Note that the fore-end cap has a lip on its rear under edge to help retain the ramrod.

34

35. *The New Land Pattern lock*

The quality of both design and finish stand out even on cursory examination of this lock. It is almost entirely of new design. The lockplate is now completely flat with a uniform bevelled edge and the pan is raised or 'semi-waterproof' and the tail of the steel is of a simpler, stronger design. The steel spring has a plain, flattened bulbous finial, and both limbs of the spring are bevelled. The cock is also flat with a bevelled edge and of ring-neck design. The jaw screw is both pierced and slotted. The comb is wider in profile, hence stronger, and the jaws are of heavier construction. The only signs of ornament—which are completely absent on some examples—are the leaf sprig at the tail of the plate and the lines on the pan bridle. Inside, a new type of mainspring is used, with a flat tip on the upper limb engaging in a notch on the pan reinforce, doing away with the older and more expensive method of screw fastening. The crown over GR and TOWER are now neatly stamped and several variations in the size of the Royal Cypher have been noted.

35

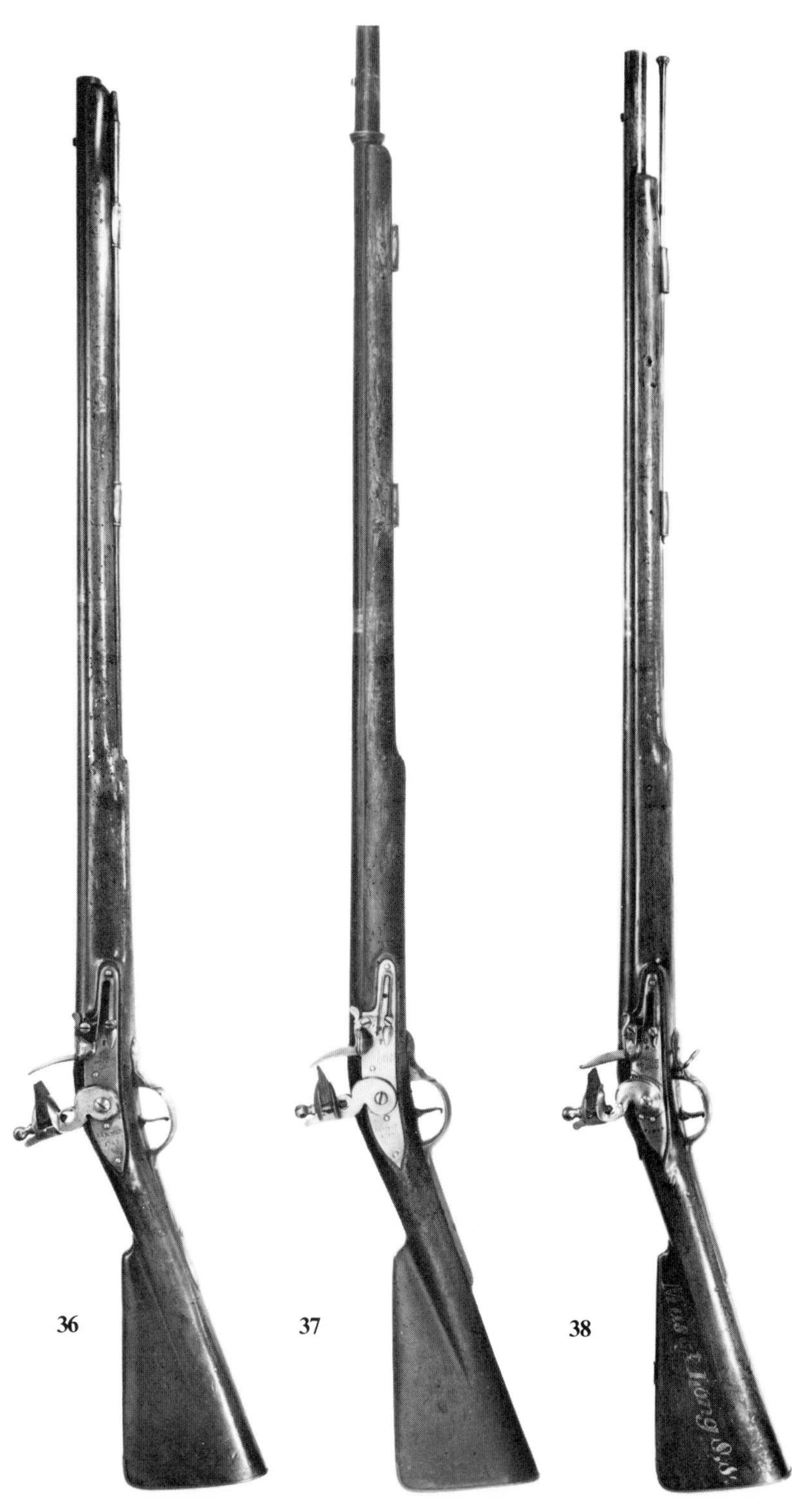

36

37

38

36. *A Sea Service Musket by James Farmer, dated 1745*

Stocked to the muzzle with no provision for a bayonet or for sling swivels, the barrel is retained by three pins. Two barrel-shaped brass pipes retain the wooden brass-tipped ramrod (tip missing). The barrel is blacked making this a 'Black Sea Service Musket' as opposed to those with ordinary bright-finished barrels. The flat lock is retained by three sidenails, and the lockplate measures $7\frac{5}{8}$in × $1\frac{1}{4}$in. The flat brass sideplate is flush with the wood. The Sea Service Musket was made in this general pattern until *c.* 1760, when the conventional rounded Land Pattern lock came into general use. On those weapons which can be substantiated as Sea Service arms the barrel length varies between 36in and 38in. With the exception of the sideplate, the pattern of the furniture remained constant until the end of the flintlock period. Steel ramrods gradually replaced wooden ones during the 1780s. Close examination shows this arm to be as well made and finished as the Land Pattern of the same date. *Overall length $51\frac{7}{8}$in, barrel length $36\frac{1}{4}$in, calibre 0.78in.*

37. *Sea Service Grenade-launching Musket by James Farmer, dated 1743*

This example is stocked to $4\frac{3}{8}$in of the muzzle, the ring support for the grenade cup being 4in from the muzzle. The barrel is retained by three pins and is blacked rather than bright. The brass-tipped wooden ramrod is missing. There are no sling swivels; it was not until 1752 that the Admiralty decreed that in future all Sea Service Muskets should be fitted with them and also made to accept a bayonet. The thickness of the barrel of this musket, and of that in Plate 36 indicates that these were deliberately forged barrels of an intermediate length and not cut-down Land Pattern barrels. *Overall length 53in, barrel length $37\frac{1}{8}$in, calibre 0.78in.*

38. *A Sea Service Musket, c. 1780*

It is stocked to $4\frac{1}{2}$in of the muzzle, the barrel being retained by the usual three pins and the upper swivel screw, missing on this example. Two barrel-shaped brass pipes retain the steel ramrod, the lower pipe having a small spring riveted inside to hold the rod and prevent it rattling. The overall lines of the Sea Service Musket have not altered from the 1740s although the front of the guard bow has now been pierced and fitted with a sling swivel and the fore-end has been shortened to allow the use of the regulation socket bayonet. A standard Land Pattern rounded lock is used and the sideplate is of the post-1775 Land Pattern (or Marine & Militia type). None of these Sea Service Muskets have a trigger plate, the trigger working on a plain slot in the wood, and the barrel tang screw fastens into a square iron plate let into the wood just ahead of the trigger. As well as the weapons in Plates 36 and 37, this is a Black Sea Service arm. The identical musket with a bright barrel was known as the 'Bright Sea Service' Musket, and the two types were issued as required by various ships, in approximately equal numbers. *Overall length 53in, barrel length 37in, calibre 0.78in.*

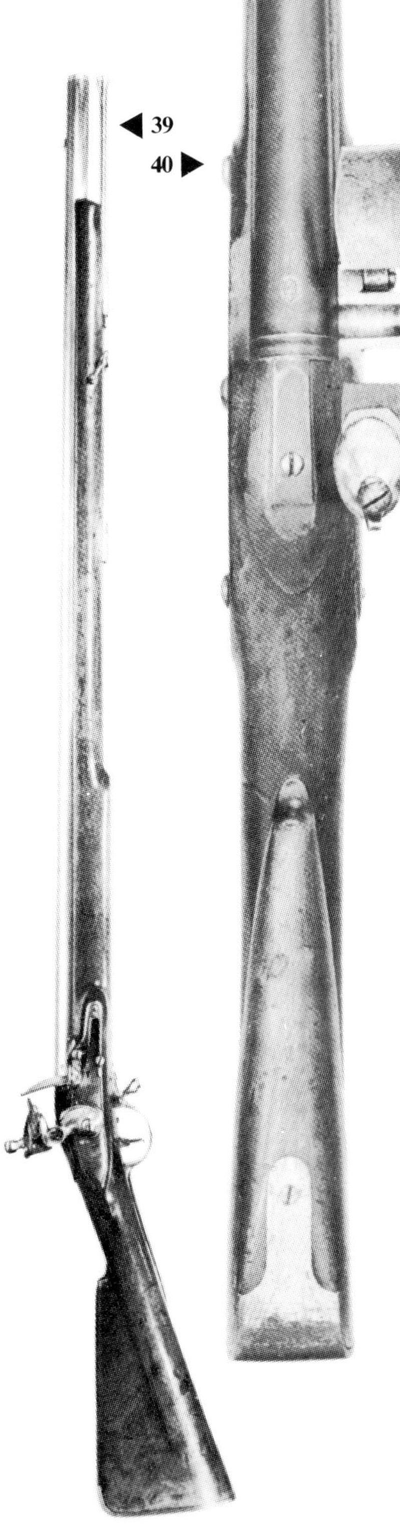

39. *An India Pattern Sea Service Musket, c. 1810*

This is stocked to $4\frac{3}{8}$in of the muzzle and the barrel is retained by the standard three pins and the upper swivel screw. Two barrel-shaped brass pipes identical in pattern to those in Plate 38 retain the steel ramrod, but in this case the upper rather than the lower pipe has the rod-retaining spring—probably not a significant variation. The India Pattern Sea Service Musket was made with swan-neck as well as ring-neck cock, under the same conditions as the army model. The sideplate of the India Pattern Sea Service Musket is the flat Land Pattern or Marine & Militia style—whichever term one chooses. Note that the bore size of the Sea Service Musket, regardless of period of manufacture, is 0.78in rather than 0.76in or 0.75in. This difference is measurable with a calibre gauge and applies for the entire series. *Overall length 53in, barrel length 37in, calibre 0.78in.*

40, 41. *Sea Service Musket furniture*

The top breech view of an early example shows the typical form of the buttplate used throughout the entire period and also the form of the breech carving and shape of the barrel tang. There was no escutcheon at the wrist. The positioning of the three sidenails, the wide rounded comb of the butt, and the construction of the steel and pan are all typical of the flat-lock pattern used until about 1760. The buttplate is of heavy gauge brass. The trigger guard, also from an early flat-lock example, is completely typical of the design used until the end of the flintlock period, except that from 1752 the front of the bow carried a sling swivel. It must be emphasized that the workmanship and finish evident in the several Sea Service Muskets examined was not inferior to that of the Land Pattern arms. Issue Sea Service Muskets should not be considered either as inferior or made-up arms.

41

42. *A Sea Service Musket flat lock of the style used until c. 1760*

This pattern is essentially a continuation of the earlier standard musket lock used during the reigns of William III and Queen Anne. The simplicity and strength of both the size and design must have recommended it for the rough usage of naval conditions. Compared with the contemporary Land Pattern lock (Plate 8) it substituted strength for weakness in structure and plain finish for elegance of execution. Note the plain spear-head pattern of the steel spring finial and that the jaw screw is both pierced and slotted.

42

Carbines

The term 'carbine' as applied to British military longarms defies any fixed definition. If length is accepted to be the criterion we find a variety of weapons with barrels of various lengths between 16 and 42inches all considered and described as carbines. The other possibility—bore size or calibre—also falls by the wayside when it is noted that until the middle of the century the normal 'musket bore' was standard and that it was subsequently resorted to on a number of carbines later in the century. 'Carbine bore' or 17 bore (0.65inch calibre) was an accepted term but unfortunately weapons described as carbines were made in other sizes as well. Ultimately, the description of a certain weapon, regardless of its bore size and dimensions, must be taken as written without an attempt to define it in structural parlance. The answer was and is, of course, that the term was applied according to what sort of troops were to use the arm and not to the arm itself.

The number and variety of carbines which appeared during the period under consideration came about as the result of several completely unrelated circumstances. The first of these was the latitude given to the colonels of mounted units, both cavalry and dragoons, in the arming and equipping of their men. Owing to the size of regiments of foot, and their total numbers, a far greater degree of regularity was obtained in their equipment than in the much smaller mounted units. The special purposes for which some of these units were designed was another explanation for the differences in the weapons with which they were equipped; the distinction between 'light' and 'heavy' cavalry and dragoons being a typical instance. Perhaps the most basic reason for the proliferation of the carbine after the middle of the century was the increasing emphasis placed upon the mobility of troop movements, and upon the increasing value of firepower in the rapidly developing field of linear tactics.

Before 1770 most of the carbines used in the British service would come under the structural heading of 'short muskets' since most of them had barrels of three feet and longer, up to 42inches. Indeed the standard dragoon carbine before 1770 was no more than a Short Land Pattern musket with a wooden ramrod. It was in the pre-1770 period that most confusion lay in the defining of fusils and carbines. Fusils are generally considered as light muskets of carbine bore, fitted for socket bayonets and carried by subalterns and sergeants of certain regiments at particular dates. However, during the period 1756–75 a series of 'Carbines' was introduced—some with and some without bayonets and all of carbine bore (0.65inch calibre); it thereby becomes extremely difficult in some instances, when confronted with an individual weapon, to determine into which of the two categories it should be placed.

In order at least to clarify the problem itself, if not the solution of it, a listing is given of the troops to whom carbines and fusils were to be issued, and the first appearance of reference to this fact in documentary sources:

1. Cadet's Carbine (artillery cadets, Woolwich)	*c.* 1744
2. Light Dragoon Carbine, with ring and bayonet	1756 (Plate 35)
3. Artillery and Highlanders' Carbine with bayonet	1757 (Plate 36)
4. Carbine for Horse, without bayonet	1757 (Plate 37)
5. Light Infantry Carbine, with bayonet	1758 (Plate 38)

This first grouping comprises the older carbines most resembling fusils and short muskets. Then, in the 'inter-war' period between the conclusion of the Seven Years' War in 1763 and the opening of the American War in 1775, we have the next group which includes examples of both the old and the new thought in this class of weapon:

6. Royal Horse Guards or 'Blues' Carbine	1755 (Plate 39)
7. Grenadier Sergeants' 'Fusil or Carbine' with bayonet	1769
8. Artillery Carbine	1770 (Plate 40)
9. Officers of Fusilier Regiments fusil	1770
10. Heavy Dragoon Carbine with ring and bayonet	1770 (Plate 41)
11. General Eliott's Light Dragoon Carbine	1760 (Plates 42–5)

The last of these, Eliott's, was the first of the 'new idea' in carbines no doubt brought about as the result of trials by Major General John La Fausille during 1769, which proved that the length of barrel had little effect upon accuracy. It was therefore practicable to arm units who had no need for the bayonet with weapons having much shorter barrels. The retention of the long-barrelled carbines for sergeants, artillery and light infantry was purely in order to utilize the weapon in the same manner as the musket, i.e. as a pike when fitted with the bayonet.

In order to complete the numerical listing of regulation carbines down to 1815, the following weapons must be included:

12. Burgoyne's blunderbuss Carbine	1781 (Plate 46)
13. Harcourt's Heavy Dragoon Carbine (Nock's screwless lock)	1793 (Plate 47)
14. Heavy Dragoon Pattern 1796 (Government standard lock)	1798 (Plates 48, 49)
15. India Pattern Sergeants' Carbine	1807 (Plate 51)
16. Paget's Cavalry Carbine	1812 (Plate 52)
17. India Pattern Artillery Carbine	*c.* 1813

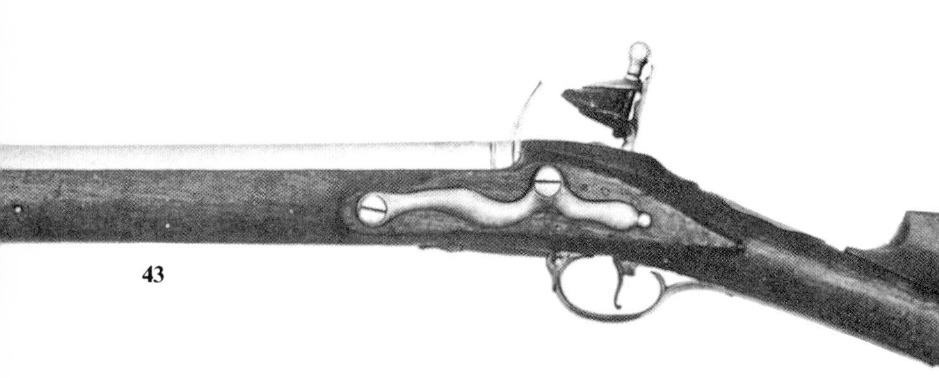

43

43, 44. *A Short Land Musket with Wooden Ramrod, for Dragoons, dated 1747*

This musket is listed as a dragoon carbine to emphasize that not until 1768 was the shorter 42in barrelled musket officially accepted as a weapon for the line infantry. It is stocked to 4in of the muzzle and there is no fore-end cap. The brass-tipped wooden ramrod is held by four cylindrical brass pipes of standard Land Pattern and the barrel is retained by three pins and the upper swivel screw. Notice the high comb of the butt and the shape of the carving round the barrel tang. The sideplate is the standard Land Pattern with a rounded contour. Comparison with plates 6–11 should clearly establish the salient features of the Land Pattern series. One exception must be noted: the carving of the stock round the lock and sideplate is simplified on this carbine and is typical of the style used from the early 1740s. An example of the earlier style is illustrated in Plate 45. This pattern of carbine, the Short Land Musket with Wooden Rod, was issued to dragoons until superseded (on paper) by a regular Dragoon Carbine in 1770 (Plate 57). *Overall length 58in, barrel length 42in, calibre 0.78in.*

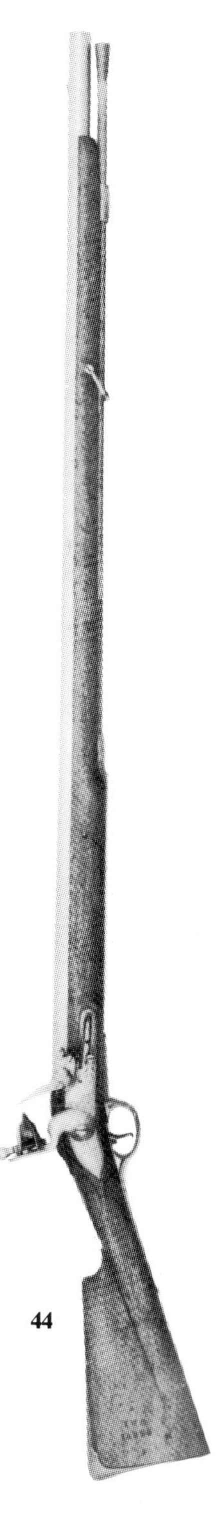

44

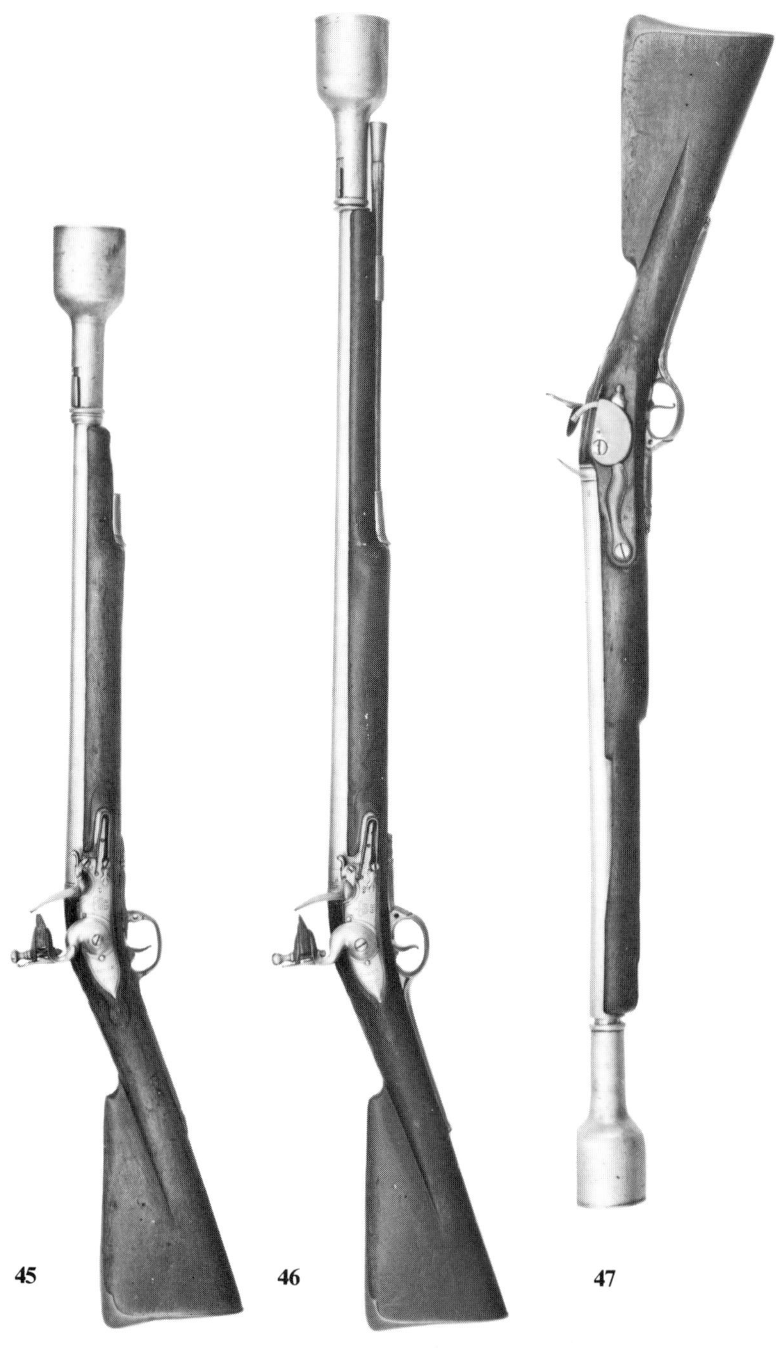

45 46 47

45. *A Grenade-launching Carbine dated 1728*

Aside from the interest in this weapon as a grenade launcher, this is also one of the earliest known Land Pattern arms which conforms to the standard pattern for this series, with the exception of the trigger guard finials. The carbine itself is obviously made from a cut down musket. The lock is shown in Plate 8. The grenade cup fits onto the barrel in the same manner as the socket bayonet and is reinforced by a ring or collar round the barrel. The muzzle reaches to the base of the cup, which measures 3in in depth by 2½in in diameter. A quadrant-type sight for judging elevation (see Plate 47) is fitted to the sideplate: as the arm is tilted upwards from horizontal an arm pivoted beneath a brass casing rises. Note the elaborate carving round the lockplate, a style continued into the early 1740s. *Overall length (with cup) 40¼in, barrel length 21⅜in, calibre 0.78in.*

46. *A Grenade-launching Carbine dated 1740*

Similar in design to the early carbine shown in Plate 45, this example is also made from a cut down Land Pattern Musket but is longer, conforms in every particular to the Land Pattern series for the date, and is engraved on top of the barrel, ROY[L] ARTILLERY. The number 13 is engraved on the escutcheon at the wrist. This is one of the latest-dated examples noted which retains the elaborate carving of the stock round the lock and sideplate. This carbine is not fitted with the quadrant sight found on the carbines shown in Plates 45 and 47. Note that the lock is made with a pan bridle. The Artillery markings on this weapon suggest that the launching of grenades by firing them may have developed as a partial substitute for throwing them, before they went out of use generally by the middle of the eighteenth century. *Overall length (with cup) 47⅝in, barrel length 28⅜in, calibre 0.78in.*

47. *A Grenade-launching Carbine by James Farmer dated 1747, showing the quadrant sight with bar raised to full extent*

The same pattern of sight is fitted to the carbine shown in Plate 45. This carbine is fitted with a specially made heavy barrel which has been turned-down at the muzzle to accept the standard diameter grenade cup. The single forward ramrod pipe is missing and there is no provision for a tail-pipe. The fitting of special sights and, in this instance, a special heavy barrel indicates that the art of grenade-launching was being developed along very technical lines. The measurements of the several grenade cups illustrated are virtually identical, their overall length averaging 6½in. *Overall length (with cup) 43in, barrel length 23⅝in, calibre 0.78in.*

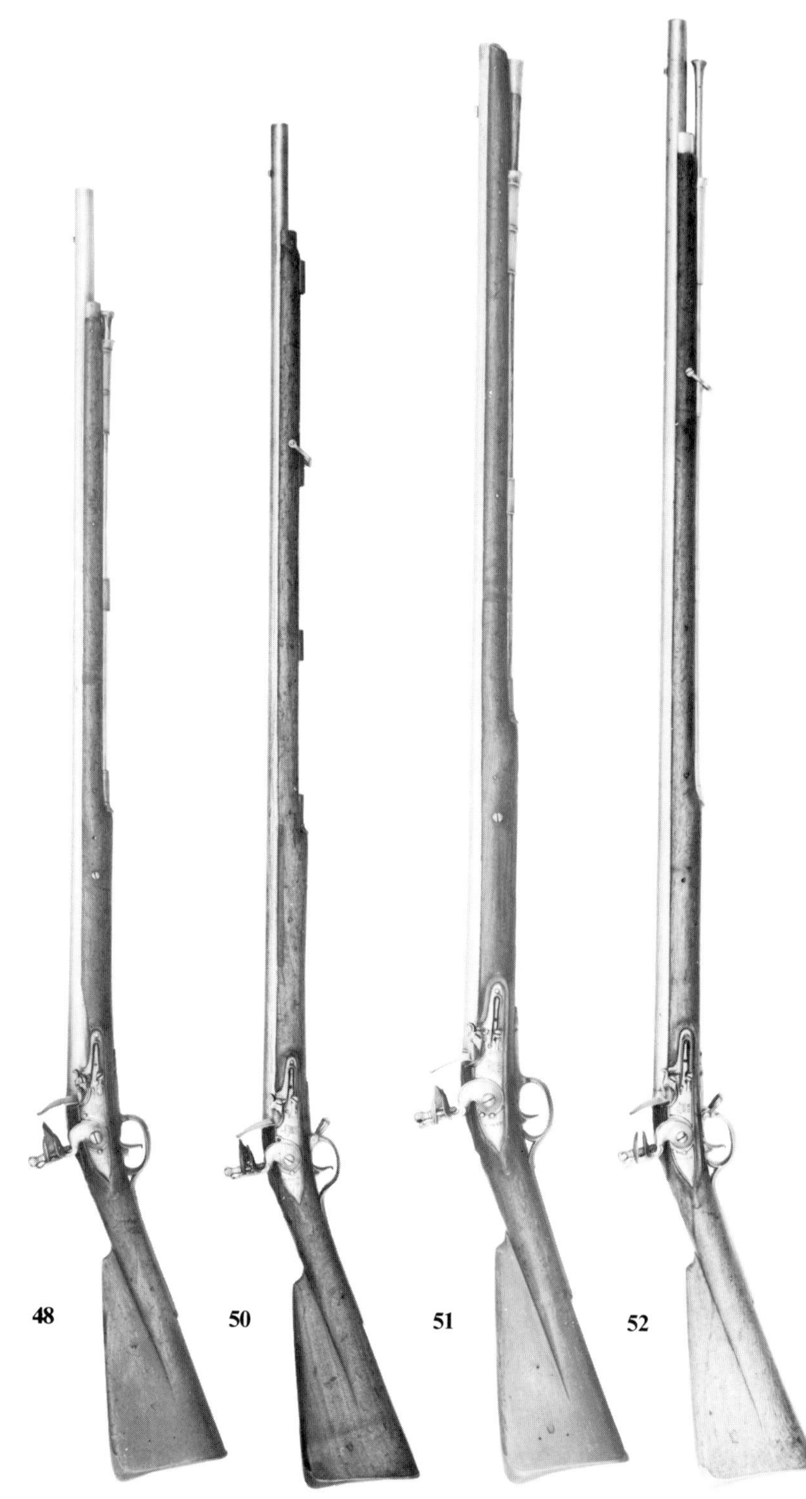

48 50 51 52

48, 49. *The Light Dragoon Carbine of 1756*

This example by William Grice, dated 1761, represents the first of a series of carbines introduced during the Seven Years War for the use of newly raised light corps. The ramrod of this example is not original and the head of the rod should lie even with the muzzle. Note the upper ramrod pipe which is made to form a long trumpet pipe by combining two shorter pipes. This would appear to be the first approach to the development of the long trumpet design which later became standard. While a sling bar has been added the standard Land Pattern sideplate is retained in reduced size. A variant form of trigger guard is used on which the forward part of the bow is pinched-in and not drilled for a sling swivel. All other furniture is of the Land Pattern made in a reduced size. The lockplate measures 6in × 1$\frac{1}{16}$in. *Overall length 51$\frac{3}{4}$in, barrel length 36in, calibre 0.68in.*

50. *Artillery and Highlander's Carbine of 1757(?)*

These particular weapons remain technically unidentified. A number of them remain at the Tower of London all bearing dates between 1757 and 1762, by such makers as Vernon, Grice, Edge, Galton and Haskins. It is quite possible that they were intended for issue to light infantry, or to the newly raised militia. They may ultimately have been issued to the Independent Companies, raised from 1759 to augment inadequate recruiting in the regular regiments. The brass furniture is smaller and of variant form to the Land Pattern and much more lightly cast and poorly finished. Contemporary comment on the quality of these troops would equate them very well with the quality of these carbines, and it is worthy of note that these companies were generally employed as light troops. *Overall length 58in, barrel length 42in, calibre 0.68in.*

51. *The Cavalry Carbine of 1757, or Carbine without Bayonets for Horse*

This example, with its undated lock and composite upper ramrod pipe, is *c.* 1765. The same pattern of sling bar is fitted as that shown on the Light Dragoon Carbine in Plate 48. A large barleycorn blade of iron is set 2$\frac{1}{2}$in from the muzzle. Note the brass-tipped wooden ramrod. The trigger guard is of the same pattern as the Light Dragoon Carbine, with no hole for a sling swivel. This carbine appears to have continued in use until the general adoption of the Eliott Carbine. *Overall length 52$\frac{1}{2}$in, barrel length 37$\frac{1}{8}$in, calibre 0.65in.*

52. *A Light Infantry Carbine or Fusil*

This pattern was introduced in 1758 and widely used in the North American phase of the Seven Years War. This particular example dates from *c.* 1780. This was standard issue for all Light Infantry companies raised from 1770. It is really a reduced proportion version of the Short Land Musket (Plate 15) and differs only in the bore size and slightly smaller dimensions of the brass furniture and stock. *Overall length 57$\frac{1}{2}$in, barrel length 42in, calibre 0.67in.*

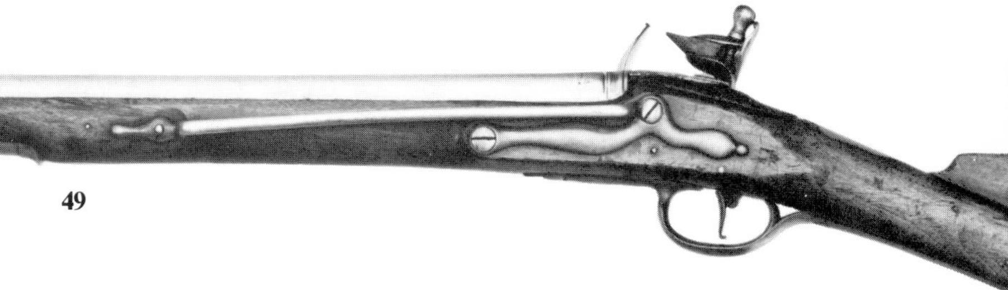

49

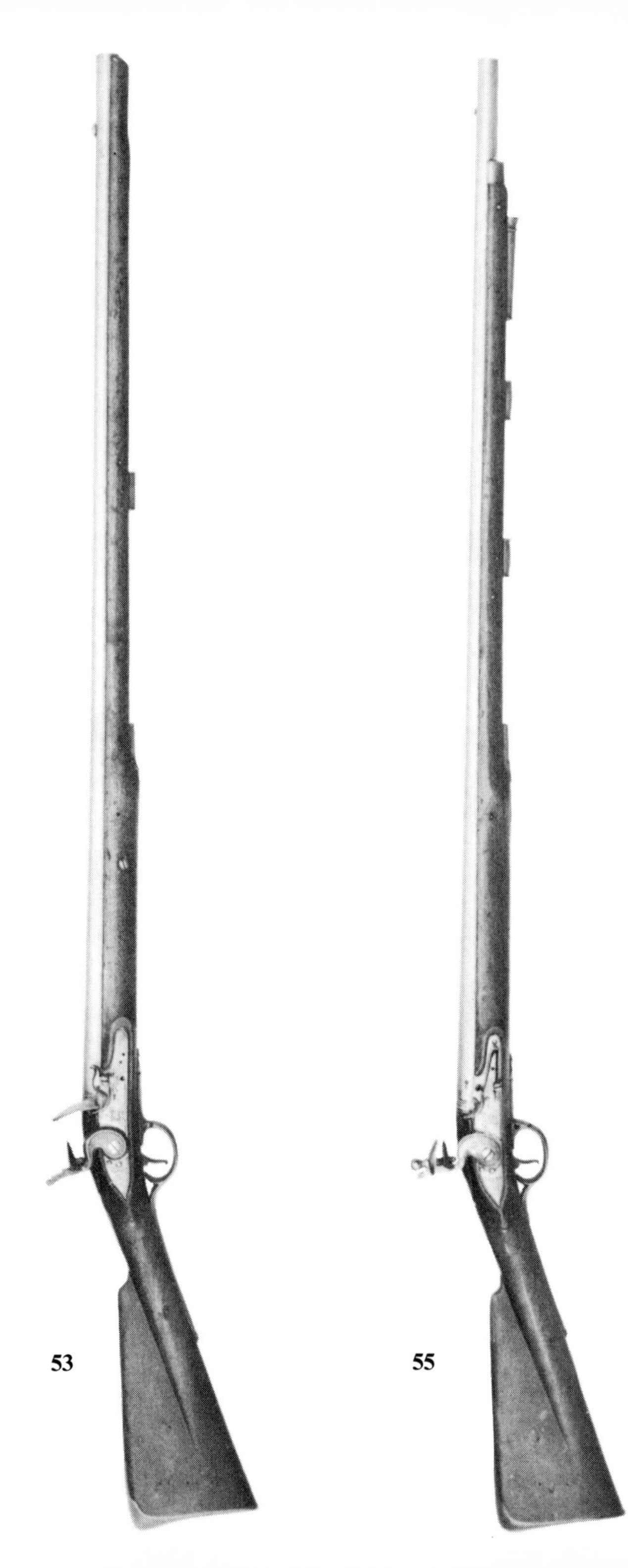

53

55

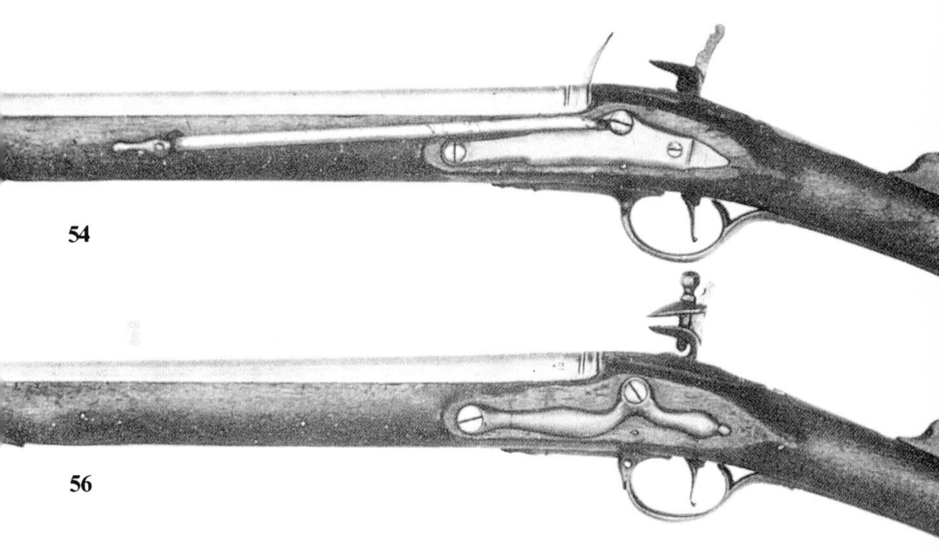

54

56

53, 54. *The Royal Horse Guards or Blues Carbine, c. 1765*

The identification of this carbine is based upon the description of it in contemporary records as having a flat lock, 3ft 1in barrel, and being of somewhat better quality than the issue cavalry carbine. The finish of this carbine is certainly superior to the type shown in Plate 51. Note the sporting-pattern sideplate, and the shell carving round the barrel tang. The sling bar and trigger guard are of the same pattern as the Light Dragoon and Cavalry Carbines, and the upper ramrod pipe (now missing) appears from the inletting to have been of the same composite trumpet pattern as the two issue carbines. This carbine is designed for a steel ramrod. Both lockplate and cock are flat with bevelled edges. *Overall length 53in, barrel length 37¼in, calibre 0.67in.*

55, 56. *The Royal Artillery Carbine, 1770*

The original pattern was made with a wooden brass-tipped ramrod. This example was made for a steel rod (not converted) and has a later style of lock, which probably dates it *c.* 1780. The brass furniture is a reduced version of the normal Land Pattern. The top of the barrel of this example is engraved ROYL ARTILLERY 1st BA . . . (Battalion). *Overall length 52½in, barrel length 37⅛in, calibre 0.68in.*

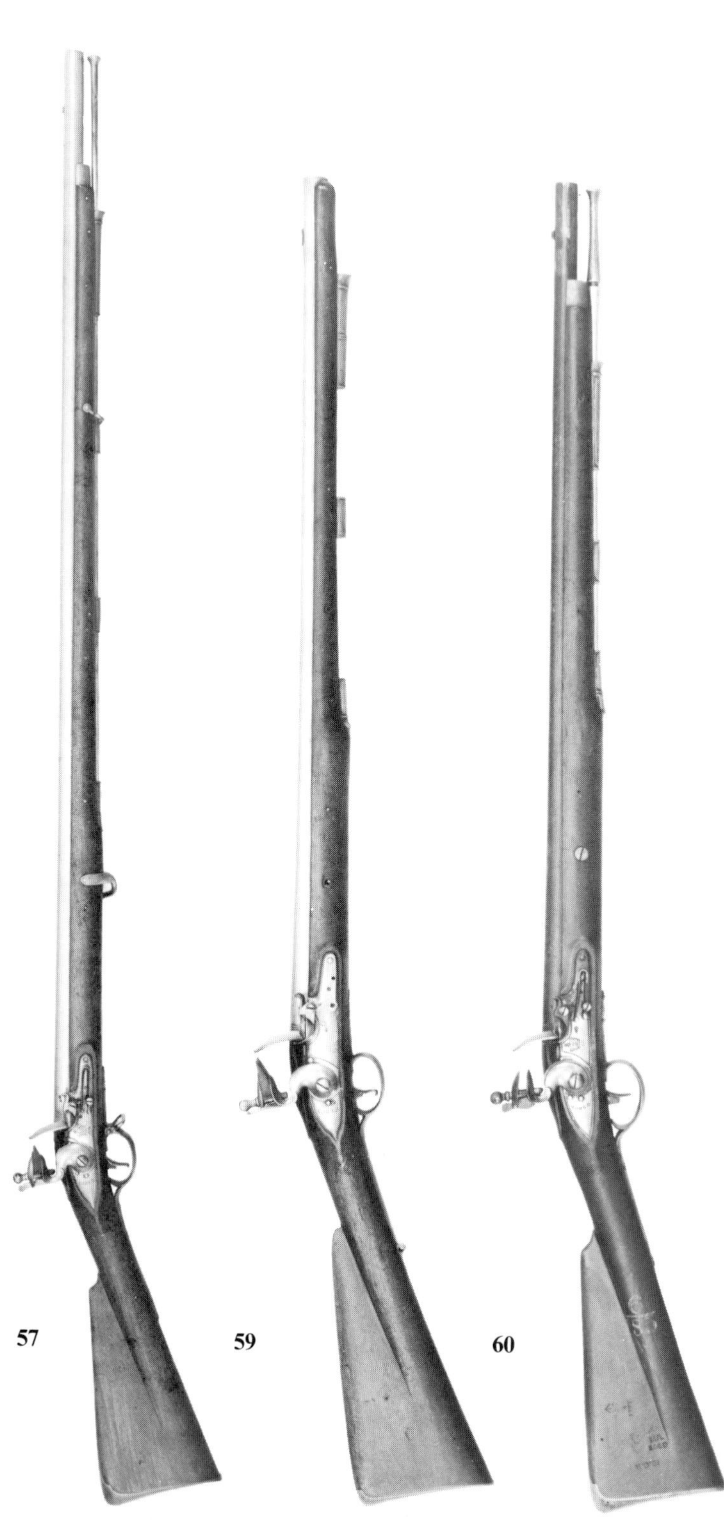

57

59

60

57, 58. *The Heavy Dragoon Carbine of 1770*

Until 1770 the Heavy Dragoons were equipped with Short Land Pattern muskets with wooden ramrods (Plate 42). With the modernization of equipment then being carried out, and the increased emphasis on mobility, it is not surprising that this carbine is much lighter in dimensions. This particular example dates from the late 1780s. The strongly designed distinctive pattern of sling bar fastens by the use of a yoke through the fore-end and has an extension at the rear held by a woodscrew in addition to the rear sidenail. The sideplate is post-1775 Short Land Pattern and the furniture throughout is a reduced size version of the standard Land Pattern. Note that the cock has the late form of comb with the curl at the tip turned outward. This pattern was originally adopted for the Horse Grenadier Guards. *Overall length $57\frac{1}{4}$in, barrel length 42in, calibre 0.65in.*

59. *The first Eliott Carbine, 1760*

It seems probable that this carbine, which is engraved on top of the barrel GEN. ELIOTT'S DRAGOONS is the one designed by Eliott for the 15th Light Dragoons, of which he became Colonel in 1759. Except in length, it closely follows the design of carbines for other branches of the service dating from this period. The upper ramrod pipe is of the composite type. Originally there was a sling bar fitted on the left side similar in pattern and dimensions to that of the Light Dragoon and Cavalry Carbines (Plate 48), and this carbine was also fitted for sling swivels. The sideplate resembles that later used on the Pattern 1796 Carbine and the Baker Rifle. The lock of this example is of the later undated type and it seems probable that it was repaired after 1764 and the original markings removed. *Overall length $43\frac{3}{4}$in, barrel length $28\frac{1}{4}$in, calibre 0.67in.*

60. *The standard Eliott Carbine for Light Dragoons, c. 1800*

This is a late example of the Eliott Carbine which was approved in this pattern in June 1773. The Eliott Carbine is immediately recognizable by the form of the ramrod and fore-end cap which are exclusive (with the exception of the very rare Burgoyne Carbine) to this arm. The rod has a swell at the throat, at the widest point of which a groove is cut round the diameter of the rod. This groove engages a lip at the front of the fore-end cap formed by cutting away a portion of the underside. The sling bar on the left side is held by the rear sidenail and a small woodscrew on the rear extension and at the front by a screw through the fore-end. The barrel is browned. *Overall length $43\frac{1}{2}$in, barrel length 28in, calibre 0.66in.*

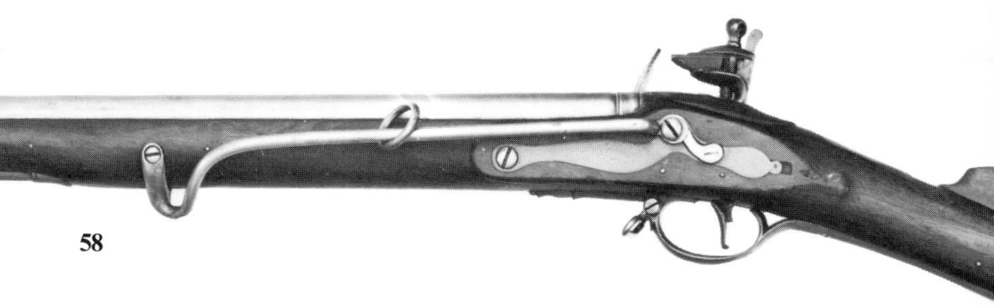

58

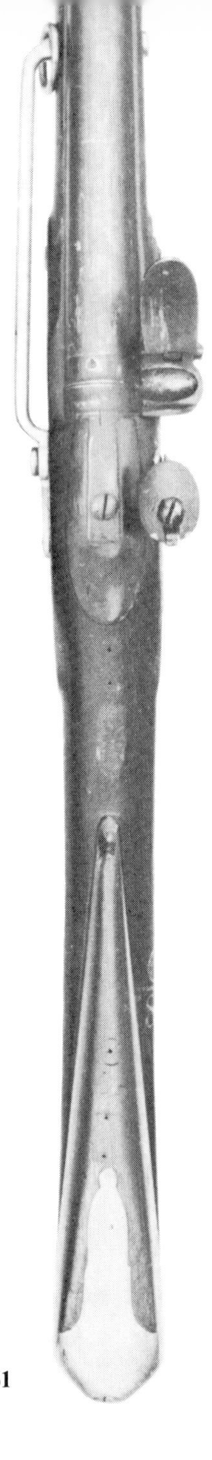

61

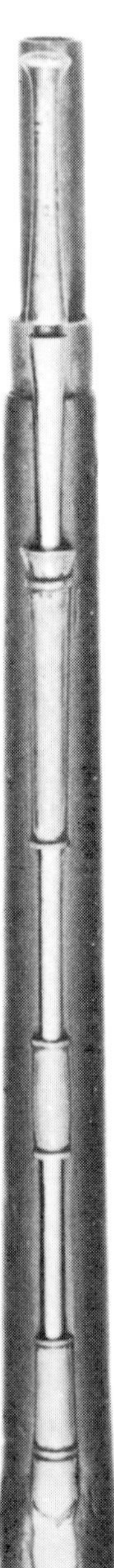

62

61, 62. *Eliott Carbine furniture*

The top view of the breech shows the positioning of the sling bar, absence of escutcheon at wrist, and the variant form of buttplate tang. The normal form of comb or handrail butt is used. The construction of the typical Eliott ramrod and pipes are clearly shown.

63. *Royal Forrester's Carbine*

Although conforming in overall outline to the standard Eliott Carbine, the Royal Forrester's Carbine has several distinctive variations. The most obvious of these is the use of the more costly flat lock and cock, and the forward fastening of the sling bar which has two screws through the fore-end securing a small base plate on the front of the bar. Note also the heavier, somewhat shorter trigger guard, and that the barrel is secured by three flat keys or slides rather than the normal three pins. The top of the barrel of this example is stamped 21st L.DS. The second ramrod pipe of this example is also a departure from the normal design, being trumpet-mouthed. The Irish Board of Ordnance was manufacturing Government pattern arms at Dublin Castle at least as early as the 1740s and the facilities were in use until closed down as a result of the Irish Rebellion of 1798. The crudely engraved lock markings of this carbine are typical of the Irish product, being a large crown over GR ahead of the cock, and DUBLIN CASTLE across the tail of the plate. *Overall length 43$\frac{3}{16}$in, barrel length 27$\frac{3}{4}$in, calibre 0.65in.*

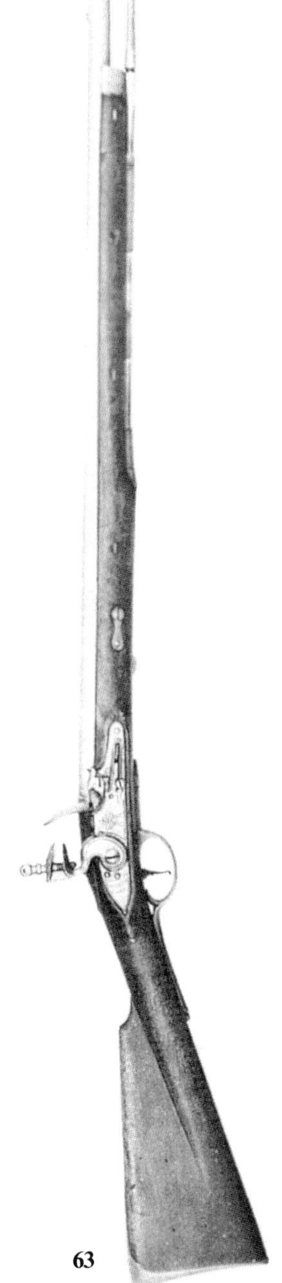

63

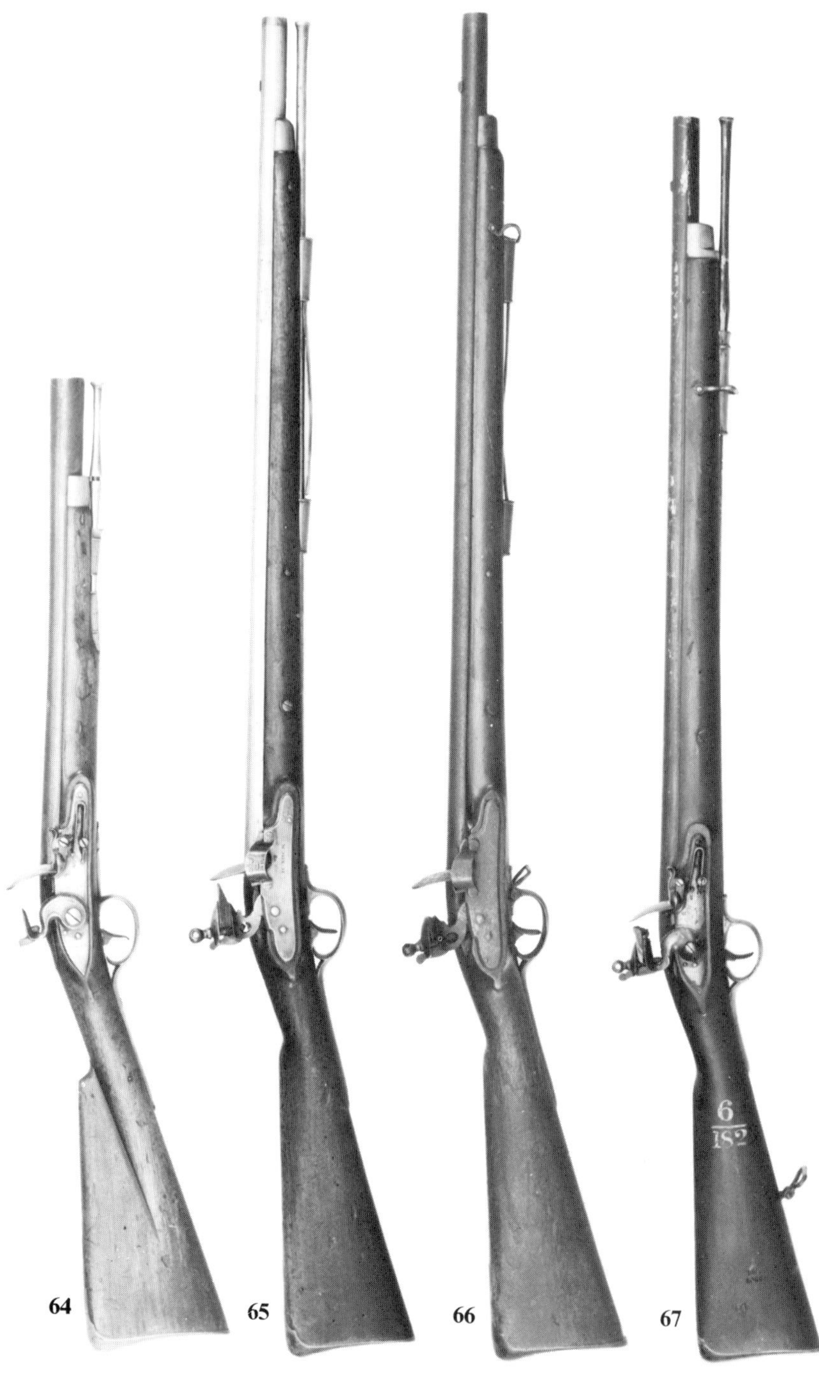

64 65 66 67

64. *Burgoyne's Musketoon or Blunderbuss Carbine of 1781*

The 'playwright General', Sir John Burgoyne, a successful and well-liked cavalry officer since the late 1750s and more recently an unsuccessful commanding general in North America, came home to England to be cleared by Parliament for the defeat of Saratoga and to be appointed Colonel of the 23rd Light Dragoons. He promptly indulged his sense of the bizarre by designing this musketoon, of which 100 were authorized to be made by the Ordnance. The distinctive features aside from its small size are the elliptical bell-mouthed barrel and the flat lock. The muzzle measures $1\frac{7}{16}$in across by 1in vertically. There is a short sling bar on the left side with a triangular form of sideplate somewhat similar to the Eliott. Eliott's ramrod and fore-end cap are utilised, as well as the pattern of the buttplate and trigger guard. The forward fastening for the sling bar was of the type used on the Dublin Castle Eliott, but this has been removed and filled in on this example. The barrel is browned and secured by two flat keys. *Overall length $31\frac{5}{8}$in, barrel length $16\frac{1}{8}$in, calibre 0.65in.*

65, 66. *The Heavy Dragoon Carbine with Nock's screwless lock, or Harcourt's Carbine*

These were first supplied to the 16th (Queen's) Light Dragoons, General William Harcourt's regiment, in 1793 on contract from Henry Nock. Aside from the lock other special features include a break-off breech, Nock's large diameter rounded-end barrel pins, a straight heavy steel ramrod held in position by a long spring riveted to the two straight tapered ramrod pipes, and a fore-end slit full length to the front of the trigger guard. The $6\frac{1}{2}$in sling bar is held by the single sidenail and by a screw through the fore-end. The stock comes to $3\frac{1}{4}$in of the muzzle and the socket bayonet for this carbine has a 15in blade. The lower carbine is a variant of this model with the holes for the sling bar plugged up and sling swivels fitted. The Pattern 1796 was made in standard musket bore in an attempt to standardize the calibre of all service weapons but it was a short-lived attempt. The barrel is heavily engraved Q L D. *Overall length 44in, barrel length 28in, calibre 0.73in.*

67. *A Heavy Dragoon Carbine Pattern 1796, with standard Government lock, c. 1798.*

Nock's lock proved too costly for large-scale contracts and the Ordnance reverted to the use of the normal pattern of lock when it placed contracts for this carbine with the London and Birmingham trades in 1798. Other changes in construction were also made including the use of standard barrel pins, omission of the break-off breech, a standard swelled button-head ramrod held by one trumpet pipe, a shorter trigger guard held by a single screw through the rear finial and cross-pinned at the front and a reduction of 2in in the length of the barrel. The fore-end is slit from its tip to the front of the trigger guard, but the channel is not so wide as on the Nock lock version. This example is fitted with standard sling swivels, the screw hole for the forward fastening of the sling bar being filled. *Overall length $41\frac{1}{4}$in, barrel length 26in, calibre 0.76in.*

69

68. *A Heavy Dragoon Carbine Pattern 1796 fitted with sling bar.*

This carbine has yet another method of retaining the ramrod. The upper barrel-shaped pipe has a short retaining spring inside (the same as used on Sea Service Muskets) and a tapered lower pipe. The heavy rod and wide slit stock of the Nock lock version are retained. The sideplate, very similar to that later used on the Baker rifle, is standard for the 1796 Carbine. The buttplate is identical to that used for the New Land Pattern arms (plate 32). *Overall length 42in, barrel length 26in, calibre 0.75in.*

69. *Nock's Screwless Lock, used on the Duke of Richmond's Muskets and Pattern 1796 Harcourt Carbines.*

Two sizes were in general use, the larger with a $5\frac{1}{2}$in plate for muskets and carbines, and a smaller $4\frac{3}{4}$in plate for rifles and pistols (the former being volunteer rifles, not Government arms). The shields were only fitted to the carbine, some muskets, and some of the volunteer rifle locks. The markings are standard. Highly praised as a military lock for more than 25 years, the only material complaint—aside from the expense of production and necessity for highly skilled craftsmen to make them—was that water could more easily enter the lock because of the internal location of the steel.

70. *The India Pattern Sergeant's Carbine of 1797.*

Carbines and fusils in the hands of NCOs seem to have lasted rather longer than those of the private soldier, as it was not until 1797 that the India Pattern was produced in a shorter lighter version for sergeants. In all respects save dimensions this is a copy of the current India Pattern musket. The furniture is not reduced in size, although the lockplate is slightly smaller, measuring $6\frac{1}{2}$in $\times$ $1\frac{1}{8}$ in. The barrel is browned. It would appear that the India Pattern Artillery Carbine was an identical weapon to this with a 39in barrel. *Overall length 52in, barrel length 37in, calibre 0.65in.*

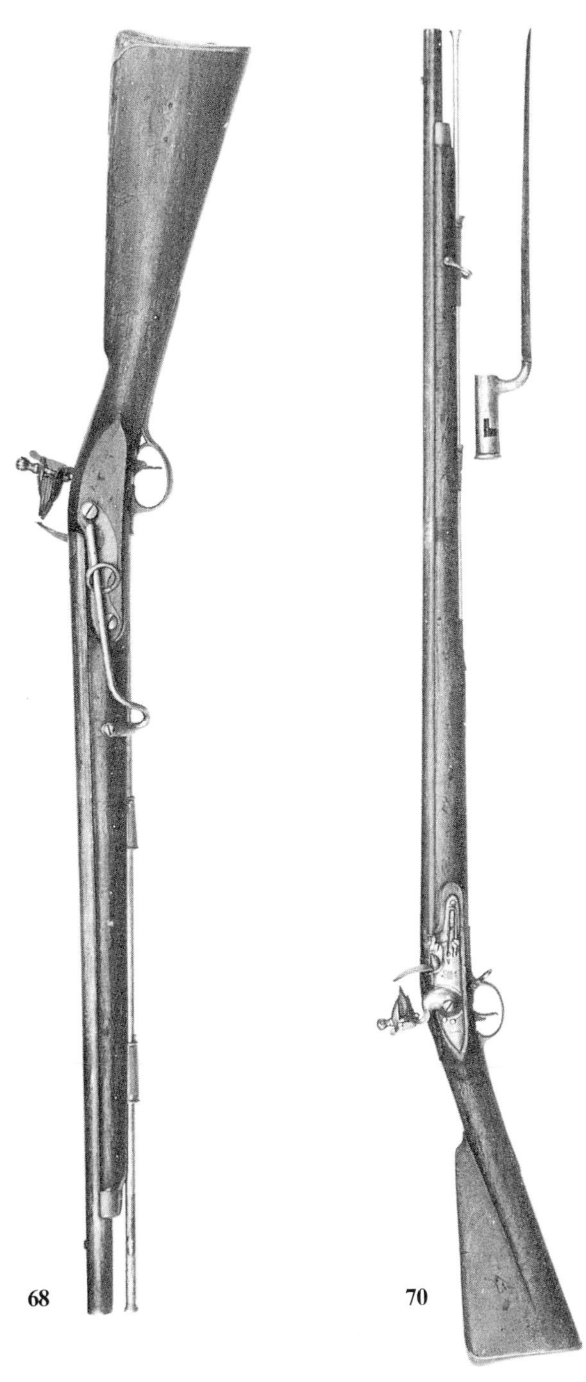

68

70

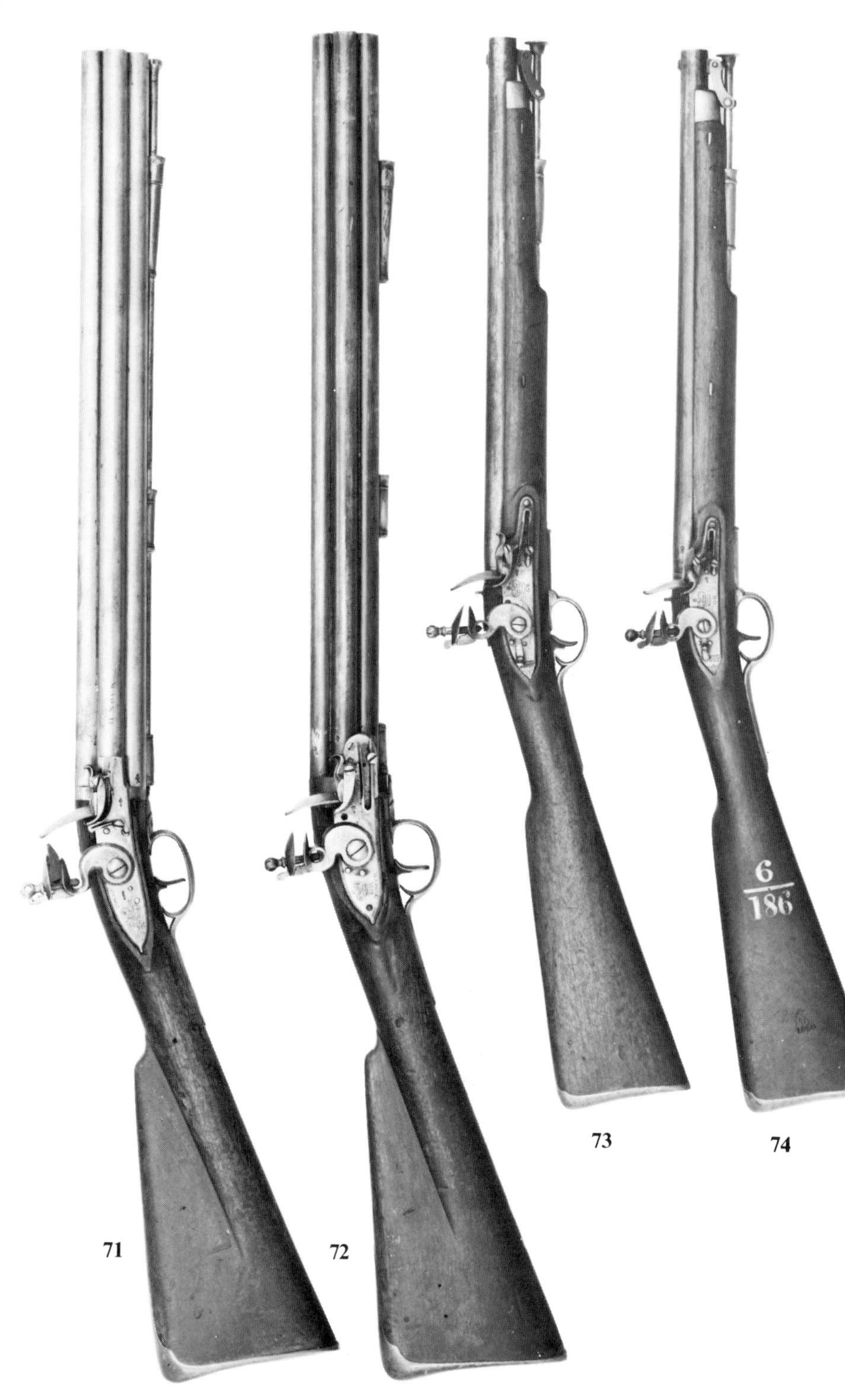

71 72 73 74

71, 72. *The Nock Volley Guns.*

Two models of this formidable weapon were produced, the first appearing to be the more numerous of the two. They seem to have been produced in two distinct batches, the first consisting of 500 (presumably first model) during 1780 and the second consisting of 100 (presumably second model) late in 1787. Close comparison reveals considerable differences between the two models. In the first model (shown in Plate 71) the back action lock is long and relatively narrow, with a flat swan-neck cock having the curl of the comb inwards, and the steel spring mounted in an L-shape ahead of the cock. The markings on the plate consist of TOWER along the upper edge at the rear of the cock and a crown over GR across the tail. The slight elongation of the oval form of the trigger guard bow is a visual but not a significant difference. On the second model (Plate 72) the back-action lock is shorter and wider and the steel spring is mounted in reverse to its normal position. The markings, consisting of a crown over GR over TOWER, are arranged differently along the tail rather than across it. The trigger guard is shorter, thicker and rounded in contour although the ramrod pipes are the same on both patterns. *Overall length 37in, barrel length 20in, calibre 0.52in.*

73, 74. *The Paget Cavalry Carbine, 1812.*

Although a wide variety of carbines were in use for the various branches of the mounted service during and after the Napoleonic Wars, the Paget Carbine was the primary arm of the cavalry until the end of the flintlock period, and certainly until 1815. Its distinctive features are the short length of barrel, the swivel ramrod and the bolted lock with raised pan. Two examples are shown, the upper one having a larger lock ($5\frac{1}{4}$in × 1in) with a curled toe on the steel, while the lower example has a small lock ($4\frac{1}{2}$in × $\frac{11}{16}$in) with a plain rounded toe to the steel. The use of various sizes of lock, all made to the same basic pattern, is the only significant variation encountered in the production of the Paget Carbine which was in service from 1812 until the late 1830s. Note the backsight block on the barrel tang. *Overall length $31\frac{3}{8}$in, barrel length 16in, calibre 0.66in.*

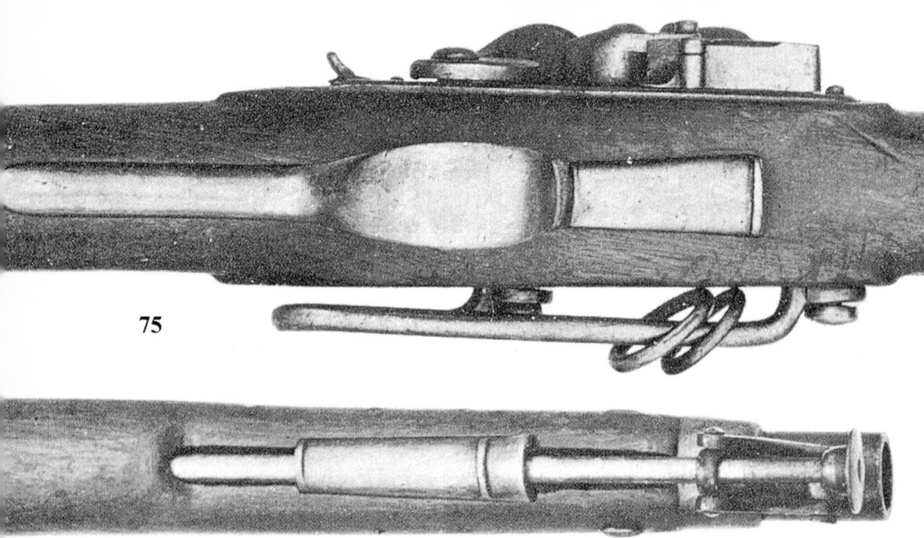

75

76

75, 76, 77. *The lock and furniture of the Paget Carbine.*

The Paget lock represents one of the most modern forms of flintlock used on a regulation British weapon. It approaches closely the accepted form for sporting gun and rifle locks of the same period, with its flat ring-neck cock and raised pan. The markings are standard. A small number of examples have been noted with rollers on the steel springs, but these may well be contemporary replacements. The toe of the steel is either as shown or curled up. The sliding bolt let into the lockplate behind the cock bolts the tumbler in the half-cock position. The design of the ramrod and the long swivels are clearly shown. Note that the barrel is retained by two flat keys and the shape of the single pipe. The sling bar is held by the two side-nails and there is no sideplate.

77

Rifles

The early history of the use of the rifle in the British service, prior to 1800, is sadly dimmed by the lack of documentary information and, as this volume deals only with issue weapons, we must confine ourselves to the period beginning with 1800, when the first regulation rifle was adopted into the British service as the arm of the 95th Regiment of Foot—later known as the Rifle Brigade—and for portions of the 60th Regiment and other special units.

Brief but inevitable mention must also be made of the Ferguson rifle, as it was issued to one special corps of British regulars which saw service between May and October 1777, during the American War. There is documentary evidence to prove that one hundred military pattern Ferguson breechloading rifles were made for the Ordnance during 1776, that they were issued to the corps known as Ferguson's Riflemen which operated during the Philadelphia Campaign of 1777 and that the corps was disbanded after the wounding of Major Ferguson at the Battle of Brandywine in September of that year. General Howe had the rifles put into store in New York City. Ferguson's rifles vanish in the autumn of 1777.

Whether it was the lessons learned in the American War which subsequently led to the formation of a special rifle corps and the adoption of a service rifle for the British Army is debatable. First and foremost is the elementary observation that twenty years is a very long time for human nature to retain any lesson taught by history, particularly an instructive or unpleasant one. Continental armies had included corps of riflemen for most of the eighteenth century and, while the value of a permanently constituted Rifle Brigade must have been highlighted by the psychological success of the American riflemen, it is probably much closer to the truth to attribute the establishment of such a body on a permanent basis in the British service to evolution and contemporary pressures rather than illuminating hindsight.

Between 1793 and 1800, throughout almost the entire period of the French Revolutionary Wars, the requirements of the British service for riflemen were met by a conglomeration of small independent foreign units variously armed with Continental rifles mostly of German or Dutch manufacture. A few rifles of Continental pattern were made by Birmingham gun makers, but they can hardly be considered as British rifles. Most of these foreign units were mounted and their weapons what we would consider as rifled carbines. By 1798 a supply of some 5,000 Prussian rifled muskets had been bought by the Ordnance and, during the entire period, the pressure had been steadily growing for the establishment of a permanent British rifle corps to eliminate the confusing piece-meal arrangements then prevailing. Serious steps were taken in this direction during late 1799 and, early in 1800, both rifles and men were being sorted out. The 95th Regiment (Rifles) was established with effect from 25th August 1800.

The Baker rifle with which the Rifle Brigade was armed in 1800 may claim the longest continuous service of any British service rifle—more than forty years with only minor modifications in design. It was also the rifle which saw the longest wartime service of any British rifle, beginning with the thirteen years of the Napoleonic Wars from 1803 to 1815. During the first fifteen years of its existence with which we are concerned here, the Baker rifle underwent a number of relatively minor changes in its construction once a few of the basic features such as bore size and lock style had been settled in the very earliest period. Unfortunately for the modern collector the appearance of these changes is confused and confounded by the wartime conditions under which they were introduced, compounded by the system which prevailed to begin with, and by a paucity of documentary classification. As with most other minor changes in design, nobody dealing with them thought it necessary to delineate them carefully at the time.

The unique feature of the Baker rifle was its barrel. These were made in both plain and twisted iron (in what proportions it is not now possible to determine) and were full-round for their length of 30 to 30½inches, with a very slight tapering flat for a few inches just ahead of the breech tang. Both plain and twisted barrels were finished with a reddish browning. The rifling consisted of seven rectangular grooves of equal width to the lands, making one quarter of a turn in the length of the barrel or, to use the more modern method, one turn in 120 inches.

Baker made no claim to the overall design of the rifle which bore his name and, as he was not reticent in coming forward to acknowledge his several inventions and ideas, we may safely assume that the design of the Baker rifle was the result of a combined effort based upon European ideas with British interpretations.

The earliest Baker rifles, those made between the acceptance of the design in February 1800 and the outbreak of war in May 1803, were made in both musket and carbine bore sizes (carbine bore here taken to mean 0.625inch or 20 bore while musket bore, with regard to the Baker rifle means 0.70inch calibre). The musket-bore version does not appear to have continued in production beyond this earliest period and surviving examples confirm this conclusion.

During this early period the locks used were of two different types but with the introduction of the second type, which closely followed the newly designed New Land pattern, it did not follow that the earlier pattern fell into disuse; both continued in use until the appearance of a third type *c.* 1806. The first type was simply a reduced version of the rounded lock and swan-neck cock pattern used on the India Pattern muskets of the last quarter of the eighteenth century while the second pattern, with its flat lockplate and flat ring-necked cock strongly resembled the New Land lock. These flat locks contained a number of minor variations: some had raised pans and roller steel springs, some had the small leaf-sprig engraving at the point of the tail of the plate although otherwise devoid of decoration aside from standard markings, and others had the double border lines engraved on the plate and body of the cock in the manner of the India Pattern musket lock. About 1806 appeared a third type of lock, the one which was to dominate the remainder of Baker production during the period covered by this volume. This had both a raised pan and a safety bolt let into the tail of the lockplate, and was fitted with a flat ring-neck cock. The plate itself had a stepped-down tail and the entire lock was somewhat smaller than the earlier patterns.

Baker rifle sights remained unchanged during the period, consisting of a low iron blade dovetailed into the muzzle of the barrel with the base rounded to leave only the blade showing, and a notched block backsight dovetailed into the barrel 6 to 7 inches from the breech. The block had a single notched leaf hinged to it and lying forward of the block.

The stock of the Baker rifle underwent a number of changes but the most important one, the slit-stock, did not come into common use in the pre-1815 period. The earliest rifles had a large butt-box with two compartments, the forward one being circular to hold greased patches and the after one being rectangular to hold the ball drawer and torque bar for the rammer. The large butt-box lid had a stepped or moulded outline at the front and measured $5\frac{3}{4}$inches by $1\frac{9}{16}$inches. Those for the musket-bore Baker varied slightly in design and were slightly larger. The normal butt-box had a single rectangular compartment, since after a certain date both wooden mallets and separate patches were abandoned in favour of a patch tied round the ball and combined in the cartridge as issued. The covers of these smaller boxes were round at the front and measured $4\frac{1}{2}$ inches by $1\frac{7}{16}$ inches. All standard Baker rifles had a cheekrest on the left side of the butt. Just where the dividing line between the use of the large two-compartment box and the smaller single compartment type came is difficult to determine; they were obviously used concurrently for some time. It seems logical to assume that, with the increasing pressures imposed by wartime production and the great rise in production of rifles which occurred in 1806, this was about the time when the smaller type with the simpler, cheaper, lid came into general use. The second major change which occurred in the Baker stock was the introduction of the slit-stock, in which the underside of the fore-end had a narrow slit from the end of the fully open ramrod channel to the trigger guard. Although used on a variety of weapons from the mid-1790s, its use on the Baker rifle probably dates from the post-1810 period and not until after 1815 did it become a standard feature in the construction of the Baker rifle. The design of the brass furniture was unchanged during the period and is best described by reference to the illustrations.

Production figures for the early Baker rifles are sketchy and probably incomplete but, at least for Birmingham, they may be taken as representative. The total production of Baker rifles in London and Birmingham until 1806—when a dramatic increase in production occurred—amounted to some 2,624 rifles. This presumably includes all of the musket-bore rifles as well as the carbine-bore type. The figure also included 1,700 rifles contracted in London in 1800 and 1801, and some 924 rifles completed in Birmingham in 1804 and 1805. There are no separate figures for London rifle production in these latter years.

In 1806 a total of 1,597 completed rifles were made in Birmingham, as well as 15,106 rifle barrels (which no doubt included a proportion of Baker cavalry rifle barrels) and 11,980 rifle locks. The largest production of rifles in Birmingham for any one year during the period was in 1808, when 3,296 rifles were completed; otherwise 1806 was the largest production for the component parts of the rifle. Between March 1804 and September 1815 a total of 14,695 rifles were completed in Birmingham, as well as 32,582 rifle barrels and 37,338 rifle locks. These figures, while insufficient because of the absence of figures for London production in detail, at least give some idea of minimum production. The component figures are separate from those for completed rifles and may represent the proportion of rifles set up in London from Birmingham parts; they would not include the production based upon Lewisham-produced parts, or those made in London itself.

Baker's Cavalry Rifle, 1803.

Although in dimensions and purpose this arm classified as a carbine, the rifled bore was considered a significant feature at the time of its design and introduction and it is included here. Baker submitted a rifled carbine as early as September 1801 but this weapon —believed to be similar to the standard rifle—has not yet been positively identified. However, in June 1803 the 20inch barrelled rifled carbine made its appearance and it was this weapon which was subsequently adopted for the Prince of Wales's 10th Light Dragoons. In 1806 some 3,000 were ordered to be set up and another 500 with Baker's pistol-grip stock were set up in 1813. The 1806 batch had bolted locks of the type typically found on Baker rifles, and the presence of this feature on a large number of 'new weapons' is of great value in determining the approximate general introduction date of this type of lock as opposed to the earlier forms. Another feature of interest in this context is the rounded-front cover of the butt-box.

Baker Rifles for the Life Guards, and West India Regiments, 1801.

Ezekiel Baker supplied an unspecified small number of rifles for the Life Guards. Eight London gunmakers supplied a total of 800 rifles for the West India Regiment, 400 with buttboxes and bayonet bars, and 400 without either.

Life Guards Rifled Musket-bore Carbine, 1812.

One hundred of these rifles .75 calibre carbines with twist-iron barrels and bayonets were ordered late in 1812, and were set up by the trade. The rifling was Baker-type, carried out by Gill and Arnold, both of Birmingham. These probably closely resemble P/1796 Carbines.

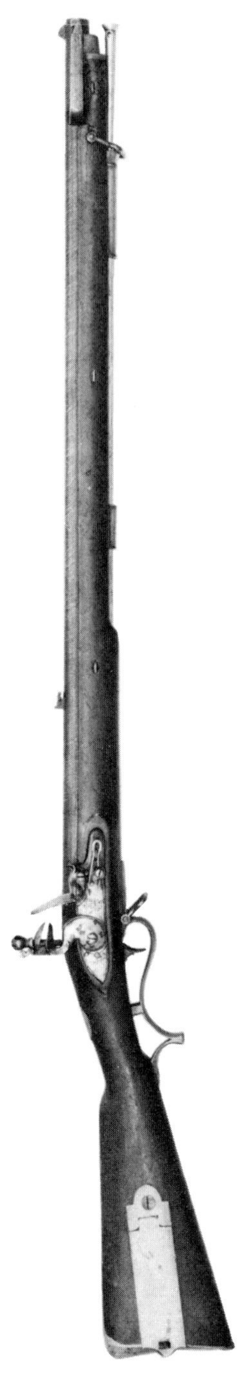

78. *A musket-bore Baker Rifle, c. 1801.*

The barrel is rifled with seven rectangular grooves making $\frac{1}{4}$ turn in the length of the barrel. The browned twist barrel is retained by three flat keys and the upper swivel screw. The blade foresight is somewhat higher and has a rather thicker base than those found on later examples. The backsight is dovetailed into the barrel $6\frac{3}{4}$in from the break-off breech, and has one notched leaf hinged forward. The rounded lock with its swan-neck cock is of the first pattern used for the Baker rifle, and conforms closely to the standard British military lock of the late eighteenth century. The lock-plate measures $5\frac{1}{4}$in × 1in and, in place of the usual TOWER, stamped across the tail is the contractor's name WHEELER. This example has a detented tumbler. The distinctive brass cover of the butt-trap measures 6in × $1\frac{5}{8}$in, and the trap itself has two compartments. The forward circular one measures $1\frac{7}{16}$in in diameter and was intended to contain greased patches. The rear compartment is rectangular and was intended to contain cleaning tools. The left side of the butt has a raised cheekrest which is standard on all Baker rifles of Government issue. *Overall length 46in, barrel length $30\frac{1}{4}$in, calibre 0.68in.*

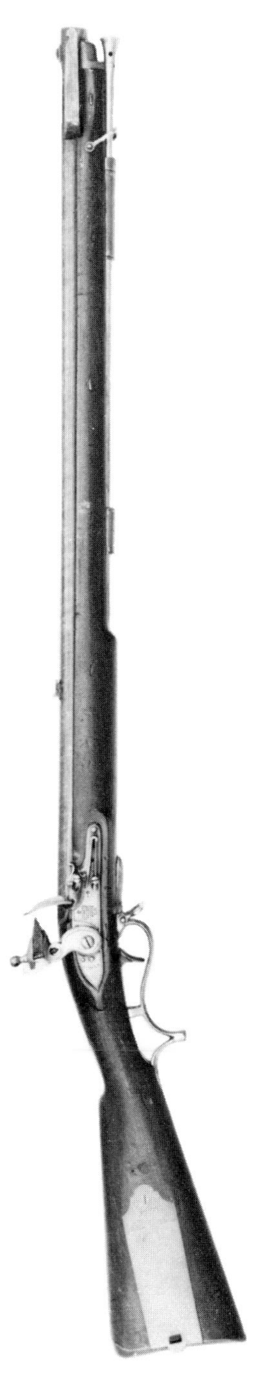

79. *A musket-bore Baker Rifle, c. 1802.*

The browned twist barrel is rifled with seven rectangular grooves almost equal in width to the lands making $\frac{1}{4}$ turn in the length of the barrel, and is retained by the standard three flat keys and upper swivel screw. The steel ramrod differs from later types in having a gradually tapering head. The foresight is a thick, low blade integral with the base. The backsight, of standard form, is dovetailed into the barrel $7\frac{1}{4}$in ahead of the break-off breech. The lock is a close copy of the New Land Pattern design with its flat, bevelled-edge ring-neck cock and raised semi-waterproof pan. The lockplate measures $5\frac{3}{4}$in $\times$ 1in. In addition to the standard TOWER and crowned GR markings, and the Government ownership mark of a crowned Broad Arrow, the plate is stamped under the pan, R & R S. The brass cover of the butt-trap is typical of the early Baker rifles but somewhat larger than most. It measures 6in $\times$ $1\frac{7}{8}$in although the internal dimensions of the two compartments are the same as those given in Plate 78. *Overall length $46\frac{1}{4}$in, barrel length $30\frac{1}{2}$in, calibre 0.70in.*

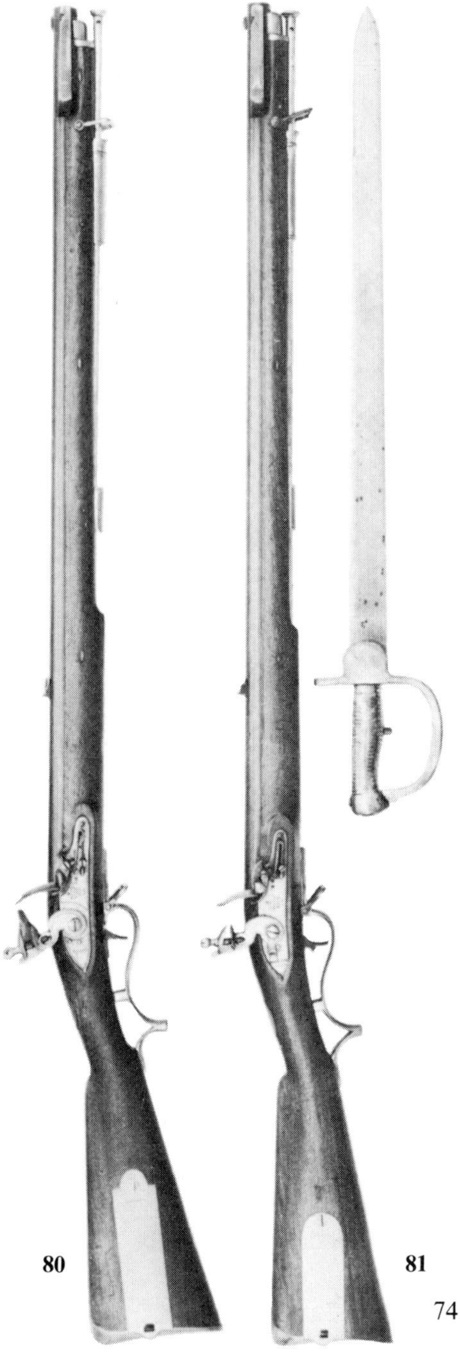

80 81

80. *A carbine-bore Baker Rifle, c. 1802.*

The plain iron barrel is rifled with seven rectangular grooves just slightly narrower than the lands, making $\frac{1}{4}$ turn in the length of the barrel (or 1 turn in 10ft). The barrel is retained in the normal way, with three flat keys and the upper swivel screw. The foresight is a curved-profile thick blade on a very thin base. The backsight, of standard pattern, is dovetailed into the barrel $6\frac{1}{2}$in from the break-off breech. The lock, while similar to the New Land Pattern lacks the raised pan, and the tumbler is detented. The fitting of a detent or 'fly' in the tumbler is a feature of early Baker rifles which was dropped on those produced after *c.* 1806. The lockplate measures $5\frac{3}{8}$in × 1in. The brass cover of the butt-trap measures 6in × $1\frac{1}{2}$in, and the trap has the usual two compartments typical of the pre-1806 Baker Rifle. The three Baker Rifles shown in Plates 78–80 are typical of those manufactured during the first six years of production (until 1805). It must be emphasized that in terms of total production they are not typical Baker Rifles, but rather they represent the developmental stages through which the arm passed before arriving at a more or less constant design which then prevailed during the period until the close of the Napoleonic Wars in 1815. *Overall length 46$\frac{1}{4}$in, barrel length 30$\frac{1}{4}$in, calibre 0.625in across lands.*

81. *A carbine-bore Baker Rifle typical of the period 1806–15.*

The browned twist barrel is rifled with seven rectangular grooves just slightly narrower than the lands, making $\frac{1}{4}$ turn in the length of the barrel. The foresight is a curved-profile tapered blade on a very thin base. The backsight is dovetailed into the barrel 7in from the break-off breech. The single notched leaf,

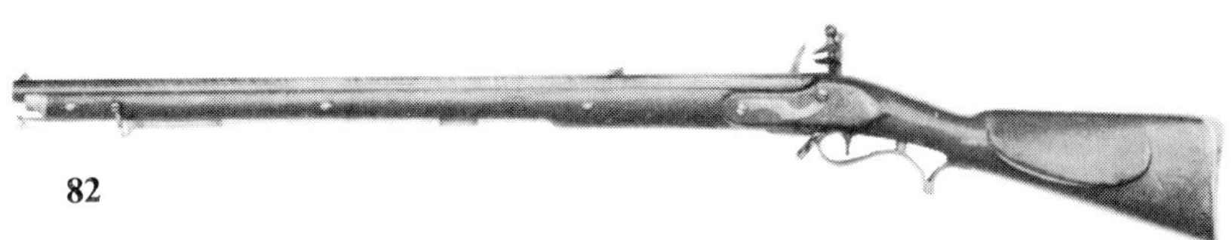

82

which is hinged forward, is thinner than on earlier rifles. The lock is one of two particular features on this rifle. It is this form which, introduced about 1806, became the standard pattern for the Baker Rifle until 1823. The roller steel spring is a replacement, as none were ever officially fitted with this refinement. The flat lockplate with its stepped-down tail, sliding safety bolt, raised semi-waterproof pan, and the flat ring-neck cock are entirely typical of the Government issue Baker Rifle of the Napoleonic War period. The plate measures 5in × 1in, and TOWER is across the lower portion of the tail stamped in small letters. The second feature which represents a significant change from earlier types and which, again, was to become standard, is the brass butt-trap cover. A plain rounded front replaces the moulded pattern and the dimensions are reduced to $4\frac{1}{2}$in × $1\frac{7}{16}$in. The trap itself is a single rectangular compartment. This particular rifle has a 'slit stock' —the bottom of the stock between the end of the open ramrod channel and the front of the trigger guard has a small slit which prevents the ramrod from jamming due to dirt or the swelling of the wood. The slit stock, as can be seen in the illustration, does not alter the outline of the rifle. It came into use about 1810, having first appeared in the 1790s, but does not appear to become either a typical or a standard structural feature until after 1815. There is no doubt, however, that some Baker Rifles of the pre-1815 period were made with slit stocks.

The sword bayonet shown with this rifle is the standard pattern during the 1800–1815 period and is generally known as the Second Model, or Pattern of 1801. The First Model, or Pattern of 1800, which was very short-lived, has a squared-off knuckle guard. A few blades were made with saw-backed edge. The blade measures 23in × $1\frac{3}{4}$in at the ricasso and is $\frac{1}{4}$in thick at the back. The backedge of the blade is sharpened for $5\frac{1}{4}$in at the point. *Overall length* $45\frac{3}{4}$*in, barrel length* $30\frac{7}{16}$*in, calibre 0.625in.*

82. *The reverse side of the standard Baker Rifle of the 1800–15 period.*

Note the form of the cheekrest and the flat brass sideplate which is flush with the wood. The shape of the brass scroll trigger guard does not change during this period, although on some rifles the front finial is rounded and on others squared-off. The slit stock generally has the squared-off guard finial. Note the position of the sling swivels and the two ramrod pipes, and the absence of a tailpipe.

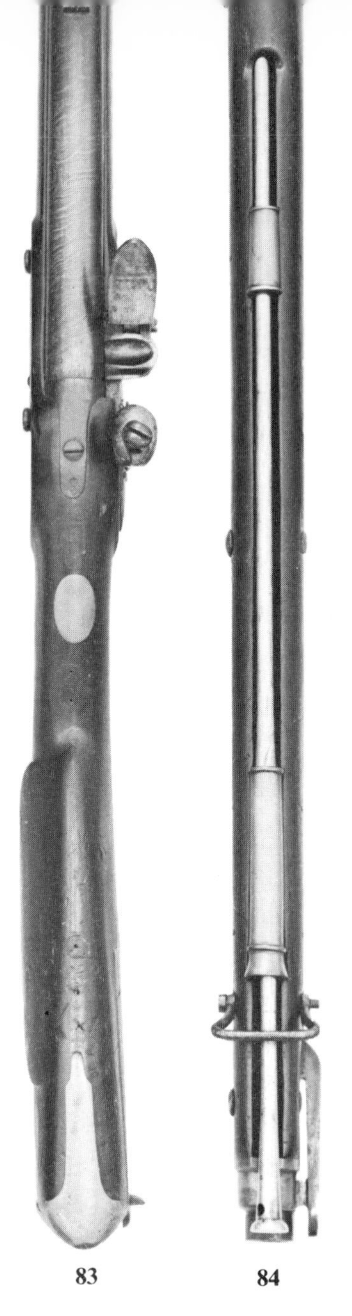

83 84

83, 84, 85. *Baker Rifle furniture*

In Plate 83 note the shape of the butt-plate tang, the form of the cheekrest and the contour of the spring which retains the butt-trap cover. The oval brass escutcheon at the wrist is held in position by the screw passing through the pillar in the central part of the scroll guard. The form of the break-off breech is standard. For a raised pan see Plate 35. The positioning and shape of the barrel keys or slides are typical; there is no tailpipe. The width of the ramrod channel in relation to the diameter of the rod itself is normal.

85

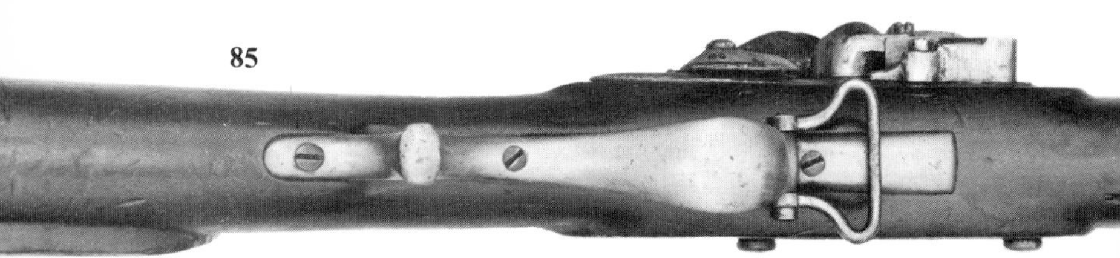

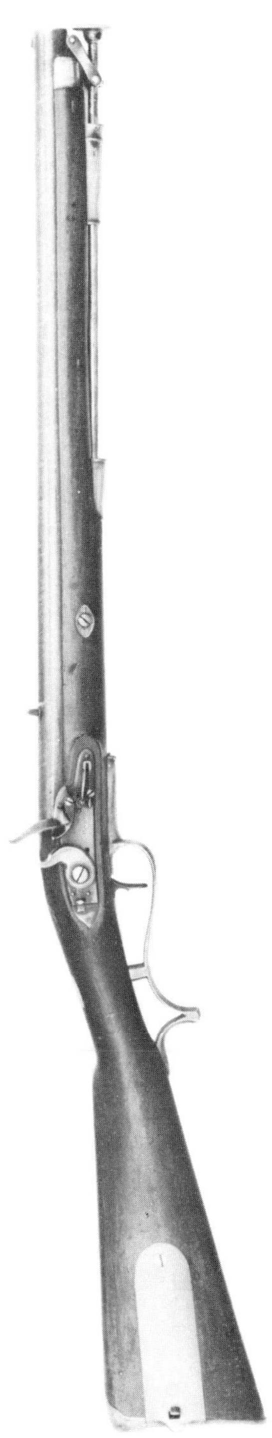

86. *The Baker Cavalry Rifle with 20in Barrel, c. 1806*

An early example of Ezekiel Baker's refined military weapons. The browned twist barrel is rifled with seven rectangular grooves making $\frac{1}{4}$ turn in the length of the barrel, and the barrel is fitted with a break-off breech. The foresight is the usual Baker Rifle type, but the backsight is a plain notched block dovetailed into the barrel 3in from the breech. The two brass ramrod pipes are both of large diameter and the front finial of the trigger guard is formed as a pipe with a retaining spring riveted inside it. The fore-end is of the slit-stock pattern. The butt-trap is a single rectangular compartment. There is a $5\frac{1}{2}$in sling bar on the left side, held by the rear sidenail and the screw through the fore-end visible in the illustration. A normal Baker Rifle cheekrest is used but there is no side-plate or wrist escutcheon. The lock is of the type which later became standard on Baker Rifles and this may be the first instance of its use. In addition to having a raised pan, sliding safety bolt and flat bevelled-edge ring-neck cock, the Cavalry Rifle lock has a roller steel spring and a hole through the lockplate so that a common nail may be used to hold the mainspring under tension while the other parts are removed for cleaning—a Baker refinement. Both barrel and lockplate are engraved E. BAKER and the barrels bear the standard Government proof marks. *Overall length 35in, barrel length 20in, calibre 0.625in.*

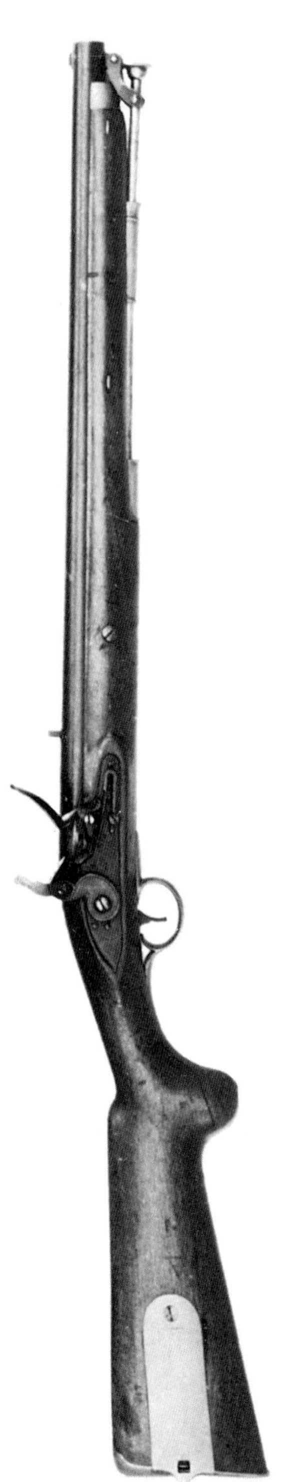

87. *The Baker Cavalry Rifle for the 10th Hussars, c. 1813*

This is actually a variation or improvement upon the rifle shown in Plate 86 and should not be considered as a distinct arm but rather a later version. It represents the first use of Baker's pistol grip stock in place of the scroll guard. Although very similar in outline to the 1806 rifle there are several important changes in detail. The form of the ramrod and its swivels is now that of the Paget Carbine. The stock is not slit. A standard Baker sideplate is used, the identical form of sling bar being retained. The trigger guard is that of the Paget Carbine, although the size of the cheekrest is reduced. An Ordnance lock of $5\frac{3}{8}$in length is used, which lacks the roller steel spring although retaining the raised pan. The tang of the buttplate is engraved in large shaded letters, X R H. A plain iron barrel is used on this particular example and the bottom of the pistol grip is held by a woodscrew from the bottom. *Overall length $35\frac{5}{8}$in, barrel length $20\frac{1}{4}$in, calibre 0.625in.*

Appendix 1
Markings on Service Issue Longarms

During the century covered by this work there were large numbers of arms manufactured which closely resembled those issued to the King's forces—often by the same firms engaged in furnishing parts or services to the Board of Ordnance—and for this reason it is necessary to identify those markings which must appear on a weapon before it may be correctly classified as a service arm. The periodic sale of old parts by the Government resulted in many locks reaching private concerns who then used them in the construction of commercial weapons, generally of low quality for the overseas markets. The presence, therefore, of a lock bearing the mark of Government ownership or inspection on a weapon of otherwise nonstandard dimensions or design should always be taken to indicate a commercial rather than a service arm.

There were three markings which served above all others to identify a Government-owned service issue weapon. The first two of them appeared on the breech of the barrel and the third on the lockplate, usually beneath the pan. These were the crown over GR over a 'Broad Arrow', formed as one stamp (Figure 1), beneath which would be found a crown over crossed sceptres (Figure 2). These two markings constituted the Government or Tower proof marks. The third stamp was a crown over a Broad Arrow (Figure 3), a symbol of Government ownership. Each of these marks was generally very deeply struck and sometimes they were not well centred, so that one side or the other was often indistinct or even missing. There were a fair number of variations caused by differences in the individual stamps made, but the patterns did not vary. The earlier markings, generally before the 1780s, were more deeply struck than the later stamps, and the crowns tended to be somewhat rounder in form. It must be noted that the crowned crossed sceptres *stamped twice* on a barrel was the Ordnance proof for *private* arms and therefore not a Government mark.

One further mark denoted ownership by the Government and this generally appeared on the right side of the butt, often stamped into the wood so deeply as to be virtually indistinguishable. This was the Ordnance Storekeeper's mark (Figure 4) of a crown over the addorsed letters GR with a date beneath. During the eighteenth century the date was normally used, but after 1806 it seems to have been dropped, although later dates are sometimes encountered. The date indicated the date at which the arm was taken into store—and for this reason it is not a reliable means of dating a weapon, since it could have been made years previously. This mark could also be found on privately manufactured arms purchased by the Ordnance in times of stress, and this condition applied to foreign arms as well. This mark should therefore be considered only as an indication that at some time in its career the weapon bearing it had been in Government Store.

It may also be mentioned with regard to the Storekeeper's mark that it does not appear to have been used annually but only periodically—so that a supply of arms could build up over several years before being officially marked.

Figure 1. Always appears in conjunction with Figure 2, being the uppermost of the two marks. Stamped on top of the breech and on later arms on the left side of the breech.

Figure 2. Always appears beneath Figure 1 on Government weapons. Privately made barrels proved by the Ordnance proof house will have this mark stamped twice, omitting Figure 1.

Figure 3. The mark of Government ownership, which is stamped on the lockplate beneath the pan.

Figure 4. The Ordnance Storekeeper's Stamp which appears, if at all, on the right side of the butt. The date is sometimes omitted and occasionally overstamped with a later date.

Appendix 2
Bayonets

The British regulation bayonet of the eighteenth century was most usually a socket pattern with a triangular blade. The few variations to be found occurred in the length of the socket and in the overall size of the weapon—depending upon whether or not it was intended for a musket or a carbine—and beyond this the differences in the bayonets were matters of individual finish and manufacturing tolerances. The bayonets were by no means interchangeable and were made to a gauge sufficiently large to take in most variations in the diameter of the barrel: some rattled and others barely fitted at all.

The bayonet issued with the Land Pattern and India Pattern Muskets had triangular blade measuring between 16$\frac{3}{4}$in and 17$\frac{1}{4}$in. The top face was flat, and the two side faces had fullers beginning approximately 2in from the reinforce at the joint of the shank and the blade. The blade itself had a maximum width of 1$\frac{1}{4}$in across the top face and the drop from the centreline of the bore to the top face averaged 1$\frac{3}{4}$in. There appear to have been two distinct lengths of socket; the longer, perhaps the earlier, averaged 4in and the shorter averaged 3in. However, the purpose of the latter pattern is obscured by the fact that both the Land and India Pattern Muskets were stocked to allow in excess of 4in at the muzzle for the socket of the bayonet. The base of the socket had a rounded reinforcing collar cut with a bridge to allow the passage of the stud on the musket barrel. The slot extended along the side of the socket for approximately 2in, when it turned through 90° and continued for a short way parallel to its original course. When fixed the bayonet blade was positioned on the right side of the piece.

Carbine bayonets conformed exactly to the pattern set for the muskets, but generally with smaller bores for slimmer carbine barrels and with smaller overall dimensions. The sockets measured between 3$\frac{1}{4}$in and 3$\frac{1}{2}$in, and specifications for the blade lengths of the various carbines ran as follows:

17in. Heavy and Light Dragoon, Light Infantry, and Sergeants' Carbines
15in. Pattern 1796 Dragoon Carbine (Harcourt's)
13in. Eliott's, Artillery, and India Pattern Sergeant's Carbines
8in. Cadets' carbines

Many carbine bayonets will be found with 'regimental markings' engraved on the socket: with rare exceptions these show rack and company numbers and the number of the regiment itself did not normally appear. As carbines were issued in much smaller numbers than the muskets, it is probable that their bayonets were not readily available—and it was therefore advisable to mark each pairing of bayonet and carbine. Bayonets of 'carbine' dimensions are known to exist with blades having measurements which do not approach within reasonable limits those given above: for these there is no explanation based upon documentary evidence.

In addition to the standard Government inspection stamps, the base of the top face of the blade often bears the name of the contractor who made the weapon, for example HILL or OSBORNE.

One conspicuous exception to the monotony of design found in these socket bayonets occurred with the introduction of the New Land series in 1802. Although the blade was virtually unchanged (the fullers began somewhat further from the shank) the socket was shorter—measuring about 3in—and was fitted with a flat retaining spring over the upper portion of the slot. The inside tip of the spring was cut with a step which dropped over the rear of the bayonet stud to provide a more positive fixing and the spring (about 2in long) was screwed onto the socket at the muzzle. This basic improvement was also applied to bayonets for the Light Infantry and Sergeants' Muskets of the New Land Pattern.

BRITISH
MILITARY LONGARMS
1815–1865

1. Guardsmen at the time of the Crimean War, from a contemporary engraving of 1854.

Background

It is true to state that the development and adoption of the rifle as a replacement for the musket as the arm of the Line infantry dominates the modern interest in the period covered by this volume: it must, however, be remembered that this development and rearming only occurred during the final fifteen years of a time during which a muzzle-loading weapon was the issue arm of the British services.

This span of a half century was predominantly one of peace, as Britain was involved in no major war between 1815 and 1853. The Crimean War of 1854–6 saw the rapid introduction and use of the rifle-musket—commenced under the most harrowing conditions of production and supply—with the resultant rapid decline in the use of the musket for regular troops. From the early 1850s a frenzy of interest in the military potential of the rifle swept the country and, with the press fanning the flames, martial ardour became the order of the next decade. Not until the largely theatrical threat of French invasion had demonstrably declined, and when the Volunteer Force had become permanently established, did this militaristic enthusiasm subside. With the rapid developments in small arms and artillery, it was perhaps the most important fifteen years in British Firearms history.

The long span of general peace which began in 1815 offered the military authorities and the gun trade the opportunity to remedy many of the faults in service weapons which had become apparent during the Napoleonic Wars, and this period consequently became one of experimentation with every type of weapon in each of the several branches of the service. Attention was given to Continental developments in ignition systems, various patterns of rifling and projectile design, with far reaching consequences. The transition from flintlock to percussion ignition took place—on paper—in 1836, while the change from smoothbore to rifle was delayed for almost another twenty years and was, even then, accelerated only by the advent of an unforeseen war.

The scope of this book does not allow the detailed examination of the large number of experimental weapons produced during this period for, as these are for the most part unique weapons, they are of primary interest only to the specialist. The Board of Ordnance's habit of authorising the production of 'trial' weapons, (sometimes of several hundred) for experimental issue to picked bodies of troops to test the attributes of some particular design has provided one difficulty. These weapons are sometimes found in private collections and do in one sense qualify as issue patterns because they have seen service in the hands of troops on active duty, and sometimes even in combat. As a result of their limited production and stated trial status, and because they were generally withdrawn after a short time, they have therefore been omitted from this study.

So far as the study of British regulation longarms is concerned, the fifty years discussed in this volume may be conveniently divided into three periods: the decline of the flintlock, the development and proliferation of the Lovell series of weapons, and the general introduction of the rifle for the entire British service. In addition, although it should not be considered as a major subdivision in any discussion of regulation arms, the last of these three periods included the serious experimentation with breech-loading arms—particularly for the cavalry—which culminated in the adoption of the Snider system for the whole of Britain's regular forces.

The decline of the flintlock occupied the years from 1815 until 1835. In the immediate postwar years there was little activity in the development of longarms, the emphasis being upon a reorientation to peacetime existence. By the mid-1820s, however, the Board of Ordnance had become revitalised and some tentative questions began to be asked, for example, about the accuracy of the Baker Rifle and the usefulness of the Paget Carbine. Some changes had already been made in the design of the Baker Rifle and its bayonet but, taking the entire period, there were almost no basic changes in the design of regulation weapons in the hands of the troops. The changes which were instigated did not affect the fundamental characteristics of the weapons and were made in the lengths of the barrel and the entire arm, with a suitable bore size selected for the particular purpose. The flintlock mechanism had reached its most advanced military form with the acceptance of the raised pan, ring-neck cock and safety bolt adopted on the Paget Carbine and some Baker Rifles from about 1808. There were no further improvements upon this general design and, in fact, the majority of the service arms did not enjoy these refinements.

Throughout the period from 1815 until the late 1840s the musket of the Line regiments was the India Pattern flintlock, vast numbers of which were also held in Store. The Guards—and perhaps some other special units—were armed with the New Land Pattern Musket, until the manufacture of the first percussion muskets in 1839. The cavalry continued to use the various flintlock carbines adopted since the Eliott, the regular cavalry armed primarily with the Paget Carbine and, for the Guards and Dragoons, the Pattern

1796 with and without Nock's enclosed lock. The 95th Regiment, known from 1815 as the Rifle Brigade, continued to carry the Baker Rifle with certain modifications on its bayonet, lock and sights, until it was superseded in 1840 by the Brunswick Rifle.

The wearing out of arms in service and the marked depletion of arms in Store were the two factors which, aside from the great fire in the Tower of London Armouries on the night of 30th October 1841, were the fundamental causes behind any of the major developments in smallarms prior to the outbreak of the Crimean War. Many new ideas such as the percussion ignition system, the two-groove rifling system, and others of far less importance were only adopted when other conditions—invariably unrelated to the significance of the idea—were suitable.

The barrels of military longarms were officially 'browned' from 1815 and the process was used on muskets, carbines and rifles made from 1815 until the middle of the 1840s. With the increasing use of plain iron for barrels of arms of other than musket type use of blueing increased, but it is impossible to assign an exact date when this process was approved for all new production of any particular arm. It would appear to be one of George Lovell's innovations, as Enfield-made longarms of all types are now found with original blued barrels of *c.* 1844—although it should be noted that not all Enfield-made arms were blued from this date. Arms made with twist steel barrels, including the Brunswick Rifle, were browned, while those with plain iron barrels were generally browned if made before *c.* 1846 or blued if made after that date. By the time of the introduction of the Pattern 1851 Rifle-musket the finish had developed to a point at which it remained until 1865, with a blued barrel and colour case-hardened lock, blued screws and a bright ramrod. When barrel bands were introduced on the Pattern 1853 these were heat-blued, and those short rifles made with iron furniture had the material colour case-hardened.

The second division into which the present study may be conveniently partitioned is that of the development and proliferation of the Lovell series of arms, extending from *c.* 1835 until 1851. Although George Lovell was not appointed as Inspector of Small Arms at Enfield until 1840, his influence became paramount in the mid-1830s and was in some ways evident from the late 1820s. His dual interests coincided precisely with the basic needs of the British service during this period: the perfection of the percussion ignition system for military purposes and the improvement of the rifle as a military weapon. In the first of these projects his success was unlimited and the basic form established by Lovell remained in use for as long as the percussion system was the standard of the services. The success of his two-groove Brunswick Rifle has suffered much at the hands of posterity but, from what contemporary evidence there is, it was a definite improvement over those which had gone before and was considered entirely satisfactory until Continental projectile developments surpassed all previous advances. To Lovell's credit he was not slow in taking a deep interest in these developments and the adoption of the Minié system was largely due to his guidance, encouragement and labour.

Although the production of experimental and trial weapons during Lovell's period created considerable confusion, his labours produced far greater uniformity and system with regulation arms than had ever before been achieved. The same size of ball for all service weapons, and hence a far greater degree of logistic simplicity, was nearly attained by Lovell's efforts—and indeed all smoothbore arms of his design would accept the same ammunition even though there were deliberate variations in the size of the powder charge for the several types. In February 1837 new bore sizes for the three basic types of service weapons were adopted, all of which were adjusted to use a 0.68in spherical ball weighing 483 grains. By slightly altering the diameter of the bore, it was hoped that the amount of windage would be increased or decreased according both to the need for accuracy and to the amount of use the type of weapon would be likely to have in combat. The muskets were largest in size at 0·753in, for they required the least accuracy and the greatest number of rounds to be fired; the carbines were smaller at 0·733in as the degree of accuracy required was somewhat higher and the number of rounds to be fired somewhat fewer, and the rifle was set at 0.704in so that maximum results would be obtained when the plain spherical ammunition was used for 'rapid firing' rather than the belted ball.

One of the most useful practices reinstated by George Lovell was the dating of locks and barrels, the latter on Enfield products only. Arms produced from about 1835 generally had a date, especially carbines and rifles. All Pattern 1842 arms had a dated lock, and Pattern 1839 arms began to be dated with regularity from 1846.

The final subdivision concerned with the muzzle-loading service weapon deals primarily with the general adoption of the rifle consequent upon the introduction of the Minié expanding projectile with a suitable rifling system. The basic design of both the Pattern 1851 and the radically different Pattern 1853 owed much to George Lovell's influence: the Pattern 1853 continued to use what were basically Lovell's designs of lock and furniture, lightened and improved in specific details. This final period saw three (if not four) types of weapons in the hands of British troops at one time: the Pattern 1839 and Pattern 1842 smoothbore series, rifled versions of these arms in limited numbers, a similarly limited number of Pattern 1851 Rifle-muskets and, finally, the Pattern 1853 arms. By 1865 the Pattern 1853 had almost everywhere been adopted, and the other types relegated to the militia, or to condemnation and sale out of Store. From the late 1850s the mounted service was issued with a variety of capping breech-loading carbines and, from the early 1860s a serious effort was made to decide upon a breech-loading mechanism suitable for the general adoption of the service. Even with the acceptance of the Snider system late in 1864, the search did not end until the adoption in 1871 of the Martini-Henry system—hammerless, self-cocking and of reduced bore.

The numerous variations in the Pattern 1853 series have been assigned model designations because—unlike earlier types which do not readily lend themselves to this interpretation—the changes made in the Pattern 1853, officially approved and promulgated, were applied to particular contracts when previous work had been completed. There was, therefore, a consciousness of specific changes both in the correspondence and in the publications of the period. Certain types were withheld from issue in order to first employ inferior designs and others were modernised when they were refurbished. Sealed patterns for most of the structural changes were set up and distributed and it is felt that, on the basis of positive proof of contemporary opinion and practice, it is justifiable to assign model designations within a larger pattern group. Some of the Lovell arms have been similarly classified, but the use of the terms Pattern 1839 and Pattern 1842 for other than the muskets has been fully explained in the section dealing with the muskets themselves.

The advent of the American Civil War of 1861–5 caused the production of more than a million Pattern 1853 arms which had no connexion with the British services and were intended for sale to Federals and Confederates alike. It is generally accepted that the majority of those produced in Birmingham went to the Federal Government while those set up in London had a better probability of purchase by the Confederate Government: there are, however, no indisputable proofs of this contention. These arms, although conforming to standard Third Model Pattern 1853 design, bore commercial proofmarks on their barrels rather than Government proofs, and lacked the small crowned Broad Arrow stamp on the lockplate and the various stock stamps denoting Government ownership—unless these markings were accompanied by Government condemnation stamps (see *Markings*). It should also be noted that very large numbers of Pattern 1856 and Pattern 1860 Short Rifles were commercially produced to arm the Volunteer Force which came into being in 1859–60. These arms were often ornate and varied considerably in detail from the regulation examples, hence giving little difficulty in identification. These arms normally had the retailer's name and address engraved upon them, although some were set up with locks originally intended for use on Government arms—and hence stamped TOWER—but without further official markings.

Muskets

From 1815 until the early 1840s—as late as 1848 for a few regiments—the standard musket of the Line infantry was the flintlock India Pattern, manufactured from 1797. It would appear that the Guards and perhaps a few selected Line regiments received issues of the New Land Pattern Musket, but it is believed that this latter model was not generally issued. In 1814, just before Napoleon escaped from Elba, the production of New Land Pattern Muskets was recommenced in the belief that peace had at last arrived and that a return to the preferred-quality arm could be made. Some 84,500 of them were set up before the end of 1817 but, with the exception of a further 800 set up at Enfield in 1823, there is no further documentary evidence of their production after 1815.

It is also debatable as to how many India Pattern muskets were set up after 1815. The records indicate that there were 722,000 muskets, of unspecified description, in Store in 1829. From this group some 488,500 muskets had been withdrawn between 1829 and 1839 and, apparently, it was not until the latter date that any great concern was shown about replenishing the supply. From surviving examples—rare though they are—it is known that India Pattern Muskets were set up as late as the first few years of the reign of Queen Victoria (Plate 2), but it seems unlikely that any great number of them were set up for issue to British troops after 1815.

In terms of strict chronology the Royal Navy may claim the honour of being the first to move with the times and accept the percussion musket. As early as November 1832 the Navy ordered 200 converted muskets with 24in barrels and a further 2,000 percussion muskets, again made from converted flintlocks, were ordered in June 1836—the length of the barrels of these not being specified. The advantages of the percussion system over the flintlock for sea service were obvious and the numbers involved were not so great compared with those involved in rearming the land services.

Although George Lovell's first pattern percussion musket, with a back-action lock and an enclosed hammer, appeared in November 1831 and although at least two hundred of these muskets were set up and issued for trials, the first regulation percussion musket to be officially sanctioned was not approved until March 1838. Not only was the musket the last regulation arm of the type to receive approval, but the initial order was only for 2,000 to be issued to the Guards.

Clearly there was still much scepticism in high places. The first order for the new percussion musket, Lovell's Pattern 1838 (Plate 7), was signed on 25th March 1839. It had been previously decided to set up 30,000 flintlock muskets to make good the deficiency of these arms in Store but on 17th May 1839 it was ordered that these should instead be set up as Pattern 1839 percussion muskets (Plate 9) and issued to the Line regiments.

The Pattern 1838 Musket was another of Lovell's brainchildren and fully reflects his perfectionist's ideas of the best possible weapons for the British service. It probably contains more structural refinements (as then understood) than any other longarm placed in the hands of British troops before the breech-loading period. The questions of their value as parts of a military weapon, and the significance of their expense, caused considerable modification to be carried out before any great number of them were produced. The design went through two major types, a 'large lock' and a 'small lock' version, and some 800 were made in 1840 with Wilkinson's chambered breech. The latest example noted was set up at Enfield and was dated 1845; it had a blued barrel, which was a finish then coming into favour for the plain iron type.

The Pattern 1839 Musket presents quite a different picture. It originated in a desire for expediency, as a means of using up a vast supply of obsolescent parts, but was at the same time intended to achieve the results of a percussion musket. In this objective it succeeded, but structurally few features of outstanding interest were presented. The most noticeable feature of the type was the variety of markings found on the lockplates, as the stock of old parts on hand in 1838 warranted the production of the Pattern 1839 concurrently with the later Pattern 1842 until 1851. It appears that *c.* 1846 the supply of lockplates began to run low and new plates were made to the old design but, of course, without the holes for the flintlock parts present on the original type. It is curious that although a backsight was fitted both to the Pattern 1842 Musket and to the Pattern 1838, no such refinement was added to the Pattern 1839 Musket and, although no details are known of the issue of the Patterns 1839 and 1842 Muskets beyond the fact that they went to Line regiments, it is certain that the Pattern 1839 must have been considered as a less desirable—possibily second-quality—weapon.

The Pattern 1842 Musket was approved on 27th October 1841 and got off to a much more rapid start than might have been expected. On the night of the 30th October 1841 a great fire gutted the Armouries and Ordnance workshops of the Tower of London destroying at least 280,000 smallarms, and therefore almost all of the recently completed percussion weapons including—amongst others—several of the early patterns of double-barrelled carbines, back-action lock Victoria Carbines, and early Pattern 1839 Muskets. Masses of flintlock arms were destroyed, making further considera-tion of that system no less expensive than the new percussion system; the existing stocks of percussion weapons were almost eliminated, thus creating the immediate need for replacement arms and the chance to modernise their design on the basis of lessons learned in the time the new patterns had been in issue. The Pattern 1842 Musket was the first result of these object lessons, and its production and introduction into the service were greatly expedited by the fire.

In addition to the obvious change in the design of the lock of the new musket, the Pattern 1842 was constructed with screws of a standard size and thread, and with a new barrel having the breech snail welded on rather than brazed. The New Land sideplate was eliminated and replaced by two circular cups with square projections on each side, which became known as 'Lovell's sidenail cups'. The barrel was held in the fore-end with flat keys which were far easier to remove and less likely to damage the wood in the process. The bayonet stud was given a slightly peaked shape and a notched block backsight, of the type previously in use on a number of arms, was fitted. Presumably the earliest of the Pattern 1842 Muskets were fitted with the Hanoverian spring-catch but very few of this model made before 1845 have been noted, and certainly the great majority of Pattern 1839 and Pattern 1842 Muskets were fitted with Lovell's spring-catch (which received official sanction in September 1844).

Unless the problem is studied on a regimental level, it is almost impossible to determine the actual service life of the several models of percussion muskets manufactured between 1839 and 1852. Events occurred in such rapid succession that the official life of a musket, set at twelve years, may in most cases be disregarded. There would obviously have been some attempt to replace the oldest arms first, but the requirements of particular units being sent on special expeditions must have created havoc in the system. The Guards and the Rifle Brigade were amongst the first to receive issues of the Pattern 1851 Rifle-musket early in 1853, but some reliefs for the Guards regiments sent out to the Crimea late in 1855 were still armed with Pattern 1842s. The advent of the Crimean War, coming as it did just about twelve years after the initial issues of the smooth-bore muskets, greatly accelerated their withdrawal from the Line regiments. It seems reasonable to conclude that by the time the troops returned home from the Crimea in 1856, few of the them would still be carrying a Pattern 1839 or Pattern 1842 smoothbore.

During the latter years of the Napoleonic Wars some significant changes were made in the design of the Sea Service Musket, although they were entirely in keeping with the overall production policies of the Ordnance and simply involved the standardisation and limitation of production variations. Earlier patterns of Sea Service Muskets (*British Military Longarms, 1715–1815*, plates 38 and 39) remained in use throughout the period of the Napoleonic Wars, but were gradually replaced by weapons which no longer included specially-designed Sea Service furniture. The length of the barrel and the Bright and Black Sea Service classifications were retained, but the arms were made entirely from India Pattern parts modified to suit the needs of the Navy. The larger 0.78in bore was eliminated and the standard size of 0.75in to 0.76in adopted instead. This changeover appears to have begun shortly after 1810. Sea Service Muskets made during the latter years of the Napoleonic Wars were of the inferior quality associated with India Pattern arms. With the coming of peace in 1815, what little new production was authorised returned again to the finer quality of the New Land Pattern. Sea Service Muskets of the 1815–30 period showed this quality clearly, for, even though they combined India Pattern and New Land parts, the finish was decidedly superior to the earlier arms of the war years.

Also during the 1815–30 period, experimentation was carried on with Sea Service Muskets of a shorter length than had previously been standard. It is uncertain whether these muskets were intended for naval issue or for other branches of the maritime service, but their quality was not equal to that of the longer regulation pattern. These short muskets were often simply cut-down military issue dating, in some cases, from the Land Pattern and there is little foundation for believing that they were intended as regulation arms. A change to a shorter barrel was clearly indicated and, when the first regulation percussion Sea Service Musket appeared (the Pattern 1839), it was made with a 30inch barrel instead of the earlier regulation 36 to 38inches. The first percussion muskets tried by the Navy in 1832 had 24inch barrels, but the length of the first large order for 2,000 percussion muskets placed for the Navy in 1836—and made from unissued India Pattern Muskets taken from Store and converted to percussion—is not known.

The Lovell Sea Service Musket, produced almost entirely in the cheaper and stronger Pattern 1839 form, made its appearance in 1840. It was not until the introduction of the Minié rifling system that the Pattern 1842 was used in quantity for sea service weapons, and then as newly produced Rifled Muskets. Few Pattern 1839 Sea Service Muskets were modernised by rifling. It is probable that the

Royal Marines were equipped with the Pattern 1839 Musket during the years that the Navy had the P/39 Sea Service Musket, and it has already been established that the marines were armed with the Pattern 1842 Rifled Musket when the infantry received the Pattern 1851 Rifle-musket.

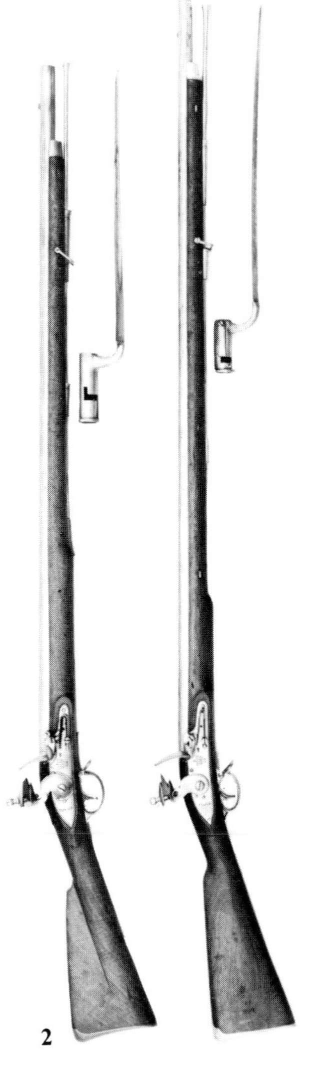

2 3

2. *India Pattern Musket*
The standard weapon of Line regiments at the close of the Napoleonic Wars in 1815, it remained so until the early 1840s, in some regiments as late as 1848. This example is *c.* 1838 and has the cypher of Queen Victoria on the lockplate. This model is fully described and illustrated in *British Military Longarms, 1715–1815*. The Artillery and Sappers were armed with an India Pattern Musket of standard design but with a 37in barrel. *Overall length 55in, barrel length 39in, calibre 0.75in.*

3. *New Land Pattern Musket.*
In addition to those manufactured during the Napoleonic Wars, some 84,500 of this model were set up between August 1814 and August 1817. It is believed that this, the most modern of British service flintlock muskets, formed the armament of the Guards regiments until withdrawn and replaced by the percussion Pattern 1838 Musket in late 1839. This musket was introduced in 1802, and is fully described and illustrated in *British Military Longarms, 1715–1815. Overall length 58½in, barrel length 42in, calibre 0.75in.*

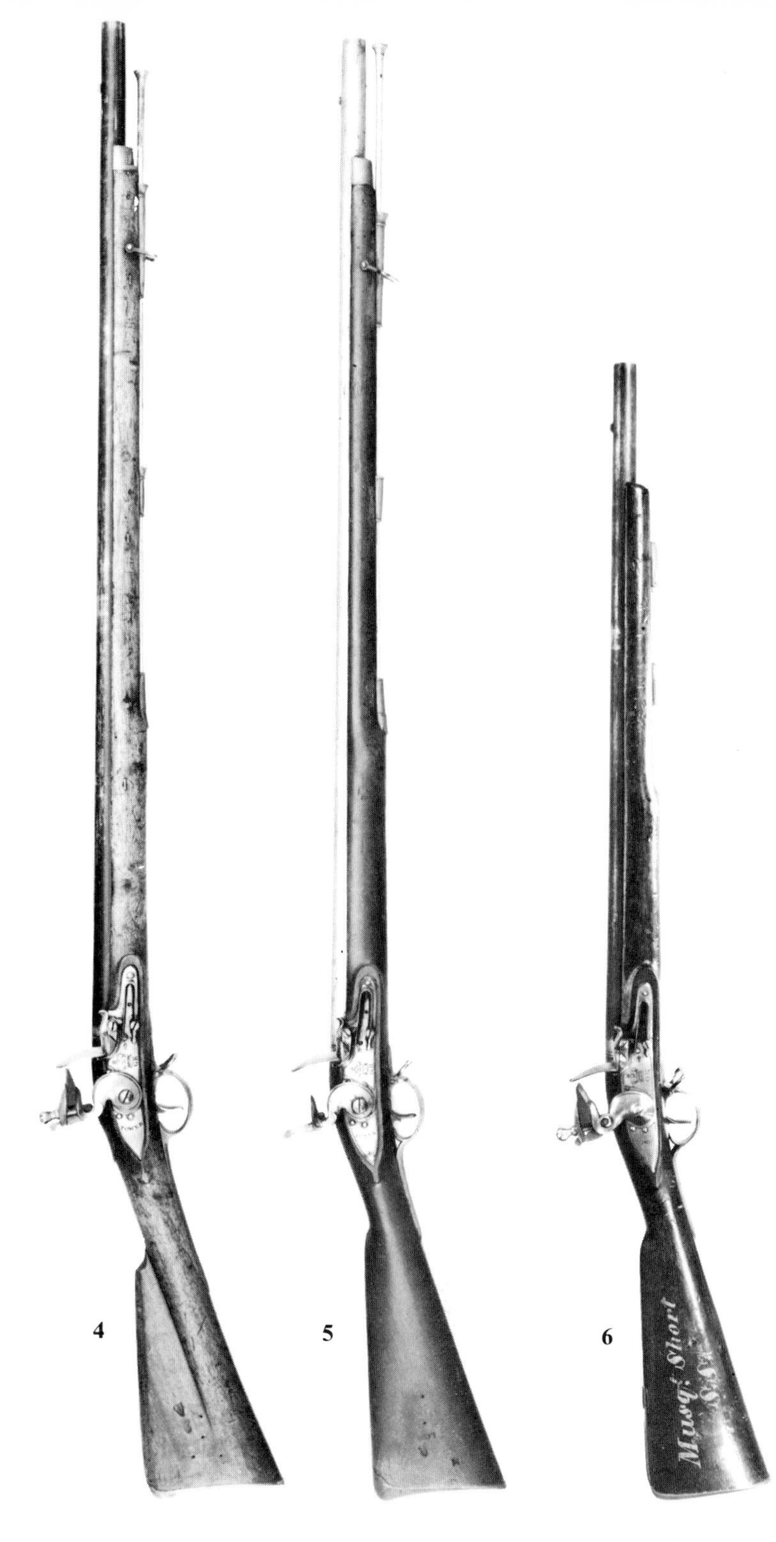
4
5
6
Musqt Short

4. *A Black Sea Service Musket of the period 1805–30.*

A shortened India Pattern Musket to which has been fitted a New Land Pattern fore-end cap, and a rod-retaining spring to the inside of the tailpipe. Staples have been driven in over the barrel pins to prevent their removal, and the barrel is draw-file finished and heavily blacked in the usual fashion. Pressure of wartime demands dictated the use of standard parts rather than the special Sea Service furniture previously used. This musket is typical of the type used for most of the Napoleonic War period and during the subsequent peacetime years until the adoption of the percussion system. *Overall length 52½in, barrel length 36⅝in, calibre 0.76in.*

5. *A Bright Sea Service Musket of the period 1815–30.*

A well-finished and obviously post-war combination of India Pattern and New Land Pattern parts, illustrating the return to higher standards of construction and finish after 1815. The barrel is a shortened India Pattern with the tip of the barrel tang rounded off. The ramrod, tailpipe, fore-end cap and lock are India Pattern, but of better finish. The design of the stock, upper and middle rod pipes, trigger guard, buttplate and sideplate are New Land Pattern. The tailpipe has a rod-retaining spring mounted internally and the fore-end has a slight swell at the tailpipe. *Overall length 52¾in, barrel length 37in, calibre 0.76in.*

6. *A Short Black Sea Service Musket, of the period 1815–30.*

Another combination of India Pattern and New Land Pattern parts, but not of the quality of the musket in Plate 5. The lock is a post-1809 India Pattern of relatively low quality. The barrel and ramrod are shortened India Pattern. The stock is basically a New Land Pattern but with a swell at the end of the external rod channel. The buttplate is a flattened and cut-down New Land Pattern. The two ramrod pipes are typical of these used on eighteenth century Sea Service Muskets, and the upper pipe has a rod-retaining spring. The upper sling swivel was mounted between the two pipes. The exact status of the Short Sea Service Musket during this period is uncertain, although it is believed that they were intended for issue to maritime services other than the Royal Navy during the flintlock period. *Overall length 42in, barrel length 26in, calibre 0.78in.*

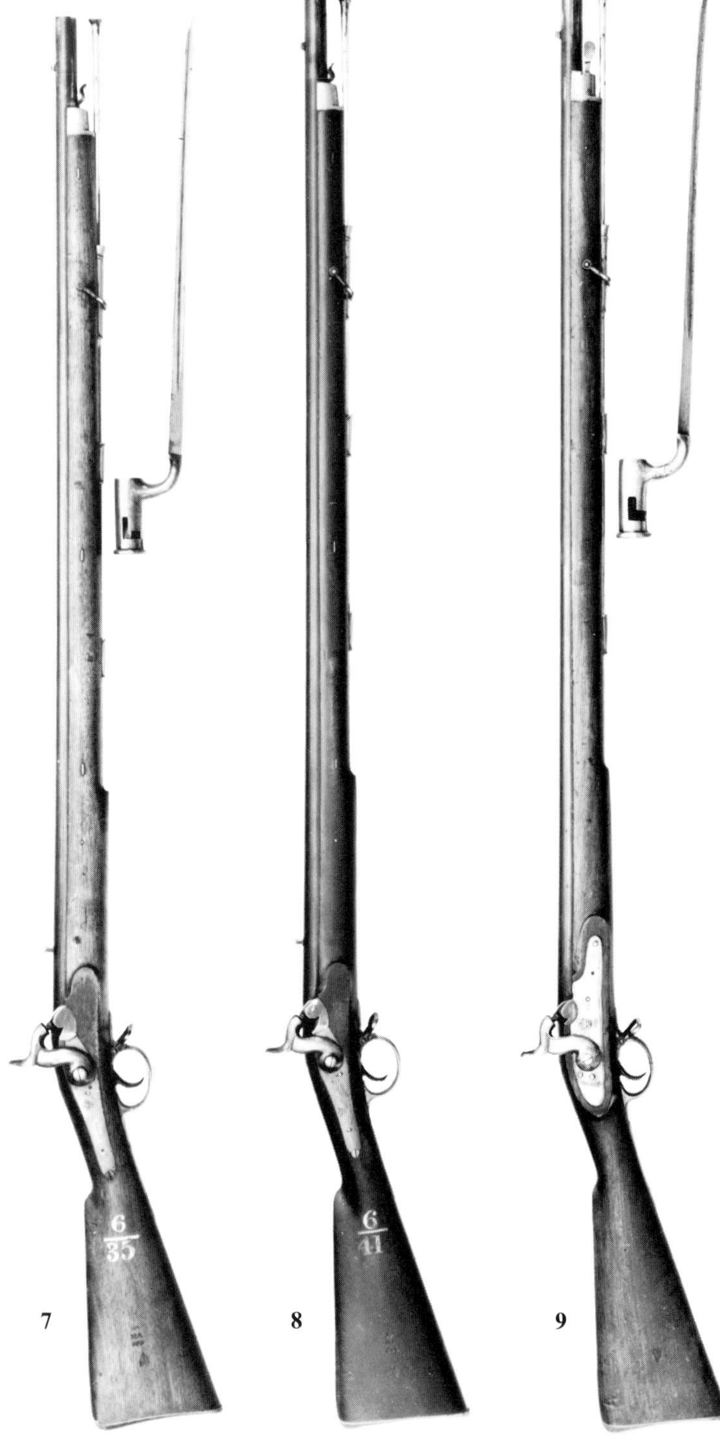
6
35
6
41
7
8
9

7. *Pattern 1838 Musket (large lock).* Approved in March 1838 and put into production in March 1839. Stocked to $3\frac{1}{2}$in of the muzzle, the brass fore-end cap being cut out to accommodate a spring-catch (known as the 'Hanoverian spring-catch') to grip the collar of the bayonet. The bayonet stud on top of the barrel is fitted with a blade to act as foresight, the first British musket so equipped. A plain notched block backsight is dovetailed and brazed to the barrel 3in from the breech and the barrel, fitted with a break-off breech, is retained by three flat keys and the upper sling swivel screw. There are three brass ramrod pipes and a straight button-head ramrod with slightly concave head. The rounded brass trigger guard is held by three screws—one through the front finial and two through the rear and the brass buttplate has a long tang with a pinched-in tip. One sidenail, with a circular brass cup, holds the front of the lock and the rear edge of the plate hooks under a woodscrew. The lockplate is $5\frac{3}{4}$in long (rather than 5in on the later 'small lock' version). The lock is not dated. This musket was officially known as the 'Musket, Rank and File, for Foot Guards, Lovell's pattern of 1838'. They were being set up at Enfield as late as 1845, and represent the most advanced designs ever adopted for a smoothbore musket in the British service. The triangular bayonet blade measures $16\frac{3}{4}$in and the socket has a plain rounded collar, gripped by the spring-catch. *Overall length $54\frac{3}{4}$in, barrel length 39in, calibre 0.75in.*

8. *Pattern 1838 Musket (small lock).* The lock used on this arm is identical in size to that used on the First Model Brunswick Rifle and the First Model Victoria Carbine. It made its appearance in March 1841 and apparently superseded the large lock on new production from that date. The description of this arm agrees with that of Plate 7, except that the lock is 5in long and the hammer is slightly smaller. The tang of the buttplate is made with a plain rounded tip and the lockplate is dated 1842. *Overall length 55in, barrel length $39\frac{1}{4}$in calibre 0.75in.*

9. *Pattern 1839 Musket.*
In October 1838 it was decided to set up 30,000 flintlock muskets to alleviate the shortage of arms in Store, pending the production of percussion arms. By May 1839 this decision had been amended to call for the production of percussion arms using the old parts: the Pattern 1839 Musket was the result. They were manufactured until at least 1851, and later examples have lockplates of new manufacture. These arms were never set up as flintlocks although fabricated from parts originally intended for flintlock arms. The earliest production, prior to the autumn of 1844, had the Hanoverian spring-catch, rather than Lovell's spring-catch as shown on this example. This musket is stocked to $3\frac{1}{8}$ in the muzzle, and the barrel is retained by three round pins and the upper swivel screw. The bayonet stud acts as a foresight and there is no backsight. The upper of the three brass ramrod pipes is trumpet-shaped, the two lower ones being barrel-shaped, and the button-head ramrod has a slightly convex head. The rounded brass sideplate is held by a woodscrew through its centre as on the New Land arms, and the tang of the buttplate is similar to the New Land with a plain rounded end. The lockplate has the holes for the steel screw, steel spring screw and stud filled—and is stamped ahead of the hammer with a crown over VR, and across the tail of the rounded plate, TOWER. The triangular blade of the socket bayonet measures $16\frac{3}{4}$in $\times \frac{11}{16}$in and the socket has a collar with a pronounced eccentric lug ('Lovell's lug') which engages the spring-catch. *Overall length 55in, barrel length 39in, calibre 0.76 in.*

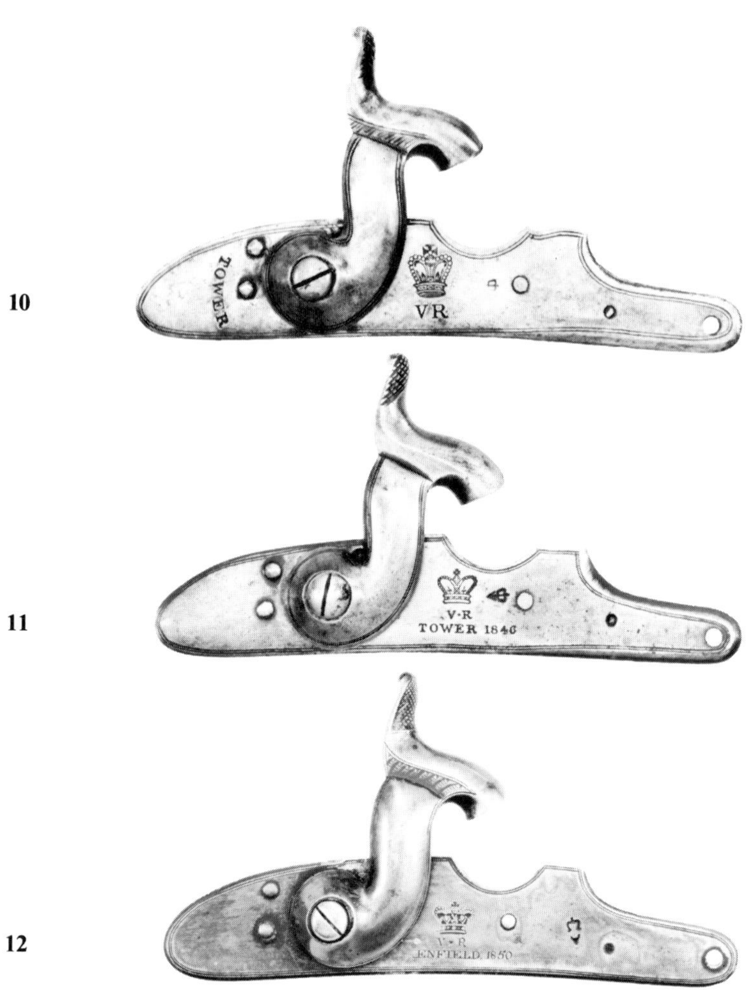

10, 11, 12. *Pattern 1839 Locks.*
These three locks indicate three periods of production of the P/39 Musket, the standard weapon of the Line regiments from the time the India Pattern was withdrawn until the issue of the P/51 Rifle-musket or, in some cases, of the P/53 Rifle-musket in the mid-1850s. Plate 10 shows the earliest type, with TOWER stamped across the tail, and the tail being still slightly rounded. The second lock, Plate 11 is dated 1846, and other dates until 1851 are known; this is still a 'converted' lock. Plate 12 is a new production lock with the latest type of markings for this pattern. New production locks are known dates as early as 1846, at which time the practice of dating P/39 Muskets apparently recommenced.

13. *Pattern 1842 Musket.*
The last of the regulation British smoothbore muskets and the first percussion musket of new production to be issued to British Line regiments, it is in design a revised Pattern 1838, using a side-action lock and omitting the refinement of a break-off breech. The barrel is retained by three flat keys and the upper sling swivel screw, and the ramrod is of the button-head type with a slightly concave head. The bayonet stud has a blade fitted on top to act as a foresight and the plain notched block backsight introduced on the Pattern 1838 is retained. The sideplate is replaced by two circular brass cups ('Lovell's sidenail cups') with square extensions on either side, a standard feature of P/42 furniture. The earliest P/42 specimens have the Hanoverian spring catch, but it appears that only a very small number were so manufactured before the adoption of Lovell's spring catch in the autumn of 1844. This pattern was set up until 1853. *Overall length 55in, barrel length 39¼in, calibre 0.75in.*

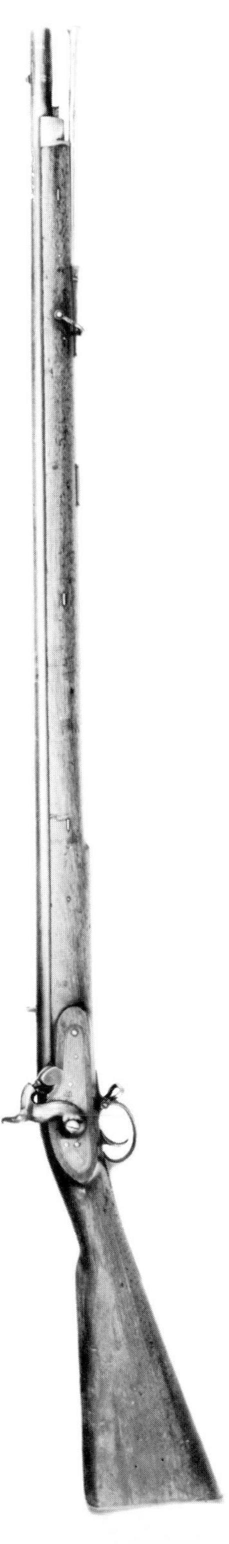

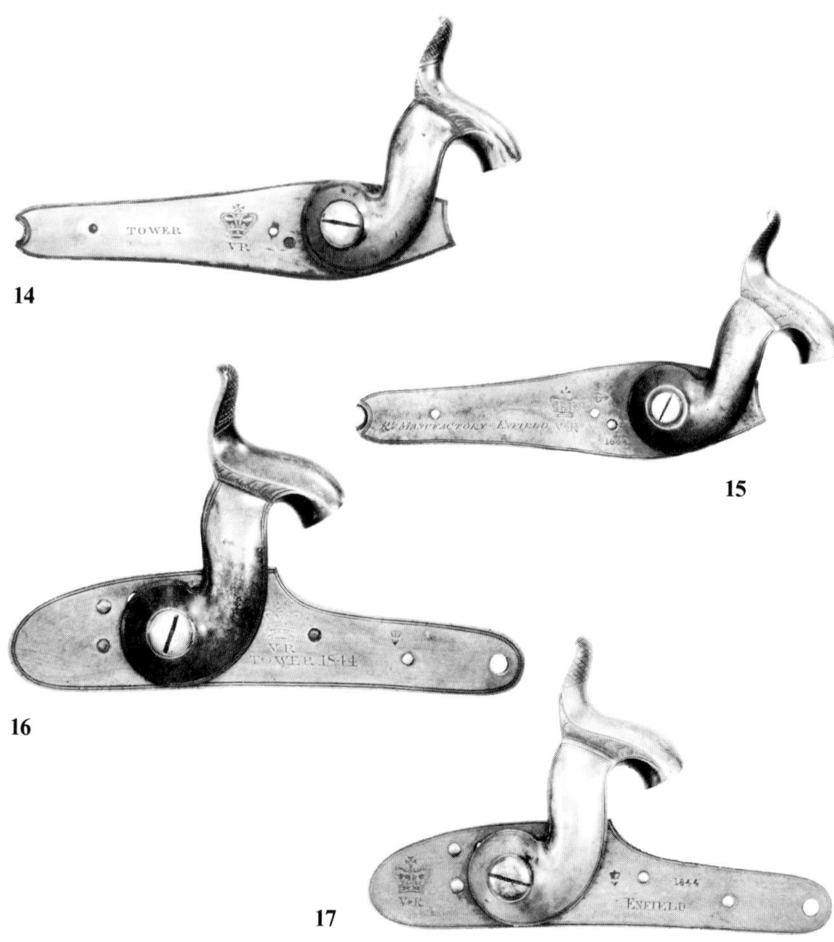

14, 15, 16, 17. *Lovell Locks.*
Plate 14 is the Pattern 1838 Large Musket lock which measures $5\frac{3}{4}$in, but is otherwise of standard design and has standard Tower markings for the Lovell back-action lock. The plate is sometimes dated inside. Plate 15 is the standard Lovell back-action lock, measuring $5\frac{1}{8}$in, with standard Enfield markings; this lock was used on P/38 Muskets, the First Model Brunswick Rifles and Sergeant of Foot Guards Rifled Muskets, and the First Model Victoria Carbine. Plate 16 and 17 show the P/42 lock used for all longarms of this model, with standard Tower and Enfield markings and decorative engraving: the plate measures $5\frac{1}{4}$in $\times$ $1\frac{3}{16}$in. Lovell's locks were highly finished and the lockplate and hammer were colour case-hardened. From 1845 the tumbler shank was changed from square to round, with a peg and slot fitting.

18. *Pattern 1839 Sea Service Musket.* This converted-parts musket is stocked to $4\frac{1}{4}$in of the muzzle and is fitted with Lovell's spring-catch. The bayonet stud acts as a foresight, and a plain notched block backsight is brazed on the forward edge of the barrel tang, just visible behind the hammer. The barrel, retained by two pins and the upper sling swivel screw, is blacked rather than browned or blued. P/39 Sea Service Muskets are by far the most common of this type and it is possible that P/42 weapons of this description were only set up after 1852 as rifled weapons. This example was set up at Enfield and the lock is dated 1845, the stock being dated 1846. *Overall length 46in, barrel length $30\frac{5}{16}$, calibre 0.76in.*

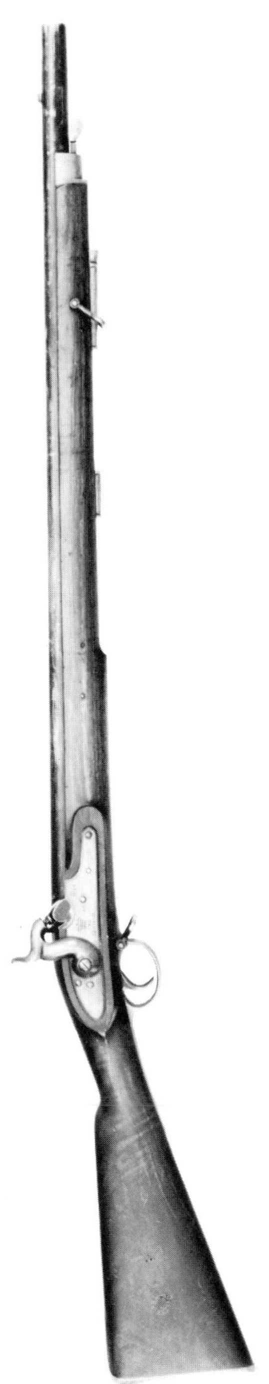

Carbines

For the greater part of the eighteenth century the carbines issued to various branches of the British service appear to have given satisfaction and it was not until the 1780s that the first serious murmurs of discontent were heard, principally of the excessive length and weight of this type of arm. Until 1812 the Eliott and Pattern 1796 Carbines had served as standards for the cavalry and dragoons respectively and in this year the Paget Carbine, with its 16inch barrel, made its debut. From this time onwards the complaints about the uselessness of the carbine increased but, until the end of hostilities in 1815, little could be done about trials with new arms. The period from 1815 witnessed a great increase both in the number of experiments with military smallarms and in the number of patterns submitted for consideration; small batches of arms were produced and issued for trials and—in general—every effort was made to improve the arms of the mounted service, but, inevitably, the development of a suitable carbine became entangled with the larger questions of flintlock or percussion ignition and of smooth or rifled bores. Indeed, when the Manton Carbine appeared the 10th Royal Hussars flatly refused to give up their Baker Cavalry Rifles. In 1827 a Board of Officers from many different cavalry and dragoon units was convened to consider ideal patterns and their deliberations continued spasmodically until 1833, by which time a mass of opinions and an imposing variety of patterns had been received. The result was the Pattern 1833 (or Manton) Carbine: a flintlock smoothbore with compromise improvements in the lock and redesigned furniture—but no improvement whatsoever in basic features over its predecessors and altogether a somewhat pointless exercise. It was obsolescent before it was approved and only 1,000 were made before the percussion era overtook it.

Throughout the period between 1835 and 1865 the history of the British service carbine was a nightmare of minor variations, small-order experimental arms, modifications to existing weapons, disagreements and disappointments over various patterns of breech-loaders and the utility of that principle and ammunition for military purposes and—finally—from 1853, a series of compromise weapons adopted pending further developments in the breech-loading field.

George Lovell's dedication to producing the finest possible weapons for all branches of the British services and his zeal for uniformity and standardization, both relative terms which must be taken in the context of the time, produced an attractive and extremely well made series of variations on a theme between the mid-1830s and the early 1850s.

The Lovell series was produced in two structural variations, one making use of a large stock of parts already on hand and the other representing completely new production. The differences lay primarily in the construction of the lock and breech area, as the other features remained virtually uniform with only a few minor differences. One point must be strongly emphasized for, although for purposes of identification the two types are designated as Pattern 1839 and Pattern 1842, these dates apply only to the musket in the original context. The structure of the carbines' breech was not specified even though most types were made in the two designs. Hence what are here called the Pattern 1839 Sergeant's Carbine and the Pattern 1842 Sergeant's Carbine were considered during the 1840s merely as the 'Sergeant's Carbine'. It is generally true to state that Pattern 1839 arms were made up using lockplates originally intended for flintlocks and which therefore have the holes for the steel screw, steel spring screw and stud noticeably filled. However, from about *c.* 1846 increasing numbers of newly made Pattern 1839 plates appeared and these are known with dates as late as 1851, indicating that supplies of the original component ran out in the mid-1840s, although there were sufficient stocks of other parts to justify the production of new plates from the old gauges rather than changing entirely to the Pattern 1842. It is also very probable, although there is no documentary evidence to support the contention that there was a deliberate policy regarding the issue of weapons which made the maintenance of a two-quality system desirable. Hence it is possible that Pattern 1842 arms were issued to particular units while others were, for various reasons, equipped with the slightly inferior Pattern 1839 with the resulting concurrent production of the two patterns.

The early Pattern 1839 Carbines, as well as P/39 Muskets, had undated lockplates but, beginning in 1845, the lock markings were changed to include the date—although the Pattern 1842 series were dated from the commencement of production. George Lovell's series of carbines is listed below for convenience; they are given in order of initial approval, and the dates are those of official approval. Bracketed designations indicate the production of the two structural variations described above.

Victoria Carbine, for cavalry, First Model with back-action lock and twist steel barrel, 1836

Sergeants of the Line Carbine (P/39, P/42), 1840
Sappers & Miners Carbine (P/39, P/42), 1841
Artillery Carbine (P/39, P/42), 1841
Victoria Carbine Second Model, with side-lock and plain iron barrel, 1843
Cadet's Carbine, 1843
Yeomanry Carbine, 1844

The most confusing group of carbines made during this period was the series of double-barrelled weapons made variously for use by mounted troops in Ireland, South Africa and India. The very small numbers of these arms made, coupled with officers' own ideas being wedded to basic service patterns to produce their own personal arms for colonial service, presented a selection of carbines which is very difficult to define with any degree of certainty. Those weapons which are known to be of a pattern made and issued to Government-equipped troops are illustrated, and in each case they bear marks of Government proof and ownership.

When the principle of the expanding bullet was finally accepted in Britain, consequently making the rifled bore a practical military reality, many of the older smoothbore muskets and carbines were rifled in an effort to modernise them in an economic fashion. This programme was applied in varying degrees to different models, and it is impossible to establish the numbers of some carbines so altered. Some found today with correct Minié-pattern rifling are nowhere mentioned in available documentary material. This applies both to the Lovell series and to the double-barrelled carbines. It is, however, evident from the number of examples existing today that the process of rifling was applied primarily to Paget-pattern Carbines (previously altered to percussion) and the Pattern 1842 Musket. Other branches of the service continued to carry their smoothbore weapons until the new reduced-calibre Pattern 1853 series supplanted them. The rifling of these older arms was carried out between 1852 and 1856 and it is probable that sometime in 1854 a change was made from the four grooves used on the Pattern 1851 Minié Rifle-musket to the three grooves used on the Pattern 1853 Rifle-musket.

Before considering the carbines of the 'new era' which commenced in 1853, it would be well to mention one large category of weapons too often confused with the Lovell series of carbines. From the time the basic Lovell patterns were accepted during the early 1840s, it became standard practice for the gun trades of both London and Birmingham to manufacture arms of these patterns for commercial sale. Not that these were always exact copies of particular military types—far from it—but they used the Lovell pattern lock and furniture to produce a generally inferior quality of arm intended for the open market both at home and abroad. Dimensions were usually sufficiently different from any standard military type to allow simple negative identification, but one feature which may be generally relied upon is the presence or absence of Government proofmarks. These are illustrated in Appendix I and should be carefully considered whenever any question of possible non-Government provenance arises. It should also be remembered that in some instances ex-Government parts were used to make up these arms, but it is extremely unusual to find both a lock and a barrel bearing Government markings incorporated into a commercial weapon, and where the finish of metalwork and wood do not give the game away. One of the finest characteristics of Government weapons made during Lovell's period of office was their finish, and the low quality of the commercial product is a feature of the weapons in question: there should seldom be any confusion when the carbines are carefully examined.

The first carbine to be introduced in the rifled-bore 0.577in calibre Pattern 1853 series was the Pattern 1853 Artillery Carbine, the design of which was actually settled before that of the Rifle-musket (although the carbine design also went through several modifications in external design). The second carbine to appear was structurally a short rifle, but is included here to maintain the official designation. This weapon, the Royal Sappers and Miners Carbine, was a revolutionary experiment (using Charles Lancaster's oval-bore rifling) which succeeded beyond all expectations—except, perhaps, those of the inventor. This carbine was approved in January 1855. In 1856, exasperated by the unacceptability of several types of capping breech-loaders, a cavalry carbine, the Pattern 1856 Carbine, based upon the pattern accepted by the East India Company was approved for issue to regular cavalry. The artillery and cavalry carbines were eventually redesigned and new models of each, known as the Patterns of 1861, were produced. Like most other late-production muzzle-loading arms, these were held in Store and almost entirely converted to Snider breech-loaders.

There were three capping breech-loading carbines which may be considered regulation by virtue of having been issued in fairly large numbers to regular cavalry and dragoons and of having Government ammunition designed and manufactured for them. In order of appearance the first of these was the American Sharps Model 1855 Carbine, 6,000 of which were received between May

1856 and April 1858. These were issued to cavalry serving in India and some were still in service in the middle 1860s. There were two variations, one with a slightly longer barrel than the other. The second carbine, which went through three variations in service pattern, was that of Calisher & Terry—or more simply known as 'Terry's Carbine'. The first pattern was approved in December 1858, the second in November 1860 and the third in March 1861. Production figures are uncertain although it appears that the first pattern enjoyed the largest production; the records indicate that they were only issued to the 18th Hussars. The third carbine, Westley-Richards' 'monkey-tail' design, suffered a lengthy and tortuous introduction into the service, but ultimately enjoyed the longest active service and remained in the hands of some yeomanry cavalry regiments well into the 1880s. The production model which was considered official, and 19,000 of which were made at Enfield, was Pattern Number 5 approved in March 1866. There are several of the earlier patterns which were produced in some quantity (generally around 400 to 600) but, at the time, all were considered as experimental trial arms.

---

19. *Pattern 1796 Heavy Dragoon Carbine.*
Fully described and illustrated in *British Military Longarms, 1715–1815*, this carbine continued to be issued to dragoon regiments until superseded in some cases by the Manton or Pattern 1833 Carbine and in others by the Victoria Carbine. This post-1815 product was made with the sling bar or with sling swivels instead of the bar. The lock of this example is of the post-1823 design with a return to the rounded swan-neck cock and the rounded tail to the lockplate. Browned barrels help to identify post-1815 examples. The Pattern 1796 or Harcourt's Carbine was also set up during this later period with Nock's enclosed lock, a device which proved very popular right to the end of its quarter-century of service, and which strongly influenced the design of the final flintlock carbine, the Pattern 1833. *Overall length 42in, barrel length 26in, calibre 0.75in.*

20. *The Paget Cavalry Carbine.*
Originally adopted in 1812, the Paget Carbine continued in issue until partially superseded by the Pattern 1833 Carbine and then finally replaced by the Victoria Carbine in the late 1830s and early 1840s. It was the cause of the lengthy series of carbine trials conducted from 1827 until the adoption of the Pattern 1833, and was not apparently considered a particularly useful weapon by those who used it. The flintlock version is fully described in *British Military Longarms, 1715–1815. Overall length 31in, barrel length 15⅞in, calibre 0.67in.*

19

20

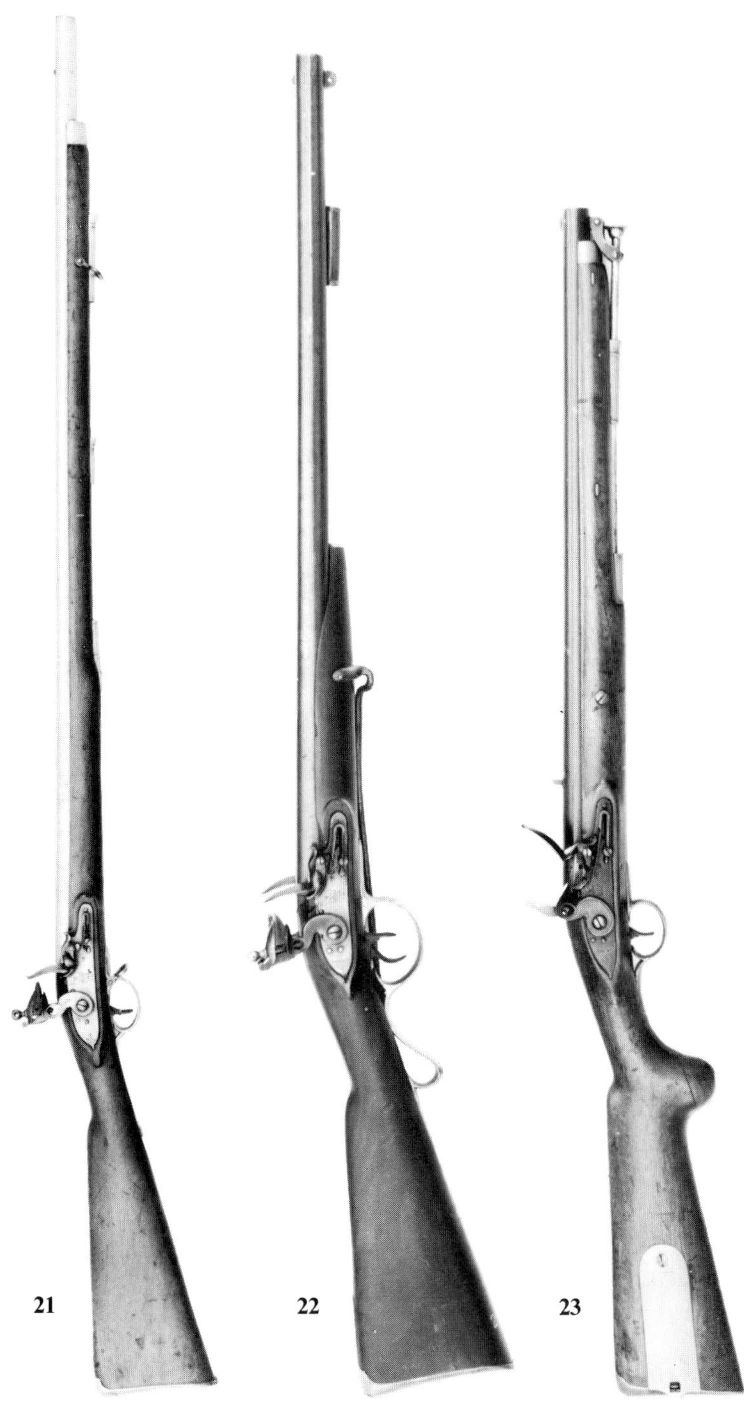

21 22 23

21. *The New Land Pattern Junior Cadet's Carbine of 1817.*
Although first designed in 1812, this carbine was not produced until 1817. It was intended for the Gentleman Cadets of the Junior Department of the Royal Military College and was subsequently adopted by the Royal Naval College and the Marine Society. It is a close copy of the New Land Pattern Musket but the sideplate, flat and with no woodscrew in its centre, more closely resembles the Baker Rifle sideplate than the New Land type. The steel spring of the lock is fitted with a friction roller. There is a brass shield-shaped escutcheon inlet on the top of the wrist, and a tailpipe of the India Pattern has been fitted. The ramrod has a button-head with slightly convex front and is made straight, without a swell. The fore-end cap does not have an extension or lip on its bottom edge. The barrel is retained by pins. The Cadet Carbine is stocked to $3\frac{11}{16}$in of the muzzle, and the fore-end has a slight swell at the tailpipe. The Senior Cadet's Carbine has a 36in barrel. *Overall length $49\frac{1}{4}$in, barrel length 34in, calibre 0.64in.*

22. *Cape Cavalry Carbine of 1822.*
The first in a series of limited-production double-barrelled carbines and the only one using flintlock ignition. This and the subsequent percussion types were intended for the use of mounted troops with police functions, both in South Africa and Ireland for, although carbines for use in India were very largely privately made arms those for South Africa and Ireland were of Government manufacture. This carbine resembles the New Land Pattern series in several main features including the locks and the buttplate, as well as the form of the butt. The scroll guard is of the pattern used on the New Land Light Infantry Musket. The locks measure $5\frac{1}{4}$in × 1in, but do not have raised pans. The sling bar is fastened at the front with a yoke, and at the rear is slotted up into the wrist and held by a heavy cross-pin. The barrels are browned twist steel, with standard Government proof marks, and are fitted with a break-off breech. For its length it is an extremely heavy and awkward weapon, measuring $2\frac{5}{8}$in across the locks. The swivel ramrod (missing on the example shown) has a large flat head and swivels similar to the Paget Carbine. A total of 252 of these carbines were set up between March 1822 and February 1824. *Overall length $42\frac{3}{8}$in, barrel length $26\frac{1}{8}$in, calibre 0.73in.*

23. *The Baker Cavalry Rifle of 1827.*
This rifled carbine was apparently only issued to the 10th Royal Hussars, their primary weapon between 1806 and the late 1830s. The first group of these carbines had been restocked in 1813 and in 1827 a further group of them were so altered, the pistol-grip having given complete satisfaction. This example is dated 1827 on the butt. The muzzle is well relieved to assist loading. The tang of the buttplate, which is of the Paget Carbine type, is engraved in large shaded letters, XRH and the left side of the butt has a cheekrest. The origins of this arm and its early production are discussed in *British Military Longarms 1715–1815. Overall length $35\frac{5}{8}$in, barrel length $20\frac{1}{4}$in, calibre 0.625in, rifled with seven angular grooves making one-quarter of a turn in the length of the barrel.*

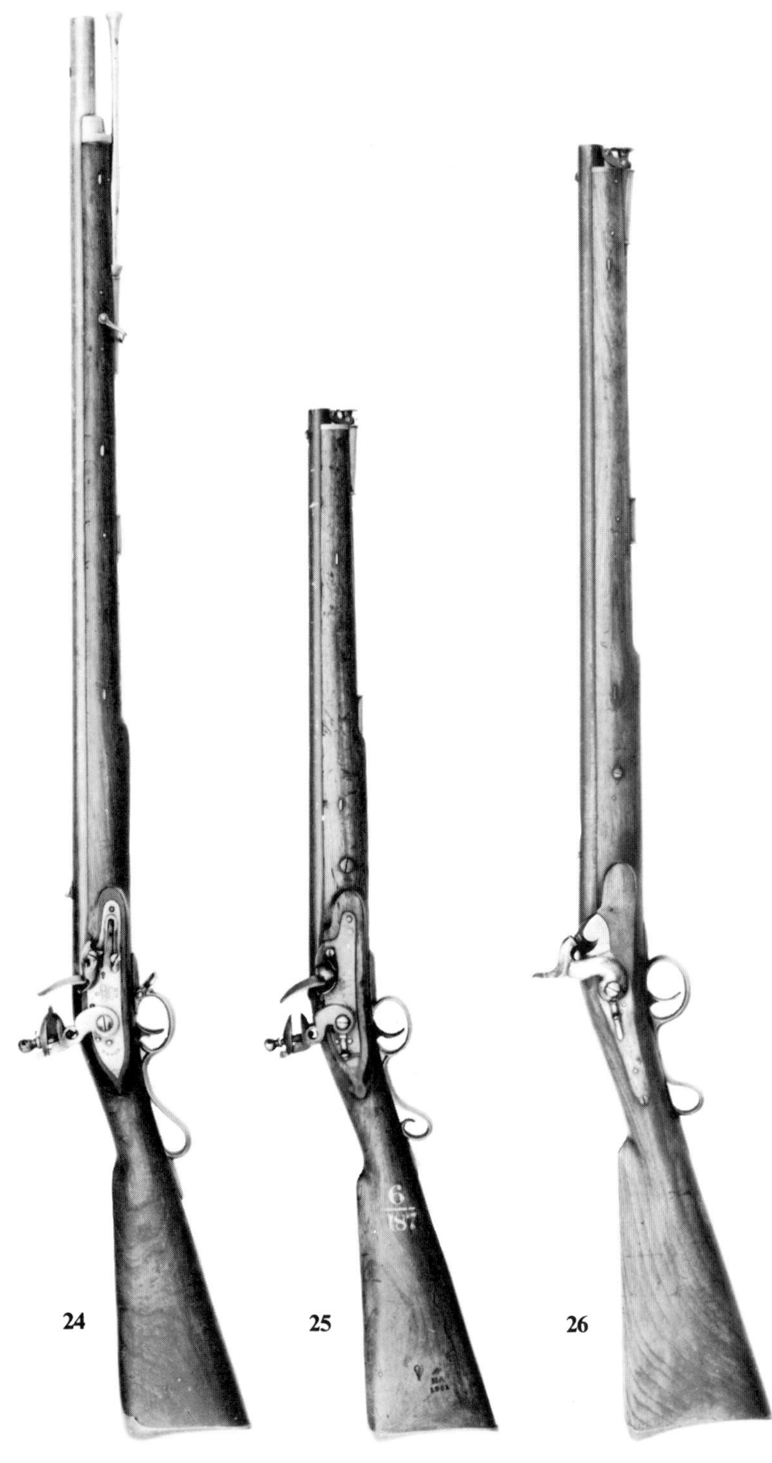

24 25 26

24. *New Land Pattern Sergeants Carbine of 1832.* This is the last member of the New Land Pattern group which first appeared in 1802, and whose entire service existence was sharply curtailed first by the exigencies of the Napoleonic Wars and finally by the economy of a peacetime military budget. These carbines are in fact Light Infatry Muskets which were cut down at Enfield in May 1832. Although intended for issue to sergeants of infantry it is questionable whether, at a time when the percussion question was uppermost in many military minds, many of these carbines were actually issued. They were—like the Pattern 1833 Carbine—obsolescent when produced. These arms are stocked to $3\frac{3}{8}$in of the muzzle and have only two ramrod pipes. The plain iron barrels are browned. In all other features they conform exactly to the New Land Pattern Light Infantry Musket. *Overall length $48\frac{7}{8}$in, barrel length 33in, calibre 0.78in.*

25. *Pattern 1833 or Manton Carbine.* This carbine represents the last officially approved flintlock longarm of the British service, and was the result of a long series of trials and experiments with various forms of carbines begun in 1827. Although it bears Manton's name both as the Master Furbisher and as the individual who put forth the final combination of features, the real credit for the several distinctive components should go to Ezekiel Baker and Henry Nock. The stock and furniture, and the short-swivel rod are connected with Baker's earlier designs, while the break-off breech and the lock are associated with Nock's military designs. The actual experimentation at the time became a contest between Charles Moore, the London gunmaker and furbisher of Hampton Court and St. James's Palaces—who copied Nock's lock in its entirety—and Charles Manton, who advocated a standard form of lock. The result was a compromise: note the flat brass fore-end plate and the trumpet pipe which fits into the lower edge of it. The rounded brass scroll guard is secured by three screws and the sideplate is of New Land Pattern with a woodscrew in the centre, but is flat and flush with the wood. The sling bar, 6 inches long, is held by the rear sidenail and by a screw through the fore-end at the front. The barrel is retained by two keys and is fitted with a break-off breech, the standing breech having a scoop-shaped backsight at its front. The plain iron barrel is browned. The lock has a raised pan and the steel spring is inside the lock, located just beneath the pan reinforce. The toe of the steel has a roller. Between July 1835 and June 1837 one thousand of these carbines were completed to the only order. *Overall length 36in, barrel length 20in, calibre 0.66in.*

26. *Victoria Carbine, First Model of 1836.*
This little-known carbine actually went into production in January 1838 and is a curious combination of earlier features and Lovell's new ideas. The short-swivel ramrod, fore-end plate, and upper pipe and scroll guard are all features of the Pattern 1833 Carbine—and were actually parts left over from the P/33. The back-action lock with the bolt for locking the hammer in the down position was Lovell's idea and so, presumably, was the method of securing the rear of the sling bar by screwing it directly into the wood. The buttplate, the break-off breech and the breech snail are all of Brunswick pattern. The browned twist steel barrel is secured by two flat keys. Production of the First Model is not thought to have been extensive. *Overall length $42\frac{1}{8}$in, barrel length 26in, calibre 0.73in.*

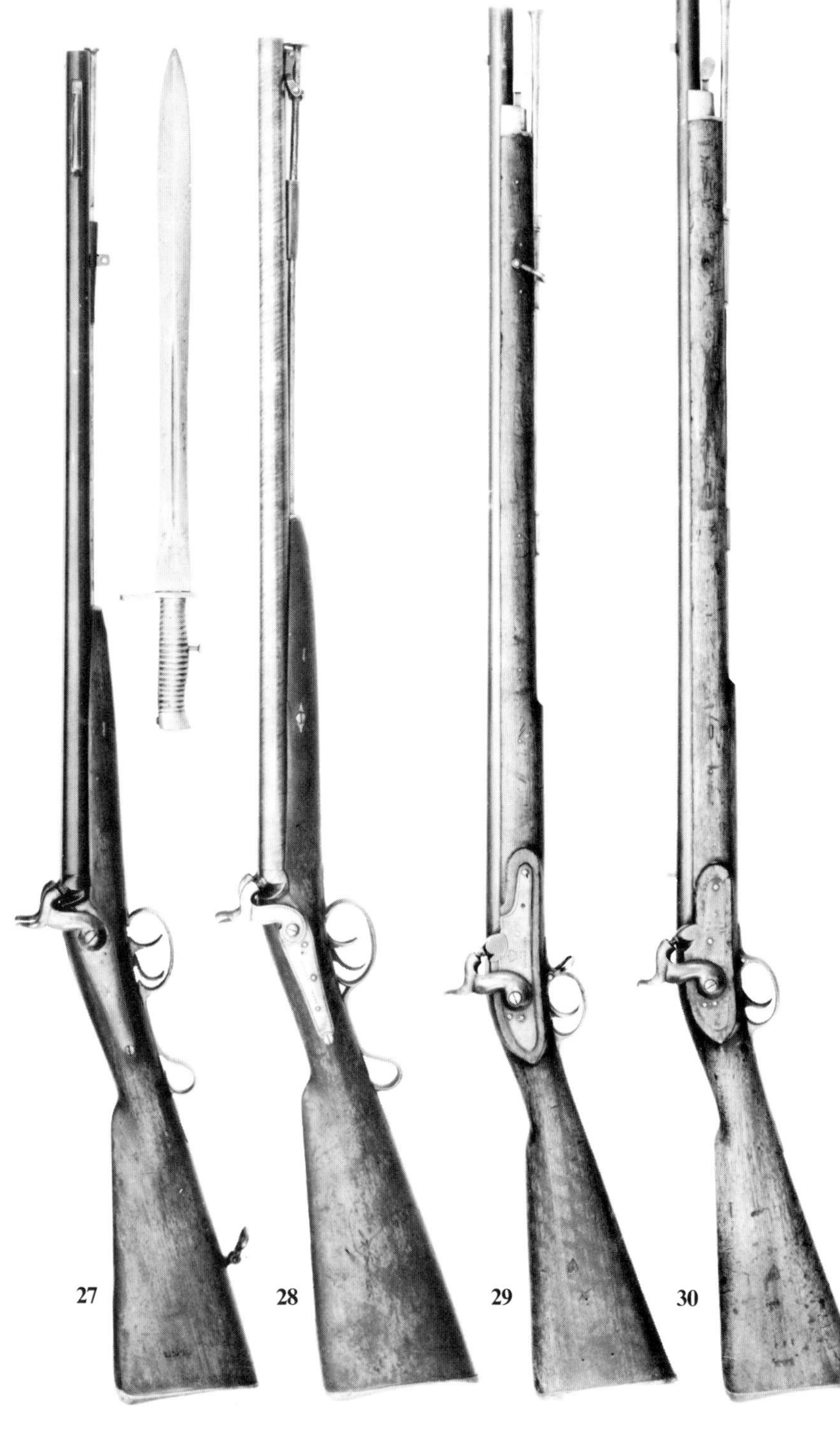
27
28
29
30

27. *Irish Constabulary Carbine of 1839.*
Constabulary carbines may be generally distinguished from Cape Carbines of the same construction by the presence of sling swivels and a sword bayonet bar, as Cape Carbines normally have a sling bar and swivel ramrod. The double-barrelled carbine approved for Irish service in 1839 originated with Tipping & Lawden of Birmingham and served as the basic pattern until double-barrelled carbines were generally withdrawn. The sword bayonet bar normally has a circular cross-section. The double-edged bayonet blade measures 16⅞in. *Overall length 42¼in, barrel length 26in, calibre 0.66in.*

28. *Cape double-barrelled Carbine, c. 1840.*
It is questionable whether there was a regulation Cape Carbine between the flintlock pattern of 1822 (Plate 22) and the rifled arm of 1854 (Plate 42) but, if there was, it is probably the weapon shown. This bears the name and address BARNETT LONDON on both locks, and the rib is engraved in script, CAPE CAVALRY. The barrels are of twist steel, browned, and bear old partially-removed Georgian proofmarks; there are no commercial proofmarks and the weapon has been sold out of Store. It has the typical features of a swivel ramrod, sling bar on the left side, scroll guard, and musket-bore. There are numerous indications of small orders for double-barrelled carbines in the 1835–45 period but, as few details are given, it is impossible to define which of them were intended for the Cape. It seems likely that the majority of Cape carbines were obtained through private channels and that only a small number were sent out by the Ordnance which ultimately served as patterns which were apparently closely followed by commercial gunsmiths. This weapon is offered as typical as it bears Government proof and ownership markings along with the salient features which distinguish the Cape from the Irish Constabulary Carbine. *Overall length 43in, barrel length 26½in, calibre 0.74in.*

29, 30. *Sergeants of the Line Carbine of 1840.*
Plate 29 is the Pattern 1839, and Plate 30 the Pattern 1842 version. Notable differences exist in construction aside from the pattern of the lock, breech snail and stock carving, including the use of pins to retain the barrel of the P/39 which were replaced in the P/42 by keys, and the absence of a backsight on the P/39. The sideplate of the P/39 is of the New Land Pattern, with a woodscrew through its centre, while the P/42 has Lovell's cups only. The sling swivels are missing from the P/42 shown. The carbine, or 'Serjeant's Musket' was approved in 1840 and is known with dates as late as 1852. *Overall length 49in, barrel length 33in, calibre 0.73in.*

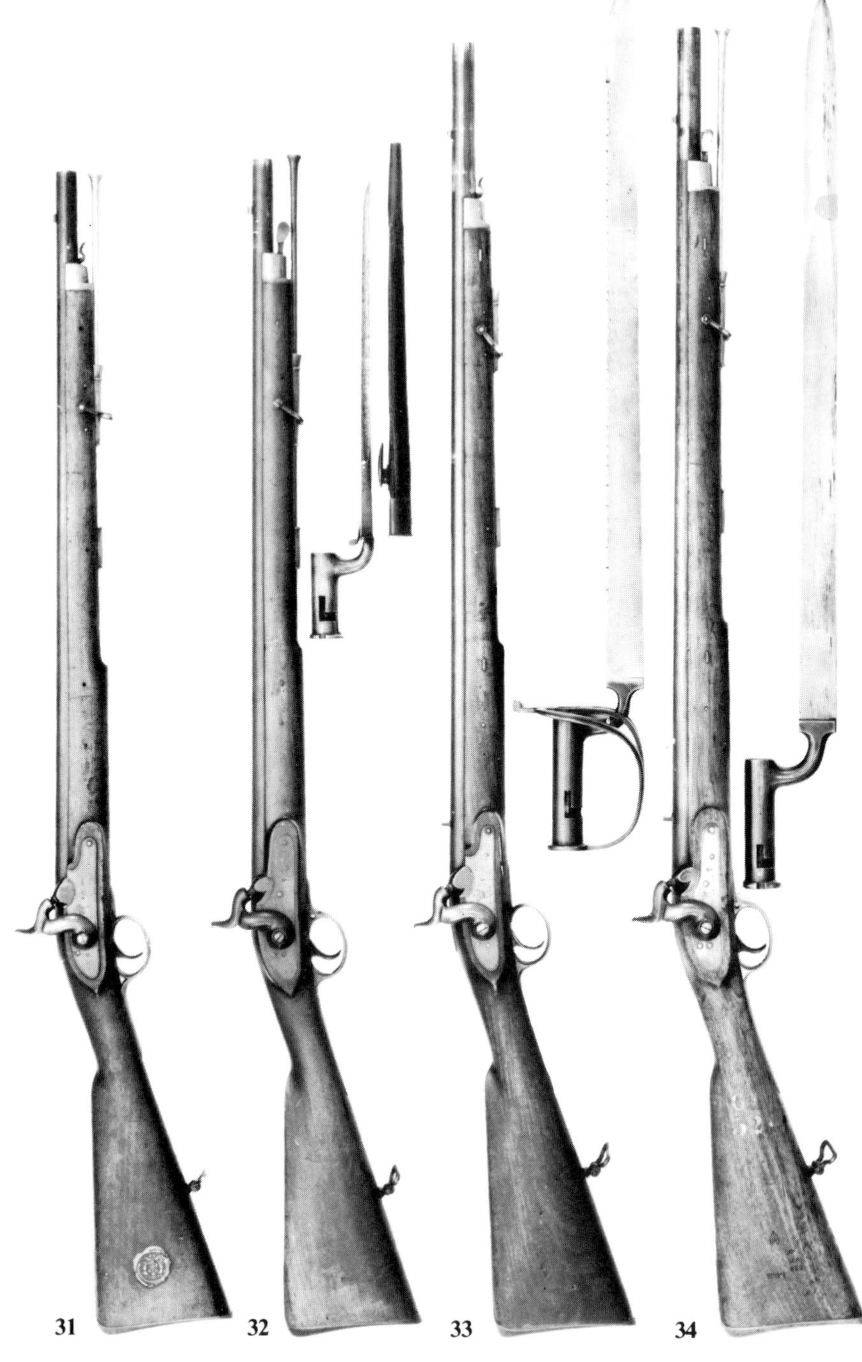

31 32 33 34

31, 32. *Constabulary Carbine of 1840.* Plate 31 is the sealed pattern of the P/39 version, and Plate 32 is the P/42 style with the special bayonet for this model. Note the use of the Hanoverian spring-catch on the P/39 and the Lovell catch on the P/42. The position of the lower sling swivel is characteristic of the Constabulary Carbine, as is the absence of a backsight combined with the barrel length and bore size. The P/42 shown here is dated 1852. The blade of the bayonet is 13in long and has a spring catch on the inside face which holds the blade firmly in its scabbard to prevent it being readily removed by an assailant. *Overall length 42½in, barrel length 25⅝in, calibre 0.65in.*

33, 34. *Royal Sappers & Miners Carbine of 1841.* Plate 33 is the Pattern 1839, with the first pattern saw-backed bayonet which was approved in March 1841 and placed in production in June 1842. Plate 34 is the Pattern 1842 type, with the second pattern of bayonet approved in January 1843. The use of keys on the P/39 and the form of the guard bow are not typical, as this example is a pattern arm. Production weapons do not have these features. The P/39 Royal Sappers & Miners Carbines are stocked to 5½in of the muzzle and the bayonet stud is filed on top to form a blade sight; the notched block backsight is brazed 2½in ahead of the breech. Those of P/42 type are stocked to 4⅝in of the muzzle, the socket of the second pattern bayonet being just this length. The blade of the first pattern saw-backed bayonet measures 24¾in × 1⅜in, while the plain blade of the second pattern measures 25½in × 1$\frac{5}{16}$in and is double-edged for 9in from the tip. *Overall length 46in, barrel length 30⅛in, calibre 0.73in.*

35. *The Artillery Carbine of 1841.*
It is questionable whether or not there is any structural difference between this and the Royal Sappers & Miners Carbine. The example from which measurements were taken is stocked to 4⅝in of the muzzle, which is identical to the P/42 RS&M Carbine but shorter than the P/39 version intended for the saw-backed bayonet. It seems probable that with the introduction of the second pattern bayonet for the RS&M Carbine on the Pattern 1842 version, the distinction between this and the Artillery Carbine disappeared. Both types were intended to take a standard socket bayonet, the difference being that for special purposes the RS&M Carbine was to have used the special sword bayonet. The butt swivel is in the same location as the RS&M Carbine. This example, dated 1848, has a blued barrel and the blade of the bayonet measures 16¾in. The Artillery Carbine was approved in September 1841 and was made in both Pattern 1839 and 1842 styles, with—as usual—no distinction being made at the time. *Overall length 46in, barrel length 30¼in, calibre 0.73in.*

36. *The Victoria Carbine Second Model, with side-action lock, 1843.*
Numerous complaints about features of the First Model (Plate 17), and Lovell's desire for uniformity, brought about the approval of this improved Victoria Carbine in mid-1843. The side-action lock used on the Brunswick Rifle was substituted for the back-action lock, and the break-off breech was omitted in favour of the plain pattern; the twist steel barrel was abandoned in favour of plain iron. The Brunswick pattern scroll guard was standardised in place of the Manton pattern rounded version used on the earlier Victoria Carbines, although this had already come into use to some extent on the examples of the First Model made after 1840. The 5½in sling bar on the left side is held at the front by a screw through the fore-end from the right side and, at the rear, it is screwed directly into the sideplate flat between the two sidenails. The Second Model Victoria Carbine was last set up in 1854 and later production examples are found with P/53 buttplates (having a screw in the tang). *Overall length 41¾in, barrel length 26in, calibre 0.73in.*

37. *The Junior Cadet's Carbine, 1843.*
In appearance the Cadet Carbine is a small-scale artillery carbine, but without the addition of a special spring catch for the bayonet. Two other features aside from its reduced dimensions distinguish the Cadet Carbine: the presence of an octagonal escutcheon of brass inlaid on top of the wrist and the positioning of the backsight 4¾in ahead of the breech, rather than the typical 2½in to 3in of other models. Approved in December 1843, this type was first manufactured in 1844 and it is believed only in the P/42 style. There is a known variation, identical in all respects but with a 33½in barrel: it is known that some of these, the Senior Cadet's Carbine, were set up at Enfield in 1846. *Overall length 42¾in, barrel length 26⅞in, calibre 0.68in.*

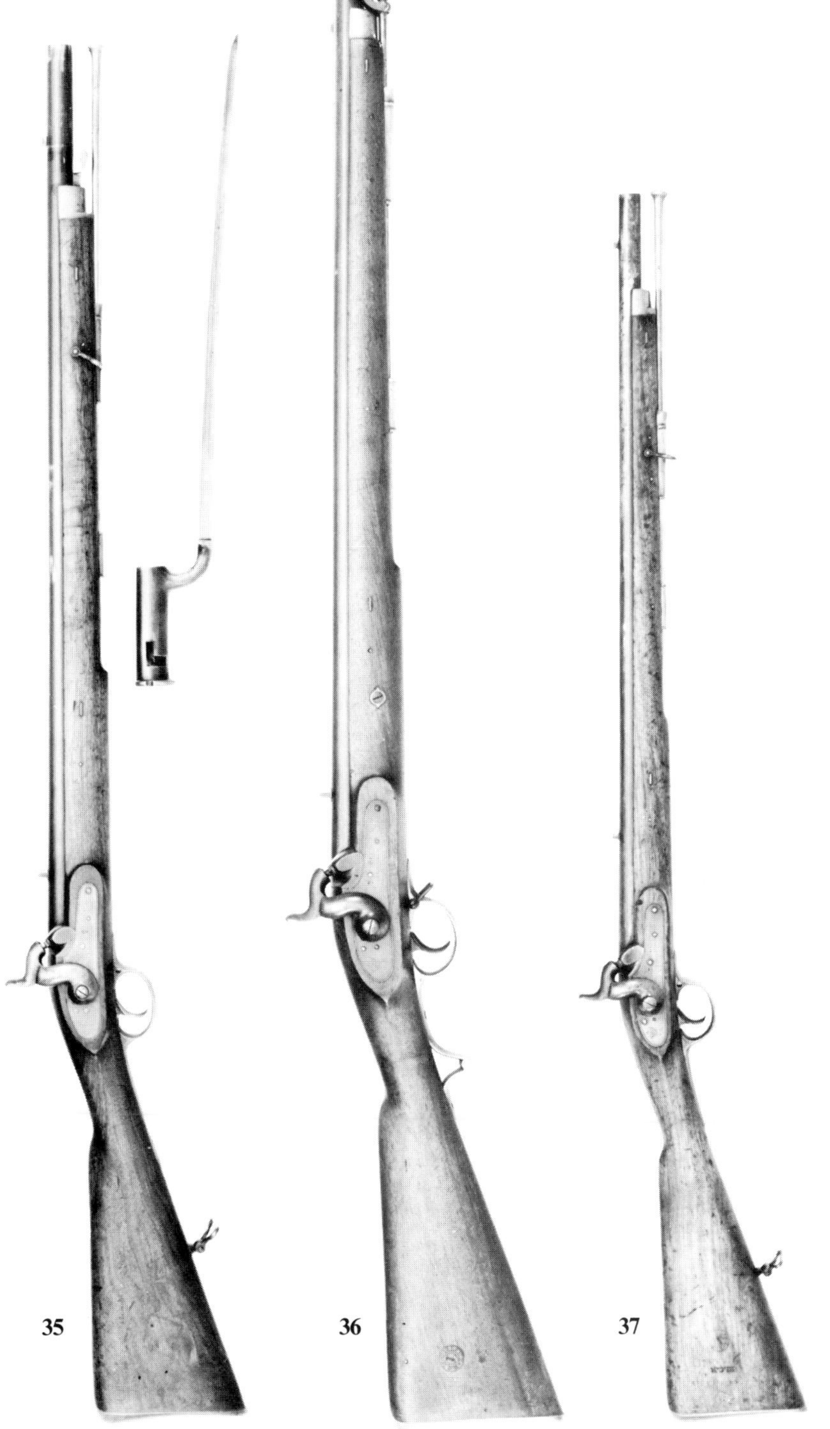

35

36

37

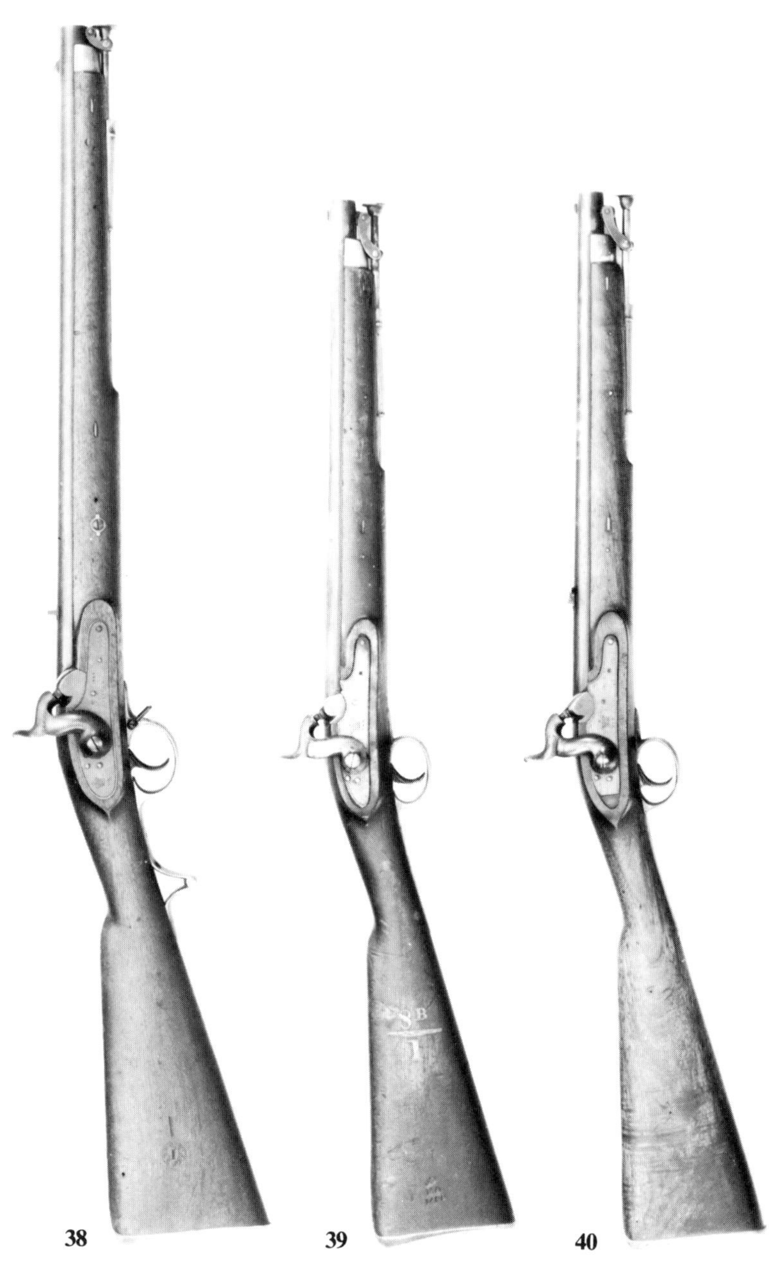

38

39

40

38. *The Yeomanry Carbine of 1844.* The Yeomanry cavalry were armed with a variety of old and new weapons concurrently, of which this P/42 arm is but one example which may be considered standard for that branch of the service. It is really a smaller version of the Second Model Victoria Carbine, for which it is often mistaken. It uses the standard side-lock having a $5\frac{1}{4}$in lockplate and has the same pattern furniture and sling bar as the Victoria Carbine; it has, however, only one ramrod pipe, and the stock is slightly lighter and smaller in size—but not sufficiently so to make necessary any change in the size of the lock or furniture. The barrels are generally of browned twist steel. One known variation has a longer sling bar attached at the rear underneath the rear sidenail, with a small extension of the bar to the rear securèd by a woodscrew. *Overall length 36in, barrel length 20in, calibre 0.66in.*

39. *Paget Percussion Carbine of 1847.* Another 'standard' weapon of the Yeomanry Cavalry came into being in 1847 as an attempt to make some use of large numbers of parts in Store for the old Paget Carbine. While some original flintlock Paget Carbines were converted to percussion, examination of large numbers of examples indicates that most of the percussion Paget arms were of new production, using older parts where possible. Some locks were completely refinished at the time of construction so that they bear the crowned V*R ahead of the hammer, while others will retain the original GR or WR cyphers. The sliding safety bolt on those which originally had them has been removed and the slot filled in. The locks, barrels, swivel ramrods and sling bars on those which have them, were the principle Paget parts usèd. New stocks, trigger guards, longer trumpet ramrod pipes and Lovell pattern buttplates were added. Most barrels will have the original Georgian Government proofmarks, but some have newer Victorian marks for non-Enfield production. Some barrel tangs bear dates between 1847 and 1851. *Overall length $31\frac{1}{2}$in, barrel length 16in, calibre 0.66in.*

40. *Paget Rifled Carbine of 1852.* The Paget Carbine was one of the several smoothbore arms which were taken from Store and rifled upon the Minié principle during the first half of the 1850s. As with the other arms, both four and three-groove rifling was used. They are generally stamped with their new calibre, '.685' on the barrel tang, but some still have only the date of original manufacture. A small block backsight, graduated to 300 yards and with two leaves hinged forward, is dovetailed into the barrel $3\frac{1}{2}$in from the breech. Paget Rifled Carbines are some of the most common of the 'rifled-up' series, and they continued in service with the Yeomanry Cavalry as late as the mid 1860s. *Overall length $31\frac{1}{2}$in, barrel length 16in, calibre 0.685in, rifled with four or three broad shallow angular grooves making one turn in 78in.*

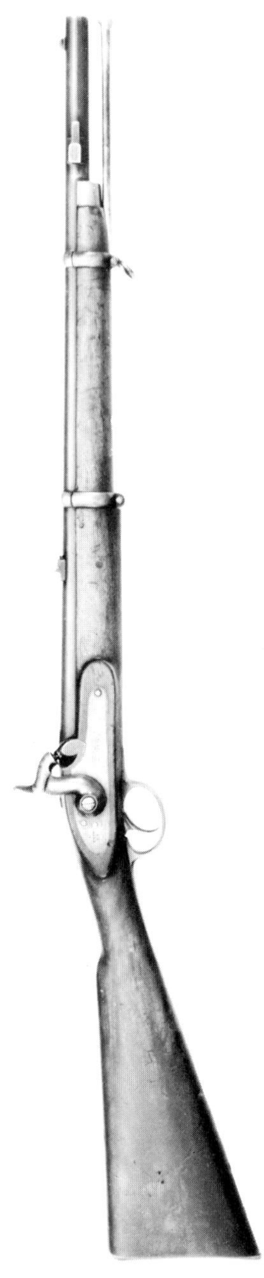

41. *The Pattern 1853 Artillery Carbine, First Model of 1853.*
The very first of the Pattern 1853 arms to be approved, the Artillery Carbine dates from January 1853, although the initial contract was not signed until October 1853 and the first contracts were not completed until December, 1854. The features which distinguish this model from subsequent types are the bayonet bar with its forward extension, the button-head ramrod with a swelled stem and the thin well-curved hammer typical of all early Pattern 1853 arms. The butt swivel is missing on this example, which is dated 1854. Artillery Carbines were also manufactured in Belgium from early 1855 and continued to be made there, in the First Model, until 1857. These Belgian contract carbines are identical to the English produce except for the markings (see Plate 72). The two leaves of the backsight are graduated for 200 and 300 yards. *Overall length 40in, barrel length 24in, calibre 0.577in, rifled with three broad angular grooves of uniform depth, making one turn in 78in.*

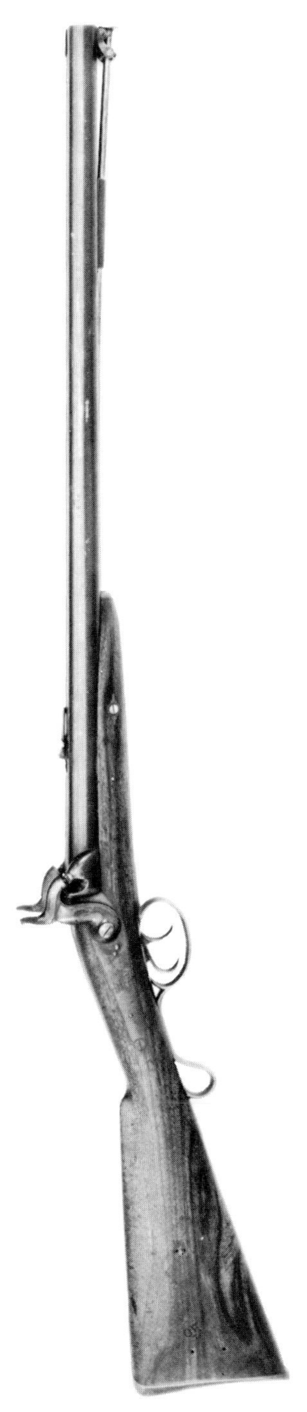

42. *Cape double-barrelled rifled Carbine of 1853.*

The last in the series of regulation double-barrelled carbines for Ireland and South Africa, there is some question of how many of these weapons were actually finished as rifled arms. It appears that various orders for a total of 500 double-barrelled carbines were in course of completion between 1851 and 1854 and, while only 50 are stated to have been ordered as rifled, it seems highly probable that most if not all of the 500 in question were ultimately rifled —and this does not include weapons of earlier issue which were called in or taken from Store and then rifled. This carbine greatly resembles the earlier Cape Carbine of 1840 (Plate 28) but the breech snails are slightly larger, a swivel ramrod has been fitted and there is a sling bar on the right side, held by a screw through the fore-end (from the right at the front) and screwed directly into the stock at the rear. The backsight bed is screwed to the rib $3\frac{1}{4}$in from the break-off and the leaf is graduated to 800 yards. The swivel of the ramrod is elliptical in shape allowing the rod to be used for either barrel. *Overall length $41\frac{3}{4}$in, barrel length $25\frac{13}{16}$in, calibre 0.733in, rifled with four broad shallow angular grooves making one turn in 78in.*

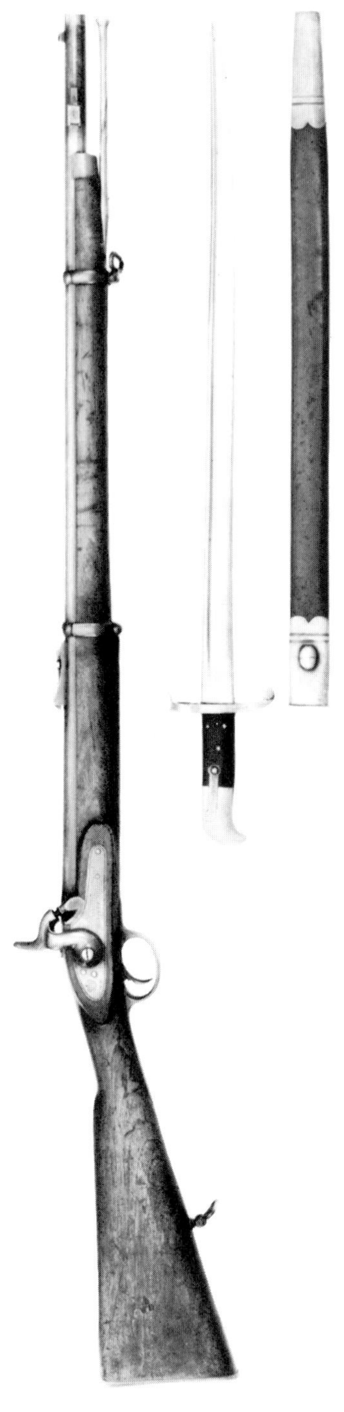

43. *Royal Sappers & Miners Carbine with Lancaster's oval-bore (Also known as Lancaster's Royal Engineer's Carbine) of 1855.*

Adopted in January 1855, Charles Lancaster had the exclusive manufacture of this weapon until November 1858 when contracts were let with both the London and Birmingham trades. The Lancaster may always be distinguished not only by its brass furniture, but by the backsight being mounted in reverse to the normal position for the Pattern 1856 Short Rifles. The bayonet bar has a short forward extension and, on regulation examples, there is always some reference to LANCASTER'S PATENT stamped near the breech of the barrel. The sword bayonet is distinctive both in blade, scabbard and hilt, as the blade has a double-edged spear-point, the black leather scabbard has brass mountings, and the pommel and guard are made of brass rather than steel. The blade measures 24in. Bayonets having this pattern blade but with steel hilt and scabbard mounts will be for Volunteer Rifles, large numbers of which were made with Lancaster's rifling. *Overall length 48in, barrel length 31½in, calibre (nominal) 0.577in. The bore actually measures 0.577in across the minor axis of the ellipse at the muzzle and 0.593in across the major axis; at the breech, where the bore has been relieved, the minor axis measures 0.580in and the major axis 0.598in. The twist of the rifling gains in rapidity from breech to muzzle, averaging one turn in 36in.*

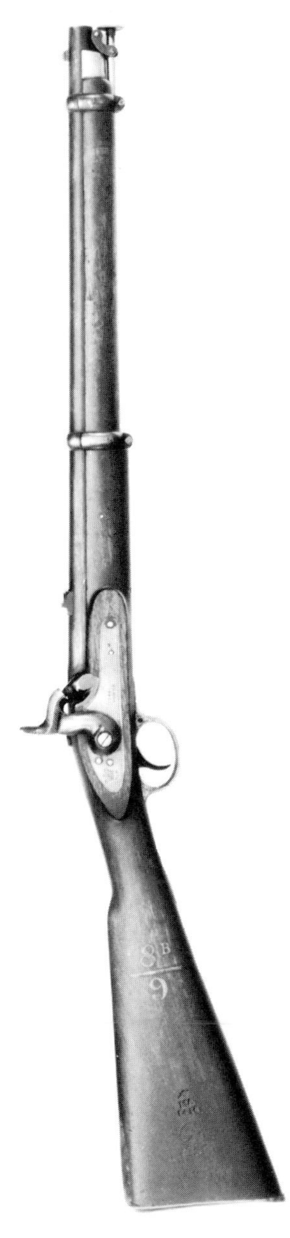

44. *The Pattern 1856 or 'East India Pattern' Cavalry Carbine.*

Because no one capping breech-loader seemed to meet the requirements for general adoption into the cavalry this pattern, based upon the P/53 series, was accepted in 1856 as a stop-gap measure for general issue pending further developments in the breech-loading field. It is distinguished by its short barrel, swivel ramrod and a sling bar on the left side, anchored by the two sidenails. These were made at Enfield and by the London and Birmingham trades but not, apparently, in Belgium. The two-leaf backsight is graduated for 200 and 300 yards. The P/56 Cavalry Carbine was placed in production in June 1857 and a large number of them saw service in India. They should not be confused with the Native Police Carbine which is externally similar, but is a smoothbore with a calibre of 0.65in, and has a plain block backsight. *Overall length 37in, barrel length 21in, calibre 0.577in, rifled with three broad angular grooves making one turn in 78in. The majority of this pattern have rifling grooves of uniform depth.*

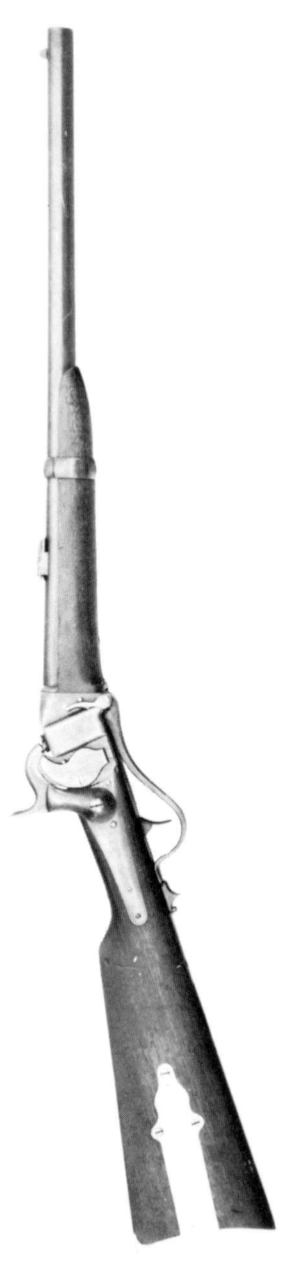

45. *The Model 1855 Sharps Carbine, made to a British Contract of 1856.* The first capping breech-loader issued in large numbers to regular cavalry was this American weapon patented by Christian Sharps of Hartford, Connecticut. They were manufactured on sub-contract for the Sharps Rifle Manufacturing Company of Hartford by Robbins & Lawrence of Windsor, Vermont. A contract of 26th March 1856 called for 6,000 carbines of this pattern, 3,000 of which were to be made with 21in barrels and the final 3,000 with 18in barrels. The 6,000 carbines were delivered between May 1856 and April 1858. The four-leaf backsight is peculiar to this model and is graduated to 600 yards. Examples of this carbine made for the British Government have British inspection stamps on the breech of the barrel and the receiver tang, and Sharps' serial number normally appears on the underside of the barrel and underside of the receiver tang. The top of the receiver tang is stamped SHARPS PATENT 1848 which refers to Sharps' original patent and is not a model designation. The magazine cover of the Maynard tape primer mechanism is stamped EDWARD MAYNARD PATENTEE 1845. These carbines were issued to five regiments of cavalry serving in India, and to their English depots. *Overall length $37\frac{3}{4}$in, barrel length (measured to the front of the receiver) $20\frac{1}{2}$in, calibre 0.577in, rifled with three broad angular grooves making one turn in 78in.*

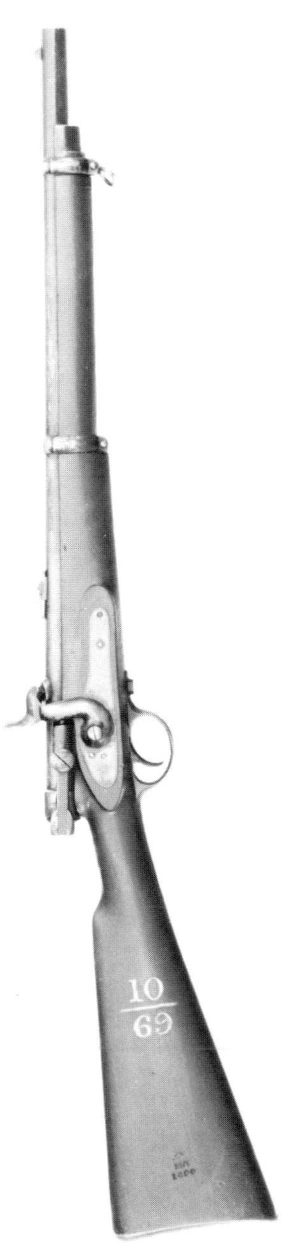

46. *Calisher & Terry's Carbine ('Terry's Carbine').*
Approved for limited issue in November 1858, the first pattern was sealed in the following month. It is distinguished from the subsequent designs by its larger bore and three-groove rifling. The example shown has iron furniture and standard Government markings on the lock-plate, which is dated 1857. The four-leaf backsight is graduated to 500 yards, and the left side is fitted with a sling bar anchored by the two side-nails. The breech section of the barrel, behind the hammer, is engraved TERRY'S PATENT. This pattern, and subsequent variations of the carbine, were issued to the 18th Hussars and despite this very limited issue they were treated, as were Sharps' and Westley Richards' carbines, as regulation arms. *Overall length 36¾in, barrel length (to front of nipple seat) 19⅝in, calibre 0.568in, rifled with three grooves making one turn in 78in.*

47. *The Pattern 1853 Artillery Carbine, Second Model of 1858.*

As with the P/53 Rifle-musket major structural changes were made upon the original pattern during 1858, based upon practical and theoretical developments since the original issue. On this Artillery Carbine these included, aside from the introduction of progressive-depth rifling, the fitting of a straight-stemmed ramrod of heavier proportions and with a slotted jag-head. The forward extension on the bayonet bar was discontinued. The fore-end cap is now identical to the design used on the Rifle-musket, the earlier pattern lacking the lower extension or lip to help retain the rod. The barrel bands are somewhat more sturdily constructed and the lock uses a heavier hammer which had been generally adopted in 1856. In addition to being produced at Enfield and by the London and Birmingham trades, the Second Model Artillery Carbine was also produced in Belgium, the lockplates generally bearing dates from 1859 until 1862. An internal change on this model is the use of Burton's spoon-spring for retaining the ram-rod, in place of Smith's roller-spring. *Overall length 40¼in, barrel length 24in, calibre 0.577in, rifled with three broad grooves of progressive depth (0.013in deep at the breech and 0.005in at the muzzle) making one turn in 78in.*

48. *Calisher & Terry's Carbine, Pattern No. 2 of 1860.*

This second type of 'Terry's Carbine' is a much more lightly constructed weapon throughout. The dimensions of the stock and the iron furniture are smaller and the rear barrel band is replaced with a key. The backsight is of the type used on the P/61 Carbines, but only graduated to 500 yards. In addition to the Government proofmarks on the breech the rear of the barrel section is engraved TERRY'S PATENT 30 BORE. The lockplate bears typical Government markings and is dated 1860. Total production of Terry's carbines for the Government is unkown, but this example is numbered 418 on the barrel. A third pattern approved in March 1861 involved only the substitution of the Baddeley barrel-band for the Enfield type. It was ordered that previous types should be altered to the new arrangement, but the number of examples extant with the Enfield band make it doubtful whether this was fully accomplished. The cleaning rod is missing from this example. *Overall length 37½in, barrel length (to front of nipple seat) 20⅛in, calibre 0.539in, rifled with five grooves with a uniform depth of 0.013in making one turn in 36in.*

49. *Model 1855 Sharps Carbine, made to a British Contract, second type.*

Of the 6,000 carbines of this pattern contracted for in March 1856, the final 3,000 were to have 18in barrels. It also appears that, prior to their being produced, a reduction in the bore size was ordered as these late short-barrelled carbines are slightly smaller in the bore. Some were also altered—apparently by the British authorities—by fitting clamping barrel bands carrying a sling swivel and also by the addition of a sling swivel through the rear of the trigger plate (in addition to the standard sling bar on the left side). Sharps' serial numbers of these later arms are in the 20,000 to 23,000 range, the earlier type with the 21-inch barrel being numbered from about 18,000. By February 1864 this second type appears to have been the one still in issue and, of the original 6,000, only 2,400 were still in Government hands—either in the hands of the troops or in Store. *Overall length 35⅜in, barrel length to front of receiver 18in, calibre 0.551in, rifled with three broad angular grooves of 0.013in uniform depth making one turn in 48in.*

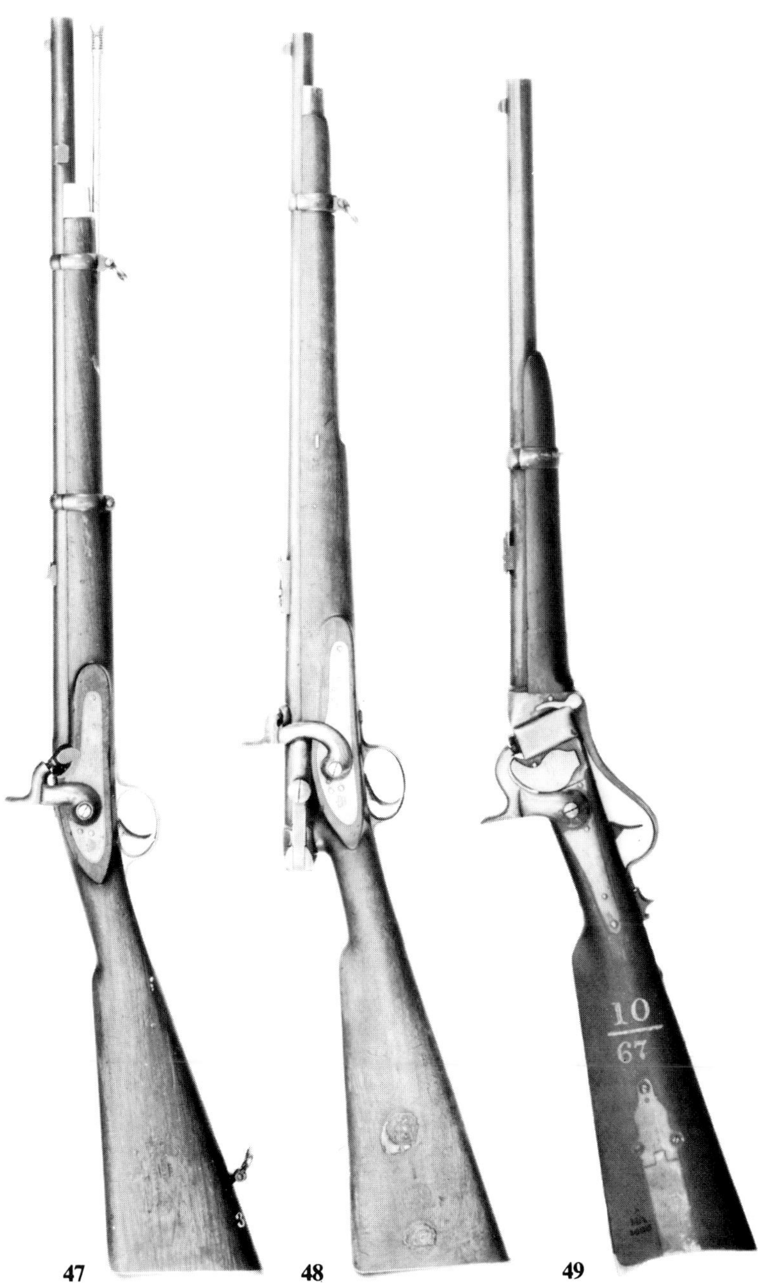

47 48 49

50. *The Pattern 1861 Cavalry Carbine.* This was approved in October 1861 and manufactured almost entirely at Enfield, therefore being interchangeable in all its parts. Only a few were apparently made by the trade. The changes from the Pattern 1856 include the introduction of the Baddeley design for both bands, the fitting of a new longer-range backsight graduated to 600 yards and the introduction of the five-groove rifling with a rapid pitch which had performed so well on the P/58 Naval Rifle. A few P/61 Carbines were made without the sling bar on the left. The black leather sight cover was authorised in May 1862 and is held by a screw on either side of the fore-end. As with most other late production Enfield arms, the P/61 Carbines were largely held in Store and converted to Snider breech-loaders. The large flat head of the swivel ramrod is missing on this example. *Overall length $36\frac{1}{2}$in, barrel length 21in, calibre 0.577in, rifled with five grooves of progressive depth (0.013in deep at the breech and 0.005in at the muzzle) and making one turn in 48in.*

51. *The Pattern 1861 Artillery Carbine.*
Approved in December 1861 and once again produced primarily at Enfield, and therefore interchangeable in its parts. The changes from the earlier P/53, Second Model, include the adoption of the five-groove rapid pitch rifling, and the same backsight graduated to 600 yards used on the P/61 Cavalry Carbine. The Baddeley rear barrel band was also adopted. *Overall length $40\frac{1}{4}$in, barrel length 24in, calibre 0.577in, rifled with five grooves of progressive depth (0.013in deep at the breech and 0.005in at the muzzle) making one turn in 48in.*

52. *Westley Richards' 'monkey-tail' Carbine, Pattern No. 5 of 1866.*
The story of the development of this system between 1858 and 1866 would fill a volume in itself. This pattern has been selected as the last of many patterns of this carbine, and the one which was produced in quantity at Enfield as a regulation arm. Although several of the earlier patterns were issued in some quantity, all were considered at the time as experimental designs. Enfield manufactured 19,000 of these from 1866, all interchangeable in their parts. The backsight is graduated to 800 yards and originally had a black leather cover the same as that of the P/61 Cavalry Carbine. The foresight blade is dovetailed into an oval sight base and the sling bar on the left side is anchored by the two sidenails. The blued iron furniture includes a butt-plate with trap for brass rod tip and a breech scraper. *Overall length $35\frac{7}{8}$in, barrel length (to hinge of breech) 20in, calibre 0.451in, rifled with eight sides forming the rifling and making one turn in 20in.*

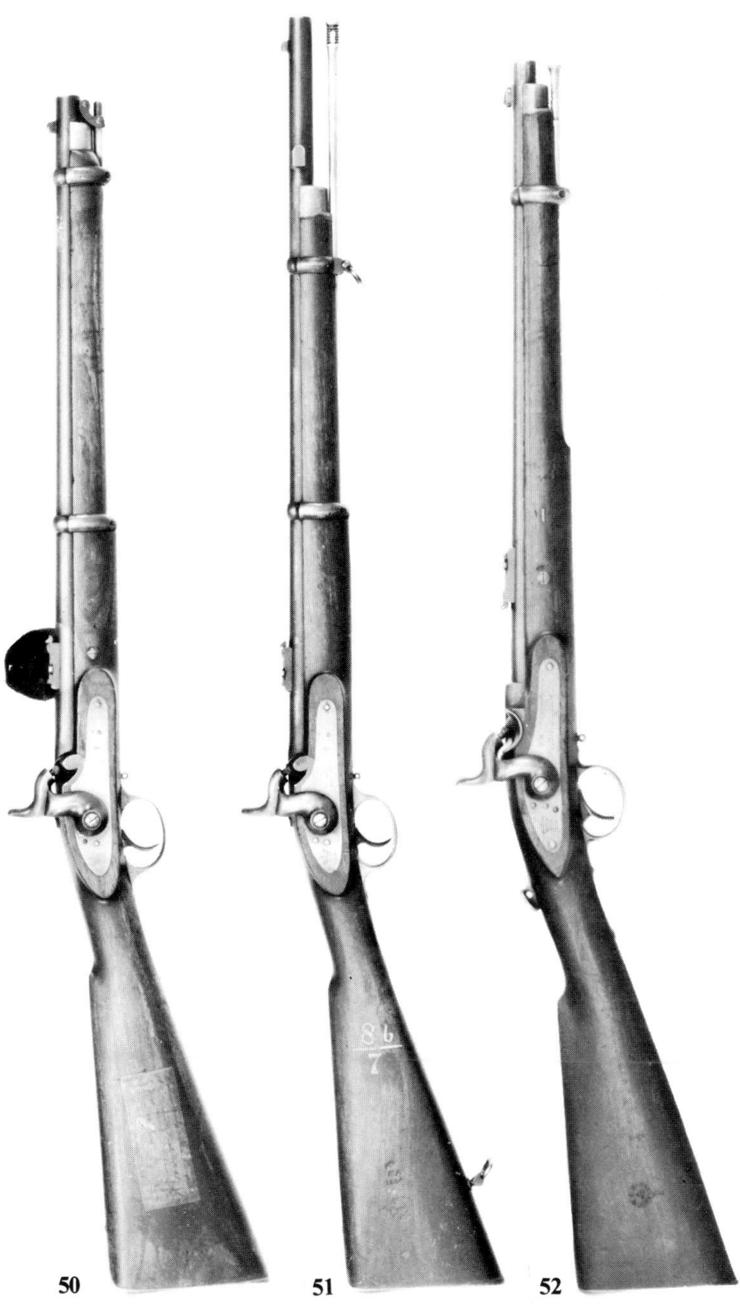

50 51 52

Rifles

From 1815 until 1840 the weapon in the hands of the Rifle Brigade and small detachments of particular temporary corps was the Baker Rifle, whose development prior to 1815 has been described in *British Military Longarms, 1715–1815*. Between 1815 and 1825 certain changes were made in the Baker Rifle which distinguish the later rifles from those of the Napoleonic period.

The most common complaint against the Baker Rifle involved the bayonet, rather than the rifle itself. While this instrument was found very handy for cutting firewood and other camp duties, the rifle could not be safely fired with it fixed and it was considered both fragile and cumbersome for its primary function. In 1815, as a result of these problems, a standard form of triangular bladed socket bayonet was adapted to the Baker Rifle. The sword-bar on the right side of the barrel was removed, the fore-end cut back to allow the fitting of the socket, and the foresight was redesigned in the form of of a high iron blade fixed directly to the barrel just above the fore-end cap. A New Land Pattern brass fore-end cap was fitted and a standard type of bayonet stud was brazed on the underside of the barrel; the socket of the bayonet was made with a short straight slot for the stud and fitted with a locking ring. These alterations were carried out on the several earlier patterns of Baker Rifle, but it is not believed that any new production weapons were set up to this design.

A second set of changes concerned yet another type of bayonet, although this time there were other alterations to the rifle. A return was made in 1823 to the bayonet bar on the right side of the barrel, and the bayonet adopted was a brass hilted double-edged dagger known at the time as the 'hand-bayonet'. The lock underwent a major change in design—for, in place of the flat lock with safety bolt, raised pan and ring-neck cock, the older form of rounded lock-plate, rounded swan-neck cock and plain pan were reinstated. The safety bolt was omitted. Another important change was made in the form of the backsight because, in place of the dovetailed block with a single hinged leaf, a plain notched block was brazed to the barrel. It was felt that the leaf was an unnecessary refinement which the rifleman was incapable of using correctly, and that for the ranges at which the Baker Rifle was intended to be used the plain block was entirely adequate, with the rifleman making the necessary visual adjustments. From the technological point of view both of these changes were decidedly retrograde, but equally obviously they reflected the considered needs of the British rifleman of the time: an interesting commentary.

The slit stock became standard on Baker Rifles from the changes of 1823, although it had been used, in an uncertain degree, on previous production dating as early as *c*. 1810. The post-1815 Baker Rifle was more often found with the slit stock than without, although it does not appear to have been added to those rifles converted for the socket bayonet. The changes made in 1823 were the last to affect the Baker Rifle, the manufacture of which continued to be based on this pattern until the final 2,000 were set up in 1838.

Although the seven-groove rifling of the Baker, with its angular grooves making a quarter of a turn in the 30inch barrel, had been proven inferior in accuracy to various other forms of rifling for some years, no change was made in the design from the adoption of the rifle in 1800 until its supersession in 1837 by the Brunswick Rifle. It was accepted that, for the ease of loading and a tendency not to foul, a slower twist must be utilised and that angular grooves were less likely to suffer damage or wear than rounded grooves. Most privately-made rifles, of Baker design externally and made after 1815, had eleven-groove rifling with rounded grooves somewhat wider than the flat-topped lands, with a twist of from one-half to one full turn in the length of the barrel. This multi-groove system was given a thorough trial by George Lovell during the experiments which led ultimately to the adoption of the two-groove Brunswick system.

As with most other arms of this period, the basic change in the rifle came about primarily as the result of reduced numbers being in Store, which called for replenishing. The Board also charged Lovell to design a new rifle upon modern principles which would then be manufactured to supply the deficit. This at first led to the redesigning of the construction of the rifle and then to the selection of the two-grooved rifling system using a patched, belted ball. The first was commenced early in 1835, and the latter completed by the beginning of 1837. The result was Lovell's Improved Brunswick Rifle, adopted in January 1837, ordered into production in March 1838 and placed in the hands of the troops early in 1840. It remained in the hands of the Rifle Brigade, the Royal Canadian Rifles and a few other units of small size, until 1853, when it began to be replaced by the Pattern 1851 Rifle-musket—the Minié Rifle.

There were two changes made to the Brunswick Rifle. The first was the change from a back-action to a side-lock. This occurred on paper in the autumn of 1841, but the earliest noted side-lock on the

Brunswick Rifle is 1844. This change also involved the omission of the break-off breech used on the back-action lock type. This major change was followed late in 1847 by a minor one in which the bayonet bar was strengthened by moving the locking notch from the front towards the middle of its upper surface, with a corresponding modification to the bayonet hilt. This change was approved in June 1848, and consequently presented three variations of the Brunswick Rifle: the back-action lock type or First Model, the side-action type or Second Model, and the variation of the Second Model with the 1848 bayonet modification. It is therefore possible to assign to these classifications more specific pattern dates, which would be 1837, 1841 and 1848 respectively: this is not, however, historically correct and neither is it defensible in terms of the methods under which these arms were produced, issued, or described by those concerned with their manufacture and use. For modern purposes it is best to keep to the use of model designations which clarify, but do not mislead.

There are three remaining weapons which utilised the two-groove Brunswick rifling system and which were constructed to resemble the Brunswick Rifle; these are the Sergeant of Foot Guards Musket (Rifled), the Heavy Navy Rifle of 1840, and the Tower Brunswick or 'Sikh Brunswick' of 1864. The first two were made in very limited numbers for the purpose indicated by their titles while the third was, by the time of manufacture, the resurrection of an obsolete system to effect a compromise between the modern rifled arms of the British infantry and the smoothbore weapons in the hands of most native Indian soldiers. As it was not issued to regular troops it does not concern us here.

The Brunswick rifling system was superseded not so much because of any inherent inferiority as by a revolutionary change in the basic conception of ammunition for the military muzzle-loading arm, a revelation which made it practical to place a rifle in the hands of the entire Line infantry for the first time. Although many people were involved in the development of the cylindro-conoidal expanding bullet, the names which were of the greatest importance were those of two French officers, Captains Delvigne and Minié. It was the latter name alone, despite his own published objections, which became popularly associated with the system.

The full history of the development of the Minié system in England has been thoroughly examined by Dr C. H. Roads in his superb *The British Soldier's Firearm, 1850–1864*, which is the standard reference for this period and which contains a wealth of detail concerning the origins of all the forms of British military firearms adopted during the final era of the muzzle-loader. The scope of the present volume allows us only to observe that the Pattern 1851 Rifle-musket, or 'Minié Rifle', was officially approved in October 1851, ordered into production in February 1852, and was first placed in the hands of the troops in January 1853. It was not until the close of 1853 that any regular issue was begun and, by the time the issue was being extended, yet another design of Rifle-musket had been approved—the final type with which this volume will be concerned.

Before describing the Pattern 1853 arms a definition must be sought of the seemingly contradictory term 'Rifle-musket.' This term is intended to make clear that the weapon indicated was of full musket length in the barrel, stocked as a musket and fitted for a bayonet, and the entire unit of an adequate length to unhorse cavalry. At the same time the bore was no longer smooth but intentionally rifled in the original production. Hence the term Rifle-musket, correctly applied both to the Pattern 1851 and to the Pattern 1853 rifles with 39in barrels. The term 'Rifled Musket' is applied where a musket was originally manufactured as a smoothbore and subsequently rifled, which primarily relates to the Pattern 1839 and Pattern 1842 designs which were rifled on the Minié system and supplied with new backsights and ammunition in the early 1850s.

The first form of rifling adopted for the expanding bullet in an English regulation longarm, the Pattern 1851 Rifle-musket, has four lands and grooves of equal width and of uniform depth from breech to muzzle. The calibre was 0.702in and the twist of the rifling was one turn in 78in, or half a turn in the length of the barrel. This type of rifling was used to modernise almost all categories of the older smoothbore arms but, with the exceptions of the Pattern 1842 Musket, the Paget Carbine, and the Pattern 1842 Sea Service Musket, the process does not appear to have been carried out in great numbers and no official designations were made for arms altered in this manner, with the above exceptions. Hence it was not unusual to find a weapon conforming in every particular to a certain smoothbore pattern, but with a four-groove rifled bore and even some form of elevating backsight. In rarer instances this alteration could have taken the form of three-groove rifling; this change was presumably made in late 1854 by which time the new 'Enfield' system, which featured three grooves of uniform depth, had been adopted and put into production.

In the short space of four years the designs of British military longarms underwent a complete change: in 1850 the soldier of the line had carried a 0.75in calibre smoothbore musket of no ballistic improvement over that carried by his predecessors of 1750 and still with the same pinned barrel but, by the end of 1855, he probably carried a 0.577in calibre Rifle-musket with a band-held barrel and using the most modern design of projectile then accepted by the military world. The changes were both rapid and complete, but the last of the series of British muzzle-loading service longarms was never really in as secure a position as had been the smoothbore predecessors. Too many discoveries were being made and publicised, and the spirit of experimentation was evident both in civilian and in military circles. Even at the time of its adoption the 'Enfield system' was seriously challenged by Charles Lancaster's oval-bore rifling, which was sufficiently successful to be adopted as the standard weapon of the Royal Sapper & Miners in January 1855. Indeed, had it not been for the imminent change from muzzle-loader to breech-loader and the further reduction in bore size—all of which were being seriously contemplated in 1862—the Lancaster system would have replaced the Enfield type for the entire series of service arms.

Four distinct variations of the Pattern 1853 Rifle-musket were issued to the Line infantry between 1854 and *c.* 1866, the details of which are explained in the captions to the illustrations. Owing to the pressure on manufacturing facilities created by the Crimean War, the Second Model Pattern 1853 Rifle-musket was also manufactured in Belgium and in the United States. The Royal Small Arms Factory at Enfield was equipped with a complete set of American machinery for manufacturing fully interchangeable Pattern 1853s, which became operational in 1858 and, about a year later a private firm—the London Armoury Company Limited of Bermondsey—commenced the manufacture of Pattern 1853s (of the Third Model) on contract from the Government. These were made with a similar set of machinery to that at Enfield and these arms are therefore completely interchangeable both amongst themselves and with Enfield-made Rifle-muskets. These were the only two sources for completely interchangeable Pattern 1853s and all the other arms were designated as 'Non-Interchangeable'.

Owing to the several military eruptions of the period which created a large demand for new arms, the several earlier models of Pattern 1853 Rifle-muskets were in issue at the same time, although there was a conscious effort on the part of the authorities to use up the older, the Belgian and the American arms first. The Fourth Model, which was made almost entirely at Enfield and by the London Armoury Company, was held in Store and virtually none issued as muzzle-loaders, while First and Second models were received into Pimlico largely between 1859 and 1862 and thoroughly refurbished. These were then issued, as the need arose, to the Volunteer Force. Both of these practices applied equally to Carbines and Short Rifles.

The term 'Short Rifle' was adopted with the first of this type, the Pattern 1856, to distinguish between the longer Rifle-musket with its 39in barrel, and the shorter Carbines with 24in and 21in barrels. It was conceived in an effort to satisfy the demands of the Rifle Brigade for a handier weapon than the long Patterns of 1851 and 1853 and which would be more appropriate to the mobility of light troops. The series of short rifles was distinguished by its 33in barrel. This was the first group of British regulation longarms to use iron furniture rather than brass, the latter material having been abandoned for these arms perhaps for reasons of camouflage, as the glitter of the brass might disclose the position of hidden marksmen.

53. *Baker Rifle converted to socket bayonet, c. 1815–23.*

This is stocked to 3in of the muzzle, with a New Land Pattern fore-end cap. The sword bar has been removed and the brazing marks are quite visible near the muzzle. A bayonet stud has been brazed beneath the barrel $2\frac{3}{16}$in from the muzzle and a new foresight of iron, higher than the older sight, has been brazed $3\frac{1}{8}$in from the muzzle. The fore-end has been shortened by $2\frac{1}{2}$in, with the upper barrel key and ramrod pipe moved back, and the upper sling swivel replaced in the same relation as the original, which is evident from the plates. Apart from these changes at the muzzle, no further alterations were made to the original arm. This alteration was approved in the summer of 1815 and they were in the hands of some of the troops by August. It is very doubtful whether there were any new production Baker Rifles made in this pattern, all those known being conversions of earlier types. The conversion itself was costly, and the carrying of both sword and bayonet was inconvenient and unpopular. It is clear that, of the many thousand rifles then in existence, not more than 2,000 were converted. The bayonet blade is 17in in length, and the socket is 3in long with a locking ring $\frac{1}{2}$in wide located just above the collar. *Overall length $45\frac{3}{4}$in, barrel length 30in, calibre 0.625in, rifled with seven grooves making one-quarter turn in the barrel.*

54. *Baker Rifle, of the final pattern adopted in May 1823.*

Two features are immediately apparent when comparing this pattern to those produced between 1800 and 1815: the use of an older design of lock—no more than a small version of that of the India Pattern—and the fixed block backsight mounted well up the barrel. The original form of fore-end and sword bar are retained and, aside from the slit stock, there are no other changes from earlier types made between 1806 and 1815. The backsight is brazed into its dovetail 7in from the break-off breech. The bayonet combines a normal triangular blade with a brass hilt, avoiding the costly conversion of the rifles. The blade is $16\frac{3}{4}$in in length and the hilt $4\frac{1}{2}$in. There are two versions of this 'hand bayonet', one being slightly heavier in construction than the other. *Overall length $45\frac{3}{4}$in, barrel length $30\frac{1}{4}$in, calibre 0.625in, rifled with seven grooves making one quarter turn in the length of the barrel.*

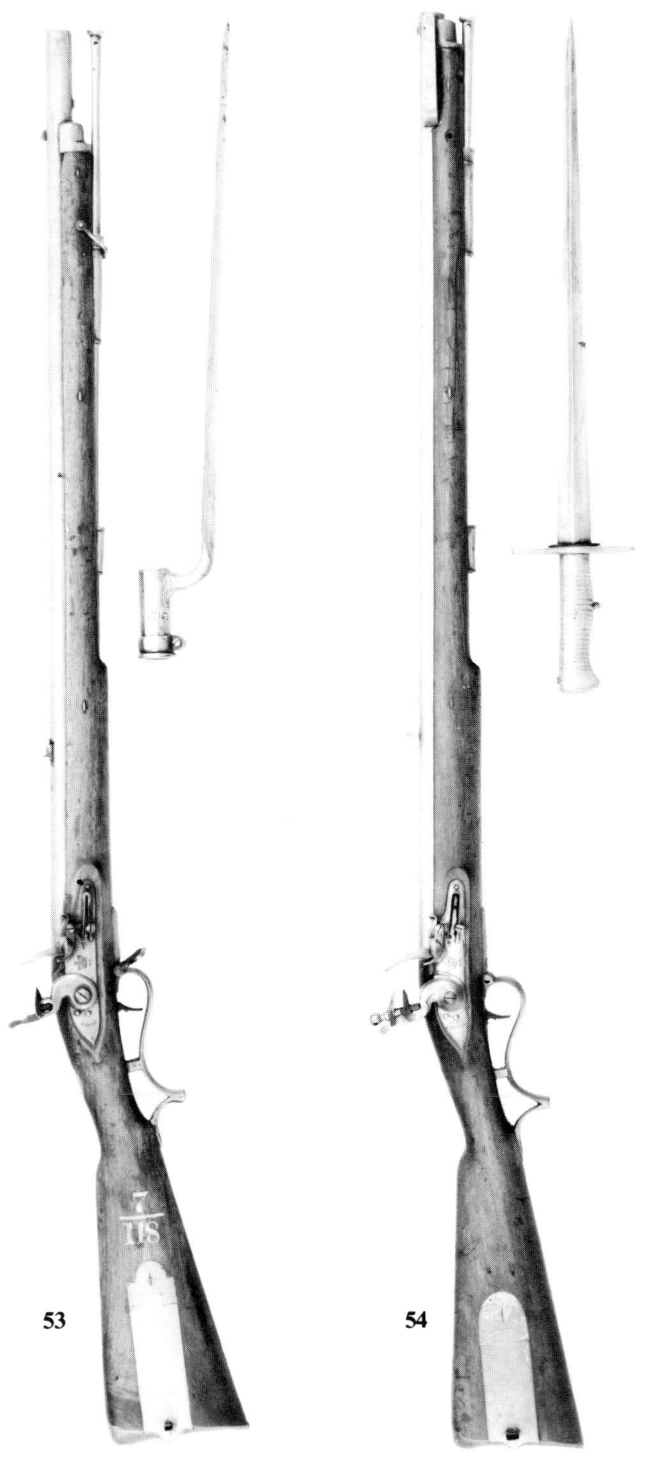

53

54

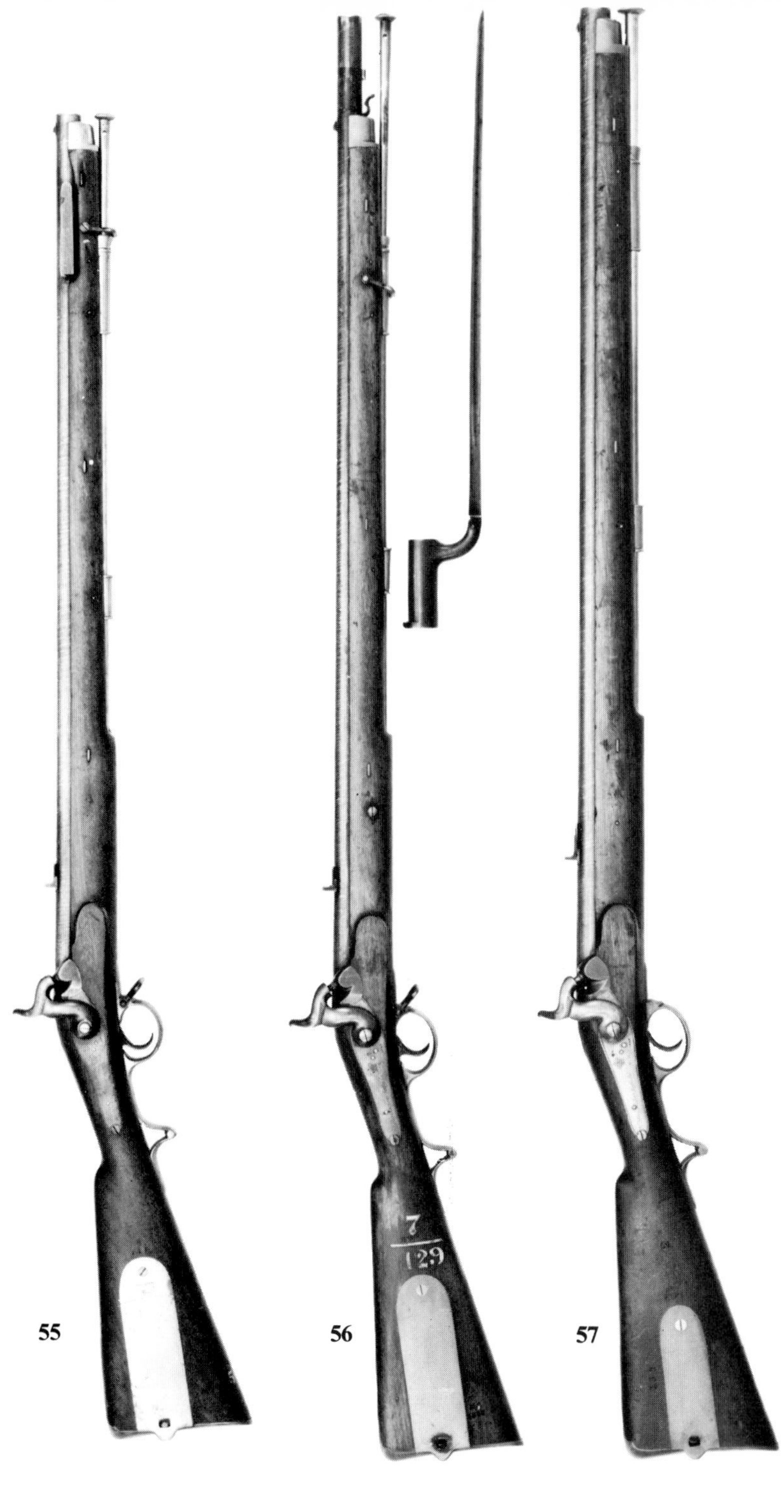

55 56 57

55. *Brunswick Rifle, First Model.*
The first percussion rifle adopted by the British Army and intended for issue to the Rifle Brigade, Royal Canadian Rifle Regiment and a few small special units. It was approved in January 1837, put into production in March 1838, and into the hands of the troops early in 1840. The rifle shown is marked as being the 817th rifle issued to the 2nd Battalion of the 60th Rifles. With certain minor variations the design strongly resembles the Baker Rifle. The bayonet bar has been moved back, a return has been made to a backsight with a folding leaf, and a larger butt-trap with two compartments is used. There is no cheekrest, and the slit stock has been discontinued. The backsight, although not graduated, was intended for use at 200 and 300 yards. The barrel is secured by three flat keys and fitted with a break-off breech. All regulation Brunswick rifles of the First Model were made with superior quality twist steel barrels. Although the side-lock was approved in August 1841, the back-action lock was used on Brunswick Rifles as late as 1845, this particular example being dated 1844. *Overall length $46\frac{1}{4}$in, barrel length $30\frac{3}{16}$in, calibre 0.704in with two wide angular grooves making one turn in the length of the barrel*

56. *Sergeant of Foot Guards' Rifled Musket of 1840.*
Structurally this is a First Model Brunswick Rifle made with a longer barrel extended beyond the fore-end sufficiently to take a socket bayonet. The fore-end is fitted with a Hanoverian spring-catch and the foresight has been moved back level with the front of the fore-end. The ramrod has been made suitably longer. All examples known have been fitted with a sling bar and ring on the left side, the rear of the bar being secured by the sidenail and the front of the bar held by a screw from the right side through the fore-end. Two hundred and fifty of these 'rifled muskets' were ordered in March 1840, and a further fifty were ordered especially for the Cape service in 1843. It would appear that ultimately all the existing arms were fitted with the sling bar and intended for issue to the mounted troops at the Cape. Several of these weapons, including the rifle shown, were set up as late as 1847. *Overall length $49\frac{1}{8}$in, barrel length $32\frac{15}{16}$in, calibre 0.704in, rifled with two broad grooves making one turn in the length of the barrel.*

57. *Brunswick Heavy Navy Rifle of 1840.*
One hundred of these rifles were set up at Enfield during 1840 for use in the fighting tops of ships of the Royal Navy. Some were still in service, mostly on Far Eastern stations, in 1862. The furniture is standard Brunswick in design, although the butt-trap is smaller than the production First Model and has but one rectangular compartment. The ramrod pipes are larger in diameter. There is no provision for a bayonet and there are no sling swivels. The backsight is of standard pattern but is fitted with three folding leaves rather than one, these being sighted to 300, 400 and 470 yards, although unmarked. A charge of $3\frac{1}{2}$ drams of powder was used with these rifles, compared with the $2\frac{1}{2}$ drams of the standard Brunswick rifles. *Overall length $48\frac{3}{4}$in, barrel length $32\frac{5}{8}$in, calibre 0.796in, rifled with two broad angular grooves making one turn in the length of the barrel.*

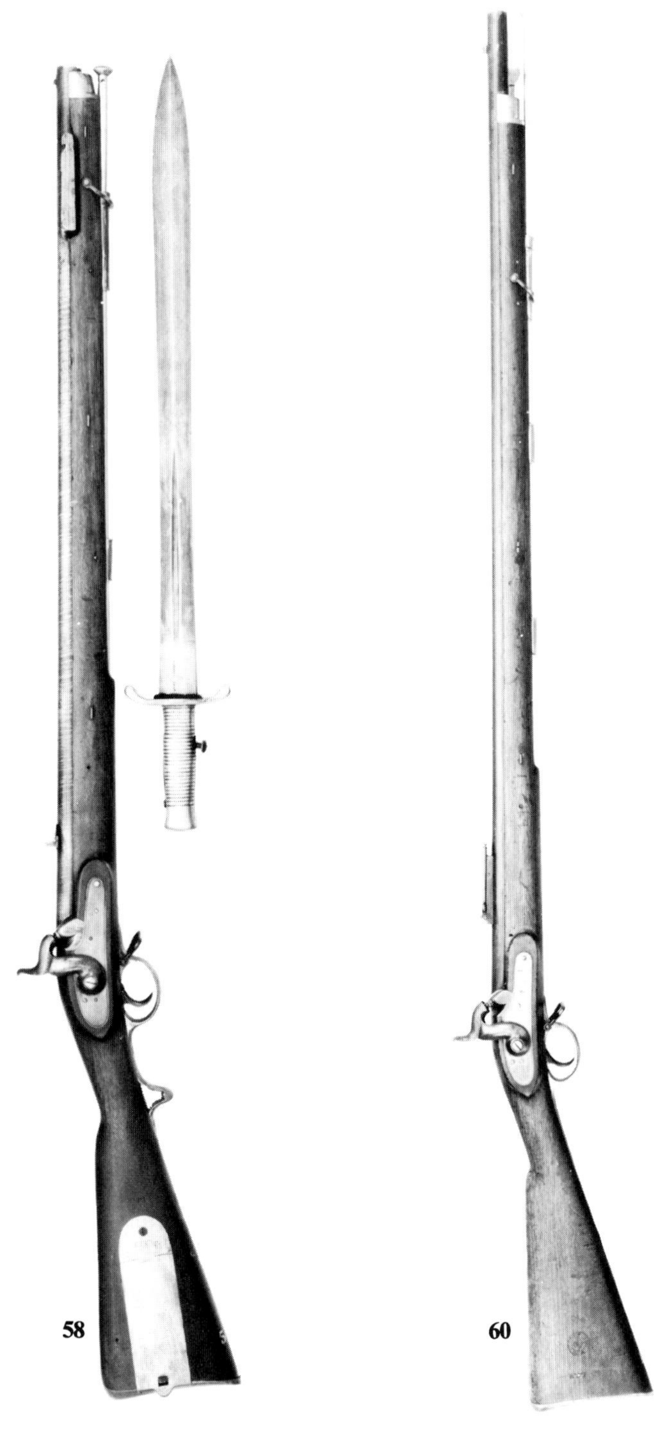

58

60

59

58, 59. *Brunswick Rifle, Second Model.*
The adoption of the side-lock in place of the back-action lock was approved in August 1841, but not until 1845 were Brunswick Rifles of this pattern produced in quantity. In addition to the change in lock type, the break-off breech was replaced with a standard breech plug and screw-fastened tang strap and some rifles of this later design were made with plain iron barrels rather than twist steel. The close-up shows a variation of the Second Model in which the notch on the bayonet bar is moved to the centre of the bar. The position of the catch and button on the hilt of the bayonet were also modified, which created a second pattern of Brunswick Rifle bayonet. This change was introduced by Lacy & Reynolds, the London gunmakers, in October 1847 and was approved for adoption in June 1848. It is probable that only the final batch of Brunswick Rifles set up in 1850 were made with this modification. The Brunswick Rifles remained in issue until early 1853, when they were withdrawn and replaced by Pattern 1851 Minié Rifle-muskets. In 1854 the Brunswicks were issued to militia regiments, who retained them in some cases into the 1860s. The bayonet for all three types has the same blade and basic pattern of hilt, the catch only changing in position and design on the late variation of the Second Model. The double-edged blade measures 22in by $1\frac{3}{8}$in and is almost always stamped with ENFIELD and a date. The brass hilt is $4\frac{1}{2}$in long. *Overall length $45\frac{3}{4}$in, barrel length 30in, calibre 0.704in, rifled with two broad angular grooves making one turn in the length of the barrel.*

60. *Pattern 1851 Rifle-musket.*
'The Minié Rifle'. The external appearance is virtually identical with the Pattern 1842 Musket, except that it is more lightly built throughout and has the large backsight with a leaf graduated to 900 yards. The same brass furniture is used and the same pattern of lock and ramrod. Locks are known dated between 1852 and 1855. This was the first rifled-bore longarm adopted for issue to the entire Line infantry as well as to the Rifle Brigade and other units who would normally carry a rifle. Officially approved in October 1851, it went into production in 1852 and was gradually issued to the troops from January 1853. Before full issue was accomplished the P/51 was succeeded —on paper—by the reduced-bore P/53, which represented an even more complete revolution in design than the P/51. Production of the P/51 appears to have ceased by mid-1855, by which time not more than 35,000 had been set up. Almost 34,000 of these were in issue by April 1855. In the true sense of the term, the P/51 was never a general issue arm, although virtually all of the total production saw service. It did not proceed further simply because of the introduction of the improved P/53. *Overall length 55in, barrel length 39in, calibre 0.702in, rifled with four wide angular grooves of uniform depth making one turn in 78in.*

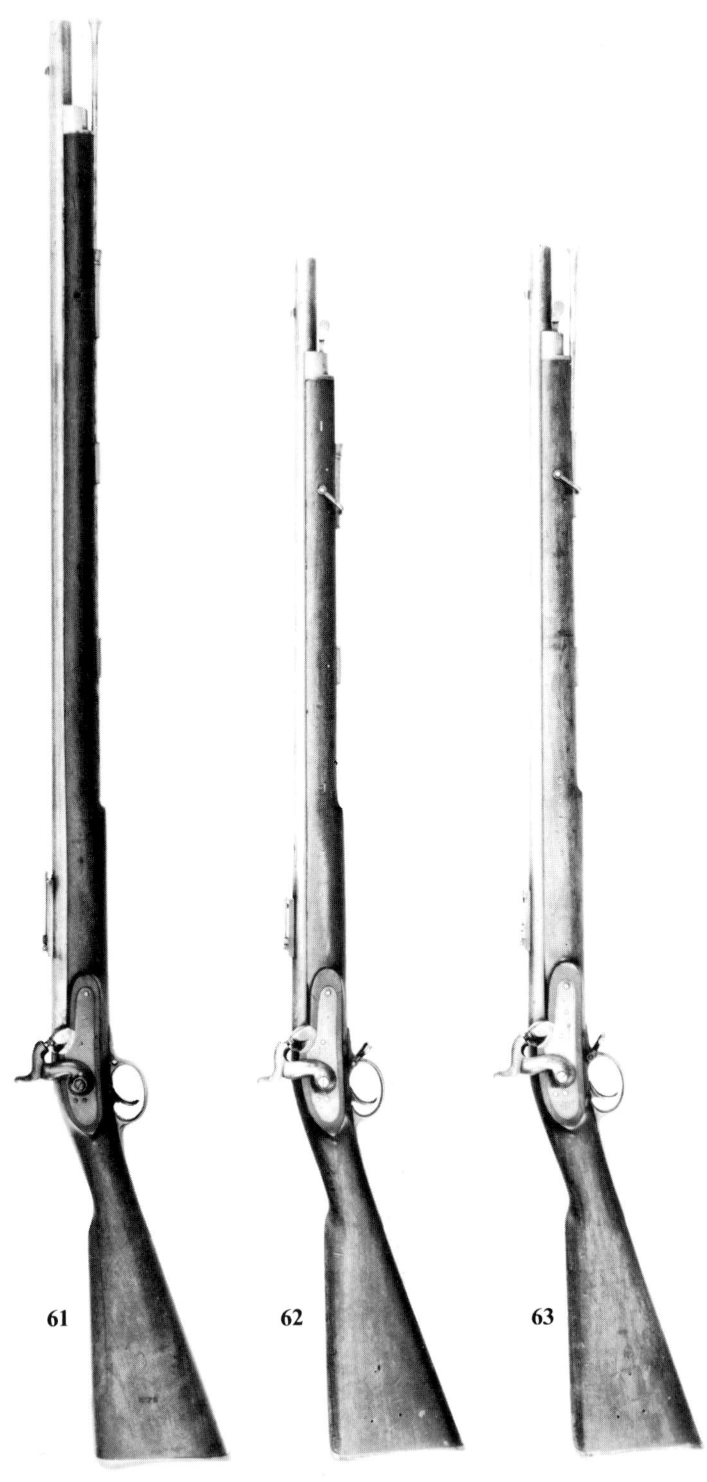

61 62 63

61. *Pattern 1842 Rifled Musket.*
Once the Minié projectile and rifling system had been adopted, it was obviously desirable to convert older smoothbore arms to the system—if possible. Originally the idea of Lieutenant-colonel Sandham of the Royal Engineers, the 'altered Pattern 1842 rifled musket' was produced for issue to the Royal Marines during the period when the P/51 was being issued to the infantry. Between April 1852 and April 1855, orders for some 26,400 of these arms were placed. They conform entirely to the P/42 Musket (Plate 13) except for the rifling, of four or three grooves, and the calibre of 0.758in instead of 0.753in. The P/51 backsight was also fitted. There can be considerable difficulty in distinguishing between this arm and the P/51 Rifle-musket. If the date on the lockplate is prior to 1851 there will be no problem, but, as Pattern 1842 Muskets were set up with locks dated 1851 and 1852, confusion still is possible. The most certain means of identification is by the measurement of the bore: the altered P/42 is approximately 0.76in and the P/51 0.70in. Weight is another criterion, although this must be accepted with reserve as considerable variations were allowed at the time. The P/42 Rifled Musket will weigh 10lb or slightly more, while the P/51 will be about 9lb 8oz. Examples of this arm with four-groove rifling may be considered earlier than those with three grooves. *Overall length 55in, barrel length 39in, calibre 0.758in, rifled with either three or four wide shallow angular grooves of uniform depth and making one turn in 78in, or half a turn in the length of the barrel.*

62, 63. *Pattern 1842 Sea Service Rifled Musket.*
With the same smoothbore origins as the P/42 Rifled Muskets, these shorter weapons were converted for the Royal Navy by rifling them with four (later three) grooves, slightly enlarging the calibre, and fitting a special backsight graduated to 1,000 yards. The first order for conversion was placed in April 1852 and they were made until 1857, with a total production of approximately 25,000. It seems highly probable that at least the final 10,000 of these were rifled with three grooves rather than four. Later examples of this arm, bearing dates after 1852, are new production rather than conversions. The P/39 Sea Service Musket does not appear to have been modernised in this manner. Plate 63 is of 'new production' and dated 1855; note the use of pins instead of keys to secure the barrel. *Overall length 46¼in, barrel length 30¼in, calibre 0.758in, rifled with four or three wide shallow angular grooves of uniform depth, making one turn in 78in.*

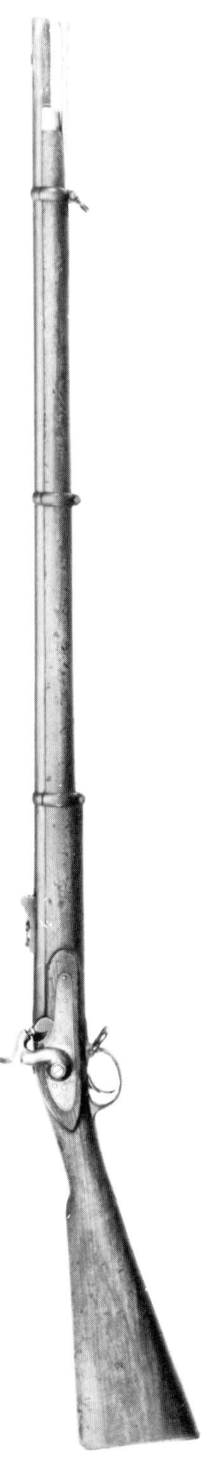

64. *Pattern 1853 Rifle-musket, First Model, the Enfield Rifle.*

The P/53 represented a major departure from many of the basic features of design accepted in British military longarms since they had become standardised. Included amongst these innovations was the use of bands to secure the barrel to the stock, an adjustable elevating backsight and the use of the swivel lock. The reduction in the size of the bore to 0.577in. was the smallest then adopted for a service longarm. The features which characterize the First Model P/53 are the screw-clamping bands, the slightly convex sides of the backsight, a button-head ramrod with a short pronounced swell, a very narrow ramrod channel slit, a narrow thin hammer with a pronounced curl to the spur and a fore-end cap which is riveted on. First Model P/53 specimen's bear dates of 1854 and 1855. *Overall length 55in, barrel length 39in, calibre 0.577in, rifled with three grooves of a uniform depth of 0.014in and making one turn in 78in.*

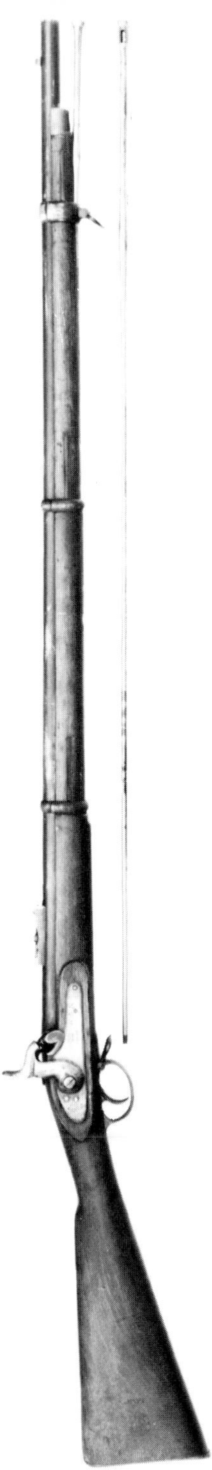

65. *Pattern 1853 Rifle-musket, Second Model.*

This arm represents one of the first examples of a weapon modified as a direct result of complaints from the battlefields. Numerous specific complaints from the Crimea resulted in the several modifications made to the basic design, which included the use of solid barrel bands secured by springs let into the fore-end ahead of each band on the right side, and a stronger hammer, the spur of which has lost its curl. The sides of the backsight are flat and the ramrod channel slit is somewhat wider. The upper barrel band is wider than the other two to assist in holding the ramrod in position. Subsequent to the basic changes made in this model a new ramrod incorporating a cleaning jag on the head was introduced on which the form and position of the swell were changed, and the ramrod channel was widened beneath the upper band rather than forward of it. Note the relative position and shape of the ramrod swells. Second Model P/53 types bear dates from 1855 to 1858, although very few were set up in the last year. There was considerable mixture of parts, particularly amongst ramrods and backsights, on the Second Model. Many were refurbished at Pimlico in 1860–2 when straight ramrods and backsight leaves graduated to 1,000 yards were fitted. Later examples of the Second Model will have Smith's roller-spring for retaining the ramrod, which proved an unnecessary refinement. *Overall length 55in, barrel length 39in, calibre 0.577in, rifled with three grooves of a uniform depth of 0.014in and making one turn in 78in. Some of the later production of this model have the 'progressive depth' rifling which came into use in 1858.*

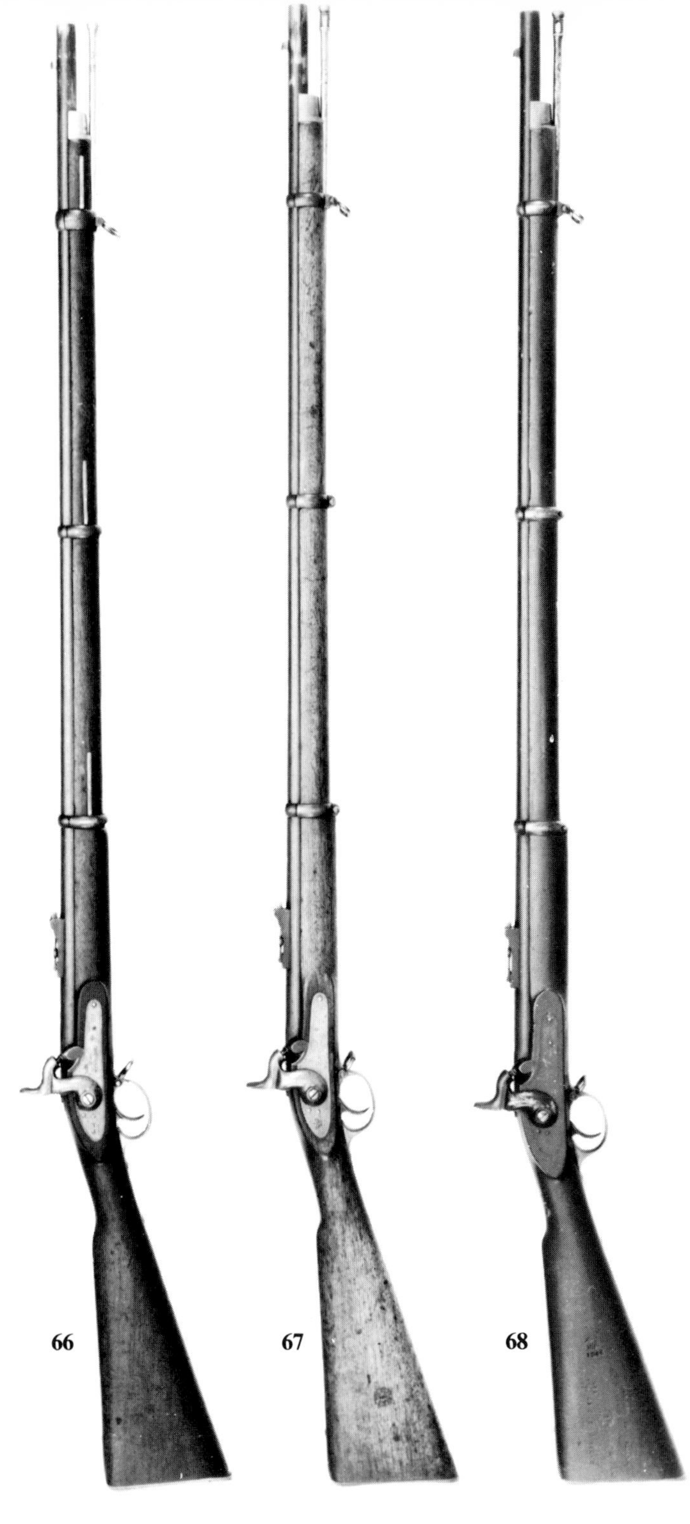

66 67 68

66. *Pattern 1853 Rifle-musket, Second Model: Windsor contract.*
Structurally this arm conforms with the standard Second Model P/53 with the jag-head swelled ramrod. To meet the demands of the Crimean War contracts were let with Belgian manufacturers and with Robbins & Lawrence of Windsor, Vermont (U.S.A.). The latter contract was for 25,000 rifle-muskets, 16,000 of which were ultimately delivered between December 1855 and June 1858. The parts of this arm are interchangeable, and the stocks are of American black walnut. Only part of the arms delivered reached England, the remainder being sold as surplus in America. Most of those received in England were immediately issued in preference to superior English-made arms (which also applies to the Belgian-made P/53), and were subsequently refurbished at Pimlico and reissued to the militia and volunteers in 1861–2. The object was first to use those arms which were considered of inferior-quality. *Overall length 55in, barrel length 39in, calibre 0.577in, rifled with three grooves of a uniform depth of 0.014in and making one turn in 78in.*

67. *Pattern 1853 Rifle-musket, Third Model.*
This is the most common style of P/53, manufactured between 1858 and 1863 by a large number of Birmingham and London contractors as well as the Royal Small Arms Factory at Enfield and the London Armoury Company of Bermondsey. It is this model which forms the bulk of those P/53 arms furnished to both combatants in the American Civil War. It is distinguished by a straight, thick-bodied jag-head ramrod and screw-clamping bands, and also by the appearance of a screw-fastened fore-end cap and a fairly wide ramrod channel slit. In order to retain the ramrod satisfactorily, Burton's spoon-spring replaced Smith's roller-spring. Some examples have backsight leaves graduated to 1,000 yards rather than the standard 900. Those made at Enfield and by the London Armoury Company have fully interchangeable parts, the locks lack border engraving and the hammers are of heavier construction. P/53 Rifle-muskets made in these two establishments have rounded-head screws securing the buttplate and trigger guard, although the other contractors used flat-head screws filed to the contours of the part. Those manufactured at Enfield after December 1859 were 1in shorter in overall length, owing to the adoption of a shorter butt of 13in rather than the regulation 14in between trigger and buttplate. The regulation was not followed by the London Armoury Company and some of the contractors. *Overall length 55in, barrel length 39in, calibre 0.577in, rifled with three grooves of progressive depth (0.015in deep at the breech and evenly diminishing to 0.005in at the muzzle).*

68. *Pattern 1853 Rifle-musket, Fourth Model.*
This model was manufactured only at Enfield and by the London Armoury Company, and is distinguished by the use of Baddeley's patent barrel bands which have the clamping screw recessed to avoid catching on the soldier's clothing. It was a refinement not enforced on the contractors. The backsight leaf is graduated to 1,000 yards, and Enfield-made examples are of the short-butt type. It should be noted that the upper barrel band is the same as that used on the Third Model, no modification being necessary with the sling swivel present. The majority of this model were never issued in their original state, but were kept in Store and later converted to Snider breech-loaders. *Overall length 54in (London Armoury Co., 55in), barrel length 39in, calibre 0.577in, rifled with three grooves of progressive depth (0.015in deep at the breech and evenly diminishing to 0.005in at the muzzle).*

69, 70, 71. *Pattern 1853 Locks.*
Plate 69 is the early type used on rifle-muskets and First and some Second Model Artillery Carbines. Note the small narrow-bodied hammer with pronounced curl to the spur. The small engraving is also typical. Plate 70 is the Standard type used on rifle muskets, short rifles and carbines. Note the broader body of the hammer with a heavier straight spur. Internally the swivel of the mainspring is also of heavier construction than the early type lock. Plate 71 is the late type used at Enfield from 1856 and by the London Armoury Company from 1860. The hammer has been made heavier still, both wider and thicker in the body. The double border lines engraved on the standard lock and hammer are omitted, as is the 'flame' engraving on the side of the head of the hammer.

72, 73, 74. *Pattern 1853 Locks, variant markings.*
Plate 72 shows the use of an italic date only, the standard marking on Belgian-made P/53 locks generally found on Second Model P/53 Rifle-muskets and Second and Third Model Artillery Carbines. Plate 73 is the Second Model Rifle-musket manufactured by Robbins & Lawrence at Winsor, Vermont. Plate 74 is the standard marking of the London Armoury Company Limited.

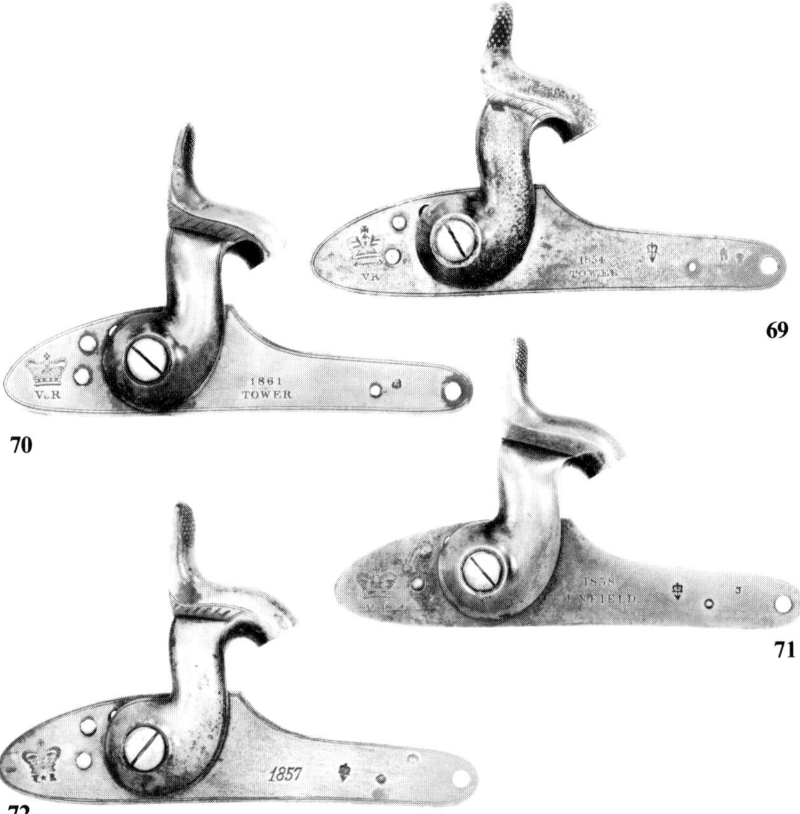

69

70

71

72

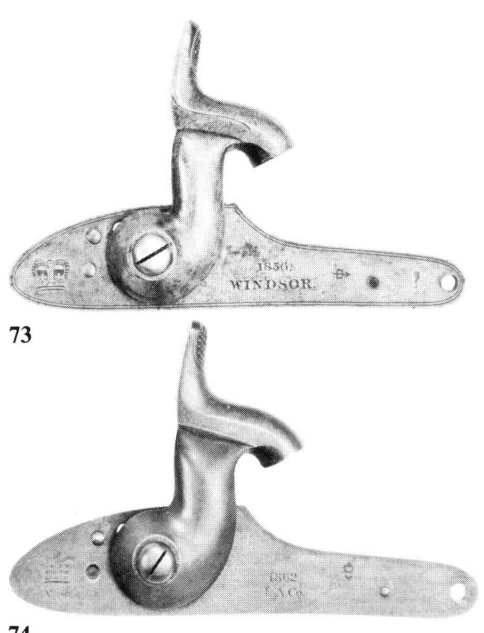

73

74

75. *Pattern 1856 Short Rifle.*
This is the most common of the four patterns of regulation short rifles, approved in January 1856 and placed in production in November 1856. They were issued to the Rifle Brigade and the 60th Regiment, the Cape Mounted Rifles, the Royal Canadian Rifles and to all sergeants of Line Regiments. They are stocked to $5\frac{3}{8}$in of the muzzle and have a bayonet bar for a yataghan sword bayonet on the right side of the barrel. The furniture is of P/53 design, of case-hardened iron rather than brass, and the lower sling swivel is screwed through the rear of the trigger guard, common to all patterns of army short rifles. The P/56 has two clamping bands retaining the barrel, and the elevating backsight is graduated to 1100 yards. *Overall length 49in, barrel length 33in, calibre 0.577in, rifled with three broad grooves of a uniform depth of 0.014in and making one turn in 78in. Those made from 1858 have the progressive rifling adopted in that year.*

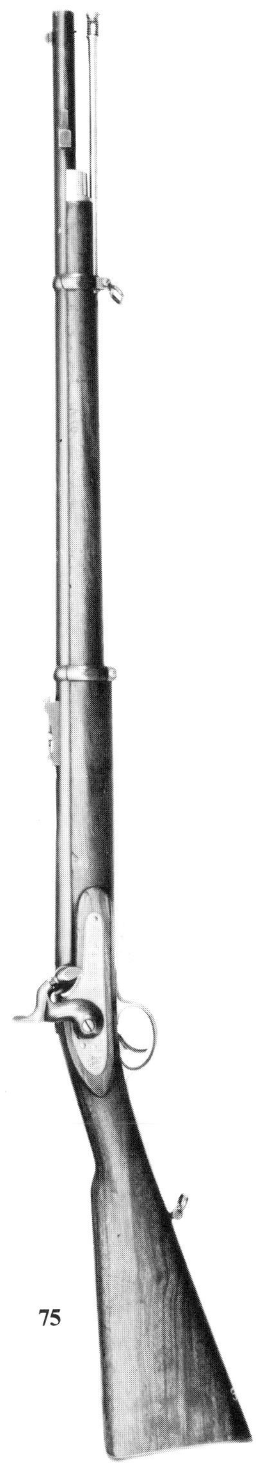

75

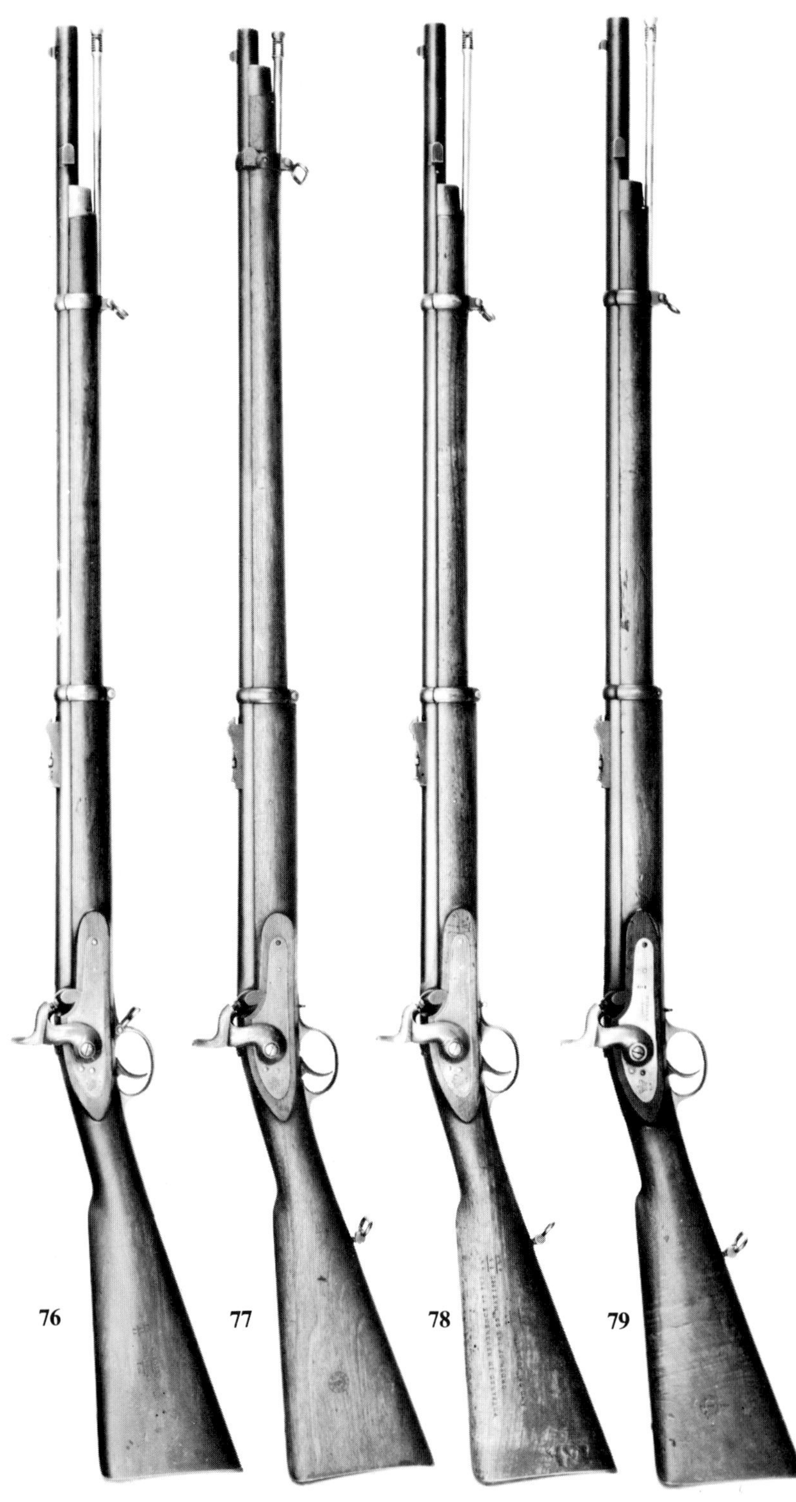
76
77
78
79

76. *Pattern 1858 Naval Rifle.*
Approved in November 1857 and put into production in December 1858, the features which distinguish the P/58 Naval Rifle from other short rifles are the brass furniture, the placing of the lower sling swivel on the front of the guard bow as on the P/53 Rifle-musket, and the use of a heavy barrel rifled with five grooves. The walls of the barrel are visibly thicker than those of the P/56 Short Rifle. The backsight is graduated to 1100 yards. In addition to those made at Birmingham, London and a much lesser number at Enfield, Naval Rifles were also made in Liège and bear typical Belgian markings. *Overall length 49in, barrel length 33in, calibre 0.577in, rifled with five broad angular grooves of progressive depth (0.013in deep at the breech and 0.005in at the muzzle) and making one turn in 48in. The weight of the barrel is 4lb 1½oz.*

77. *Pattern 1858 Short Rifle, also known as the Pattern 1856 No. 2 or the 'Bar-on-Band'.*
Approved in July 1858 and put into production in June 1859. This pattern is easily distinguished from all other short rifles by the appearance of the fore-end area: The stock comes to 1¼in of the muzzle and the upper band is wide—pinned to the fore-end by a thick cross-pin—and has the bayonet bar on its upper right side. It has a standard weight barrel with the normal three-groove rifling and in all other particulars it resembles the P/56 Short Rifle. With the general adoption of the heavy barrel the necessity for this specially equipped pattern was eliminated and subsequent designs reverted to the style established in the P/56, with the bayonet bar on the barrel. The sword bayonet for this pattern differs from that for the P/56 only in having the muzzle-ring moved further from the centreline of the hilt. *Overall length 49in, barrel length 33in, calibre 0.577in, rifled with three broad grooves of progressive depth (0.013in deep at the breech and 0.005in at the muzzle) and making one turn in 78in. The weight of the barrel is 3lb 10½oz.*

78. *Pattern 1860 Short Rifle.*
This was approved in November 1860 and put into production in 1861, although of short duration owing to the adoption of a new style of barrel band and a new powder. The true Pattern 1860 has the external appearance of the Pattern 1856 Short Rifle, but will have a heavy barrel rifled with the fast-twist five-groove system of the Naval Rifle. The backsight is graduated to 1100 yards, and the two barrel bands are of the standard Enfield design. *Overall length 49in, barrel length 33in, calibre 0.577in, rifled with five broad grooves of progressive depth, (0.013in at the breech and 0.005in at the muzzle) and making a turn of one in 48in. The weight of the barrel is 4lb 1½oz.*

79. *Pattern 1861 Short Rifle.*
Approved in August 1861, and apparently produced almost entirely at Enfield rather than by contractors. The salient features of this, the last pattern of muzzle-loading rifle officially adopted by the British services, include a backsight graduated to 1,250 yards and the use of the Baddeley pattern barrel band for the lower band of the two which secure the barrel. In all other particulars it conforms to the P/60 Short Rifle. Short Rifles of the Patterns of 1860 and 1861 appear to have been kept in Store and were very largely converted to Snider breech-loaders.

Markings

Because of the tremendous number of weapons manufactured during the entire nineteenth century from military pattern parts of both flintlock and percussion type, it is particularly important to recognise the correct Government markings on both metal and wood. The commercial market for smoothbore muskets and carbines of the India Pattern type, and of the Lovell pattern percussion weapons as well as later arms based upon the Pattern 1853, was vast and extremely well supplied by the Birmingham gun trade. Most of these arms are immediately recognisable by considerable differences in measurements from the parent type of regulation arm, but there are sufficient examples of arms closely resembling the regulation design to warrant close attention to the markings.

Until the close of the Hanoverian period in 1837 the proofmarks on Government barrels remained as they had been since 1715. The proofmark of a crowned GR over a Broad Arrow and the view mark of crowned crossed sceptres remained standard, although they were generally executed with smaller dies and were less deeply struck. In addition the Government ownership marking on the lock of a small crowned Broad Arrow struck on the forward part of the lock-plate remained standard.

During the short reign of William IV (1830–7) a new marking on the barrel made an appearance, generally in conjunction with the older Georgian proofmarks: this new mark consisted of a crowned MR, with the right-hand vertical arm of the M also acting as the vertical arm of the R. This mark was almost invariably badly struck, so that part of the M or part of the R was not present. Whether this mark was a copy of the French marking of that period, and intended to mean 'Manufacture Royal' or even 'IV Rex' is not known, but the marking does appear to be identified only with the reign of William IV and particularly with arms made at Enfield.

Regulation longarms set up by the trade during William's reign continued to use the older Georgian proofmarks.

The greater numbers of weapons set up at Enfield from the opening of the 'Lovell era' onwards make it necessary to delineate the two sets of proofmarks brought into use early in the reign of Queen Victoria. The set used at Enfield from *c.* 1838 consisted of a crowned VR as proofmark, with crowned crossed sceptres as the view. In addition, ENFIELD and a date (those noted are between 1840 and

1848) appeared. After 1848 these last two features were dropped. The crowned VR and the crowned crossed sceptres continued as the Enfield proofmarks until *c.* 1845 when the crossed sceptres were replaced by a pair of crossed pennants, crowned and with a small crown and inspector's number stamped beneath. This view mark, combined with the crowned VR proofmark, continued as the standard for Enfield barrels into the Snider and Martini period.

Proofmarks on Government barrels made by the Birmingham and London trades from the beginning of Queen Victoria's reign had a crowned TP over a Broad Arrow for proof and a crowned Broad Arrow for the view. Presumably the TP stood for 'Tower Proof'. There was normally a crowned letter, B or L over a numeral, stamped between these two markings—an inspector's mark which indicated Birmingham or London provenance of the barrel; as would be expected, the letter B was by far the more common.

Commercially-made barrels for non-regulation weapons bore the standard London or Birmingham commercial proofmarks specified by the Proof Acts of 1813 and 1855. Except on some experimental arms it was unusual to find commercial barrels which have been restamped with Government markings and therefore indicating the acquisition of the piece for Government purposes.

The indiscrimate use of inspection stamps by persons unknown at some period after the manufacture of the particular weapon makes the reliability of the stamps on the stocks of arms from this period highly suspect in most instances. The use of a stamp composed of a Broad Arrow over the letters B O (Board of Ordnance) was succeeded in 1856 by the use of a similar Broad Arrow and the letters W D (War Department) but, as the latter has been found stamped on flintlock weapons, it is obvious that at some period everything on hand was so marked and does not therefore assist in the identification of a regulation weapon.

The stamping of surnames on various parts of the stock became standard on contract weapons during the percussion period and was also found on some Enfield longarms. These occurred in three standard positions on regulation arms: on the underside of the butt behind the trigger guard strap, at the rear of the ramrod channel, and on the sideplate flat. So far as can be determined from an extensive study of weapons, comparisons, and examination of lists of persons engaged in the trade, these various positions indicate the following relationships. The name on the underside of the butt is that of the main contracting firm who had an order for the arms from the Board or the War Department. The name in the ramrod channel is that of the man or firm who supplied the stock. The name on the sideplate flat, when present, is that of the man or firm who did the actual stocking operation on subcontract from the firm whose name appears on the underside of the butt.

On Enfield-made weapons the names of G. STAINTON, J. LEADBETER, E. WANT, JAS. CHADWICK and R. CHADWICK are found on the underside of the butt, the name of the Chief Inspector or Viewer.

In common with the Broad Arrow and BO or WD stamps, the classification stamp seems to have been added at a later period than is feasible for many arms, and its use except where definitely associated with a list of classifications may be misleading. Many Lovell and Pattern 1853 arms do bear these stamps legitimately and it is therefore advisable to comment on them. In 1859 a system of Reserve weapons was set up and divided into four classifications: I–IV according to the type, age and condition of a weapon, and whether or not it had been officially refurbished. The arm was accordingly stamped on the right side of the butt with I.C.R., II.C.R., III.C.R. or IV.C.R. Yet another system called for the classification of current issue weapons on the basis of their place of manufacture and condition. These were marked with an Arabic number—1, 2, 3, or 3—below the circular stamp indicating the place of manufacture on the right side of the butt. Thus, Pattern 1853 Enfield Rifle-muskets made in the mid-1850s by the trade or in America or in Belgium, and which had been refurbished at Pimlico during the years 1859–62, were classified as Second Class arms and held in Store for issue to Volunteers and the Militia. First Class arms were those made at Enfield and by the London Armoury Company and were held for issue to regular troops only, and Third Class weapons went to regimental depots for drill purposes. Arms subsequently downgraded owing to repairs or refurbishing had both the original and a second number stamped beneath the place of manufacture stamp.

Some weapons conformed in all details to regulation arms, but bore retailers' names and addresses on either the barrel or lock—or occasionally both; these arms also had commercial proof marks for either London or Birmingham. These privately-made weapons were for commercial sale and should not be considered as regulation arms. In the unusual instance where such a weapon has a barrel bearing government proofmarks, it is assumed that the original maker of the arm had access to supplies of such barrels but, in many instances it is most likely that the barrel is a replacement. The 'legitimacy' of such weapons is always questionable. Regulation weapons of issue pattern were normally marked in a standard manner, and deviations from the standard form are always suspect—even though there may ultimately prove to be an explanation.

1

MR MR

MR VR

2

3

4

5

1. Georgian Government proofmarks from *c*. 1815 until *c*. 1830. The same component parts are used as those of 1715, but the crowns are more arched and 'taller' and the markings are smaller in size and more neatly struck.
2. The crowned initials MR or possibly IVR used on Government arms during the reign of William IV. Generally used in conjunction with Georgian markings, it was normally badly struck as shown. Occasionally this mark appeared above crowned crossed sceptres, but older marks were generally present.
3. Victorian Government proofmarks used at the Royal Manufactory, Enfield, from 1837. The crowned VR continued in use after 1865, but the crossed sceptres were superseded by crossed pennants *c*. 1844. The sceptres continued to be used for some years after this date, concurrently with others having pennant markings. The use of the date and ENFIELD has been noted between 1837 and 1848.
4. Government proofmarks for Birmingham and London-made weapons. From *c*. 1838 until 1868.
5. Later Enfield proofmarks showing clearly the use of pennants in place of sceptres, and the variation in sizes between stamps which is commonly found. These later marks are usually accompanied by smaller crowned initials immediately below the pennants, and crowned numbers as well in many cases—inspection stamps.

Addenda

Muskets. Study of the documents suggests that the designation 'Pre-Land' should be dropped in favour of 'Ordnance Pattern' and 'Regimental Pattern' muskets, since these reflect the two basic sources from which a variety of designs for infantry arms originated. Until the 'King's Pattern for Land Service' of 1722, the origins of arms design were so diffuse, and frequently outside of the Ordnance's control, that to tie the design to a concept like 'Pre-Land Pattern' to 'Land Pattern' creates an erroneous idea of continuity in the design and production methods that existed before the general re-armament of the British Army in 1739–41.

Within the British service (horse and foot) until 1739–41 could be found a variety of muskets and carbines made by private London contractors. These included Lewis Barber, Joseph Clarkson, D. Cooke, Joseph Farmer (these two from Birmingham), James Freeman, Thomas Phillips, Charles Pickfatt, Richard Sinckler, and Thomas White. Plate I/5 shows how far the designs could vary from that of the King's Pattern shown in plate I/6. Some of these arms never underwent Tower proof, and may never have passed through the hands of the Board of Ordnance, until they were finally exchanged for 'King's Pattern' arms. In addition to this miscellany, there were the several Ordnance patterns produced by the contractors within and around the Tower, to the specifications of the Board. The most notable of these during this period was the 'ketch lock' or dog lock pattern introduced in 1703 and produced until about 1710.

The first muskets to be produced under the new 'Ordnance system' were known as 'the Pattern of the 10,000'. These have flat locks without bridles, iron furniture (including the Sea Service muskets) and wooden rammers. They were marked 'Tower' and dated between 1715 and 1722. Since many regiments were already equipped with the various patterns of Regimental muskets, many of these arms were not issued until the mid-1730s!

New evidence indicates that the Guards Regiments were armed with iron-mounted muskets with steel rammers before 1739. Whether these were modified versions of the Pattern of the 10,000 or still another, more elaborate, design is not yet known.

Steel ramrods began to be fitted to the muskets of the Line regiments from January 1748 (although ten battalions serving in Ireland had received them in 1726), and conversions continued into the 1770s. New-production with steel rammers also began in 1748, apart from the 'special cases' already known. A new-pattern nosecap, first referred to in 1755, probably appeared at the same time as new-production steel rammer muskets.

Referring to the Lock Changes on page 18, a New Pattern Lock, made to gauges, was introduced in 1756, which ended the 'banana' profile of lockplate. The appearance of the tear-drop feather-spring finial probably coincides with the introduction of the new Short Land Pattern furniture in 1768. The double border-line engraving on the top jaw and the back of the steel disappears officially in 1778.

The Pioneers were given a musket in 1803, but this was no more than an India Pattern Musket with a 37in barrel (possibly plate II/4). There are no further orders after 1804. Marine muskets prior to 1756 continue to create problems in identification. We know that when new regiments were raised they were armed with some of the Ordnance-pattern muskets purchased in Liège in 1740–1. There are orders for Marine muskets in 1746, but without details. It is reasonable to assume that when these 'ad hoc' units were raised they received a musket with a 46in barrel and Land Service lock, fitted with a Sea Service stock and furniture. Steel rammers were fitted to new production Sea Service muskets from the late 1780s, and from 1802 all were fitted with the India Pattern Lock.

Carbines. The list on pages 47 and 48 has been completely revised to read as follows, and this information should be applied to the captions:

1.	Cadet's Carbine & bayonet (Woolwich artillery)	*c.* 1744
2.	Lord Loudoun's light infantry Carbine & bayonet (J. Barber)	1745
3.	Duke of Cumberland's Dragoons Carbine & bayonet (J. Barber) (design adopted for Horse Grenadier Guards 1755)	1746
4.	Artillery Officer's Fusil & bayonet	1750
5.	Artillery Carbine & bayonet (altered from cavalry carbines)	1752
6.	Royal Horse Guards ('Blues') Carbine	1755 Pl. I/53–4
7.	Artillery Carbine & bayonet, new production, stronger (also issued to Highland regiments and light infantry)	1756 Pl. I/50
8.	Carbine for Horse w/o bayonet, 'home stocked' (i.e. right to the muzzle)	1756 Pl. I/51
9.	Light Dragoon Carbine & bayonet	1756 Pl. I/48
10.	Elliott's Light Dragoon Carbine (altered to steel rods 1772)	1760 Pl. I/59
11.	Royal Forrester's (21st Light Dragoons) Carbine & bayonet (taken over by Burgoyne's L.D. in 1764)	1760 Pl. I/63
12.	Hale's Light Dragoon Carbine & bayonet	1760
13.	Artillery Carbine & bayonet	1770 Pl. I/55–6
14.	Heavy Dragoon Carbine & bayonet	1770 Pl. I/57–8
15.	Light Infantry Fusil (Carbine) & bayonet	1770 Pl. I/52
16.	Serjeant of Grenadier's Carbine (Fusil) & bayonet, 39″	1770
17.	Elliott's L.D. Carbine & bayonet, new pattern	1773 Pl. I/60–2
18.	Nock's 7-barrelled Volley Gun, first pattern	1780 Pl. I/71
19.	Burgoyne's blunderbuss Carbine	1781 Pl. I/64
20.	Nock's 7-barrelled Volley Gun, second pattern	1788 Pl. I/72
21.	Harcourt's Heavy Dragoon Carbine (Nock's screwless lock)	1793 Pl. I/65–6
22.	Royal Horse Artillery double-barrelled Pistol-Carbine, with detachable butt (H. Nock)	1793
23.	India Pattern Serjeant's Carbine & bayonet	1797 Pl. I/70
24.	Heavy Dragoon Carbine, Pattern 1796 (Ordnance lock)	1797 Pl. I/67–8

25. Duke of York's Carbine, 21″ brl, flat lock (H. Nock) 1800
26. New Land Pattern Senior Cadet Carbine & bayonet 1802
27. 'Paget' Cavalry Carbine 1812 Pl. I/73–7
28. New Land Pattern Junior Artillery Cadet's Carbine & bayonet 1817 Pl. II/21

Rifles. The rifle entered British service in May 1746, when 50 were purchased, apparently abroad, for the aborted expedition to Louisbourg. These rifles remained in Store until 12 were issued (along with breast- and backplates), for the use of the engineers attached to the Braddock expedition in 1755. One account has the engineers with the van of Braddock's troops at the Monongahela, just where rifle-equipped troops should have been. This appears to be the first combat-use of rifles by British forces. In January 1757, Col. Prevost of the Royal American Regt. was repaid for 300 rifled barrel carbines with steel rammers *and bayonets* that were intended for the use of H.M. troops in North America. It is this group to which frequent references are made throughout the French and Indian wars. It is apparent from these references that the rifles were issued to selected individuals in several of the regular British regiments serving in the North American conflict during 1758. They do not appear to have been issued to provincial rangers. Note that they had bayonets, unlike all of the rifles—except the 100 Fergusons—obtained during 1776. The evidence points overwhelmingly to an European, rather than to an American, stimulus for the issuing of rifles to the British Army, probably at the behest of the then Commander-in-Chief, H.R.H. the Duke of Cumberland. As in so much of his tactical thinking, he followed the Prussian example—Prussia having introduced rifles in 1740. In 1762, for the expedition against Havana, the British engineers were issued with 10 rifled carbines. In this same year, the Ordnance purchased 5 breechloading rifles of two different screw-plug systems from gunmaker John Hirst (at least one is still in the Tower), and 20 rifles — system not specified, but from the price almost certainly breech-loaders — were ordered from Hirst late in 1763. It appears that the rifles in Ordnance hands were sold off in 1763. They had to start again in 1775.

Basically, 1,000 rifled barrel guns were to be obtained for the use of the troops in North America. Of this number, there were delivered during 1776: 200 made in Hanover by Heinrich Huhnstock; and from Birmingham, 200 made by Benjamin Willets, 200 by Mathias Barker, 200 by Galton & Son, and 200 by Grice & Son; a total of 800 British-made and 200 German-made muzzle loading rifles, plus the 100 Ferguson breechloaders, of which 25 each were supplied by Grice, Willets, Barker and Galton. This much is fact, and that 100 of the Hanoverian-made rifles were sent to America, 50 each to Howe and Burgoyne. While it seems certain that most of the rifles went to America, at present there is no documentary proof of this assertion. The 16th Light Dragoons carried some rifles supplied to them by their Colonel, William Harcourt, but there are no further details. Of all these rifles from 1746 to 1776, only the solitary military Ferguson at the Morristown New Jersey National Park Museum and a single example of the Hirst 1762 breechloaders have been positively identified. There are several 'suspects' for some of the others.